AL-NAJM BAYN AL-NUJOOM

A Star Amongst
the Stars

The life and times of the great companion
Jabir ibn Abdullah al-Ansari

By Jaffer Ladak

A Star Amongst *the* Stars
ISBN 978-1-927930-27-4
Written by Jaffer Ladak
Edited by Arifa Hudda

Published by Islamic Publishing House – www.iph.ca – iph@iph.ca

Cover Design and Layout by the Islamic Publishing House

The rewards of this book are dedicated to leading community servants of the Ahl al-Bayt ﷺ

Marhum Ma'alim Mustafa Mawjee

Marhum Ma'alim FidaHusayn M H Khaki

Marhum Feeroz Ali Jagani

Marhum Kassam Jaffer

Marhum Riyaz Anwer Rajabali

Marhum Amirali MohamedJaffer Nasser Lakha

Marhum Gulamali Mohamed Hussain Dewji

&

Marhum Ma'alim MohamedHusayn Kermali

May they be with Jabir b. Abdullah al-Ansari in the presence of the holy Prophet Muhammad and his pure progeny.

Contents

Author's Introduction

In 1979, Dr. Ali Shari'ati wrote, "In order to understand any religion, one must study its God, its Book, its Prophet and the best individuals whom it has nurtured and raised."[1]

Two questions arise from this statement. First, why should we extend our appreciation of a religion to its followers and not curtail it to the study of its God, revelation and Prophet only? Secondly, why should one not study the worst, most ill-natured people or even the diverse spectrum of its followers in order to understand the religion itself?

As for the first question, for a religion to be followed, it must extend to those beyond its divine characters - in this case its God, revelation and Prophet. A religion is, by its nature, seeking to attract those who are uninformed about it, offering something greater to its potential adherent than one already enjoys. The study of its God will yield His Divine characteristics and drive a sense of purpose within creation. The revelation will convey communication from the Divine and connect the created with a sense of guidance and access to the Divine. The Prophet will reflect the Divine sources in his character and knowledge, his actions thereby demonstrating the perfect form of life. Through this tri-union of sources that makes up a religion, its followers will receive nurturing and become a human being. Therefore, understanding what a religion has to offer can be perceived by what it produces. Observing the greatest of its adherents is thus a marker for what the religion envisioned itself to offer to the world, and a standard for what others can also become.

---

[1] *Sociology*, p. 205.

Given that a religion seeks to infuse its adherents with the blossoming of the intellect, meritorious characteristics and spiritual fulfilment, its producing of people who are far from these virtues suggests that such people cannot truly be following the religion properly, and thus they should not be portrayed as a means of understanding the religion. It is not to say that such people should not be studied, indeed they should be, however if for example, the religion aims to produce a generous person but an adherent becomes a miser through the same religion, then either the religion is faulty in its method of nurturing such characteristics, or the adherent has not engaged properly with the religion correctly.

In today's era, this is a particular challenge for the Muslim community, that although there are a few in number, they are large in their effect, who are claiming to practice Islam, but they are the very worst version of what it should produce.

One may argue that if a religion can be interpreted in such ways as to produce such ignoble people, then there is something essentially wrong with that religion or the way in which it can be interpreted. This argument however, cannot rightly be levied against the religion itself, because returning to the above, the religion, when practiced as it intended to, will produce people of great intellect, virtue and merit. Therefore, in response to the second question that why did Dr. Shari'ati not suggest studying illegitimate claimants of practising a religion so as to properly understand it, would be equivalent to studying a person who falsely claims to be a doctor in order to understand medicine.

Amongst those who should be considered as one of the most virtuous and exemplary in the history of Islam, a person by which to understand the religion better, is the great companion of Prophet Muhammad ﷺ - Jabir b. Abdullah al-Ansari, may Allah be pleased with him and elevate his station. Arguably no companion in the history of Islam has cumulatively contributed as much as him, and certainly no companion has seen the extent of what Jabir[2] b. Abdullah al-Ansari has. His legacy remains up until today to the

---

[2] Not to be confused with another Jabir in the same era, by the name of Jabir b. Yazid al-Ju'fi. Jabir al-Ju'fi was also a prolific narrator who is recorded as having said: "I have narrated fifty thousand traditions," and in another "ninety thousand narrations." For further information, refer to *Mo'jam Rijal al-Hadith* of Ayatollah Syed al-Khoe'i, vol. 4, p. 19.

extent that many of Islam's theological, devotional and jurisprudential practices are a result of his narrations - moulding both the intellectual, as well as the spiritual traditions of Islam.

Nurtured by the hands of seven infallible members of the holy Ahl al-Bayt ⚌, Jabir was blessed by learning directly from Prophet Muhammad ⚌, her eminence Lady Fatima al-Zahra ⚌, the Commander of the Faithful Imam Ali b. Abi Talib ⚌, and Imams al-Hasan, al-Husayn, Ali b. al-Husayn Zayn al-Abideen, and Muhammad al-Baqir ⚌, dying a few years before the birth of Imam Ja'far al-Sadiq ⚌. This makes Jabir the longest living companion of the holy Prophet ⚌, partaking in a full eighty years worth of servitude to Islam. From this blessing of a life with the immaculate Ahl al-Bayt ⚌, his knowledge and understanding of Islam was such that he used to give seminars, and teach in the Masjid of Prophet Muhammad ⚌[3] and he was amongst the foremost compilers of prophetic traditions authoring the non-extant *Saheefah Jabir b. Abdullah al-Ansari.*[4]

Jabir had a special relationship with the Prophet ⚌ which was unique amongst the companions. Jabir states, "From the time that I accepted Islam, the Messenger of Allah never prohibited me from attending any of his assemblies. Whenever he saw me he would smile."[5] His loyalty and devotion to the holy Prophet ⚌ and his immaculate family ⚌ reached such a level whereby Imam Ja'far al-Sadiq ⚌ is narrated to have said regarding the Qur'anic verse, 'I do not ask any reward except love of my closest relations' (42:23) that "I swear by Allah, no one was loyal to this right except seven people: they are Salman, Abu Dharr, Ammar, Miqdad b. Aswad, Jabir b. Abdullah, the retainer of Allah's Messenger, and Zayd b. Arqam."[6]

Among the biographical accounts of the companions can be found in the book 'The men around the Prophet and his holy family' by Sheikh Fawzi Aal Sayf. The author praises Jabir with the following words: "Jabir b. Abdullah al-Ansari participated with the Messenger of Allah ⚌ in all of the activities during the Prophet's battles except for Badr and Uhud, as he was demanded by his father to stay with the women in order to look after them. In

---

[3] *Tahdhib al-Tahdhib*, vol. 2, p. 43; *Al-Isaba*, vol. 1, p. 214; *The Life of Imam Muhammad al-Baqir*, Baqir Qarashi, Ansariyan, 2003, p. 490.

[4] *Usul al-Hadith*, Abd al-Hadi al-Fadhli, Markaz al-Ghadeer, 2010, p. 63.

[5] *Shamaa'il*, Chapter on the Laughing of the Prophet ⚌, Tirmidhi, Hadith 4.

[6] *Tanqih al-Manqaal*, vol. 1, p. 200.

submission to his father, he became one of those who always accompanied the Messenger ﷺ and one of those who was taught personally by his own hand - and this is why he is one of those who knew and memorised abundantly from the Prophetic way (*sunnah*).

He used to witness that a number of the companions were distracted by trading in the markets; but instead, his commerce was to continuously talk to the Messenger of God ﷺ and gather as much as possible from his knowledge. He observed directly what a fortune they had lost and he did not miss any occasion from which he could benefit from the Prophet's ﷺ speech.

When the Messenger of God ﷺ died, he would try and track down and follow[7] his traditions - those that he did not hear directly (from the Prophet ﷺ) by travelling to different places in order to get a true (correct) tradition about the Prophet."[8]

Through many narrations, Jabir provided a first-hand insight into the formative period of the Medinan community and the intriguing relationship between the Ansar and the Muhajiroon, the former of whom he belonged to. In researching these aspects, I often became astonished at the extent of the sacrifice and generosity of the Ansar toward the Muhajiroon and their mutual assistance towards each other. It has become for me, a blueprint towards a socio-economic structure and an ideal that the modern world needs to emulate, something I aim to explicate in my commentary where appropriate.

Sheikh Aal Fawzi continues his eulogy of Jabir stating, "His company to the Messenger ﷺ and his tracing his ﷺ steps (practices) have made him accurately define the direction of the right path after the death of the Messenger of God ﷺ and so he became one of the faithful companions of Amir al-Mu'mineen Ali b. Abi Talib ﷺ."[9]

Therefore, Jabir plays an integral role in disseminating much of Islam's theology and Qur'anic exegesis. Notable aspects include his interactions

---

[7] Sheikh Aal Fawzi used the word ya-ta-ta-ba'a from the root taa'bi'. In the Holy Qur'an, Allah ﷻ quotes Prophet Ibrahim ﷺ as a metaphor for Prophet Muhammad's companions stating, "Whosoever follows me (ta-bi-'ani), he is certainly from me" (14:36) - suggesting that as Jabir continued to follow the Prophetic tradition after the Prophet's death, he was and remained 'from' the Prophet ﷺ.

[8] *Rijal Hawl al-Rasool wa Ahli Baytihi*, p. 222.

[9] Ibid, p. 223.

with the holy Prophet ﷺ, his recounting the 'Event of the Cloak' or *Hadith al-Kisa*, the salutations of the Prophet to Imam al-Baqir ؏, being the first person to perform visitation rites, or *ziyarat*, to Imam al-Husayn ؏ after his martyrdom in Karbala, and the conveyor of Ziyarat Ameenullah, the devotional salutation narrated by Imam Zain al-Abideen ؏ to Imam Ali b. Abi Talib ؏ at his grave. As the honourable reader will, Insha-Allah come to find, this is but a tip of the iceberg in terms of the contributions made by Jabir who has thousands of narrations about or attributed to him.[10]

Most striking is his relationship with the fifth Imam, Muhammad b. Ali al-Baqir ؏, arguably in its own way as unique as that of Imam Ali ؏ to the great disciple Kumayl b. Ziyad. I say disciple because in both cases it denotes a devotee who is of unique status in the eyes of one's teacher. From Jabir's perspective, despite his age, experience and high spirituality, he is someone ever thirsty for knowledge, and is time and again refashioned at the hands of Imam al-Baqir ؏.

Jabir's longing and wailing for Imam al-Baqir ؏, blind in his old age, is the perfect metaphor for a devotee to emulate in the era of the occultation of Imam al-Mahdi ؏.

Amongst the most important historical aspects of their relationship was its social perception, subtly influencing the people of Medina to understand and accept the lofty status of Imam al-Baqir ؏ during the precarious post-Karbala and pre-Abbasid period. Initially Imam al-Baqir ؏ is perceived as reliant on Jabir as a source of knowledge and Jabir's student, but as Jabir and al-Baqir ؏ continue their interactions, Jabir shifts this dynamic, utilising the people of Medina's trust in him, to demonstrate loyalty and submission to the divine authority of Imam al-Baqir ؏. He soon becomes the open student of the fifth Imam, leveraging support for al-Baqir ؏ without compromising the Imam's ؏ safety with the rulers of the time.

The first element of this unique relationship was the cause of Etan Kohlberg's study, 'An unusual Shi'i Isnad' stating, "What makes Jabir of particular interest from the standpoint of Shi'i *hadith* is the fact that he sometimes appears in the *isnad* between the fifth Shi'i Imam, Muhammad al-Baqir and the Prophet. As such he seems to be the only companion in

---

[10] Etan Kohlberg estimates 1540 narrations from him being recorded in Sunni sources, 210 of which are in *Sahih al-Bukhari* and *Sahih Muslim*. See (1975), *An Unusual Shi'i Isnad*, Israel Oriental Studies 5, 1975, pp. 142-9.

Shi'i literature from whom an Imam has transmitted."[11] Kohlberg also notes, "There are also cases where the fourth Imam 'Ali Zayn al-'Abidin transmits from Jabir." and "Jabir appears at times between al-Baqir and Ali (b. Abi Talib)." I will refer to Kohlberg's study while suggesting that Kohlberg understood only elements of this sagacious practice.

I have attempted to collect many of the narrations of Jabir, but also narrations of the Ansar given in order to provide a greater scope of his experiences and immediate community. Moreover, given that Ansar is used in its general collective sense, Jabir's actions would have coincided with their actions giving us further insight into the practices and events of his life.

Amongst the aims of this work is to demonstrate to the Muslim and non-Muslim readership, the role and precedence that the companions have in the history of Islam. Up until today, there is a misconception which has been spread out of ignorance - especially promoted in online forums or social media discussions - that the Shi'a turn away from *all* companions of the Prophet ﷺ. This of course is not correct, in fact the noble companions are greatly praised and we seek from Allah ﷻ to be counted in their stations. It is hoped that this work will go some way to addressing this query.

This explains the reasoning behind the name of this book - "A Star Amongst *the* Stars." A popular narration among some of the Muslim communities is the tradition, "My companions are like the stars - whichever of them you follow, you will be guided."[12] The Shi'i school rejects this *hadith* for four main reasons. The first is that proper guidance emanates from an immaculate Imam, chosen by Allah ﷻ and not a fallible companion. The Qur'an has a specific series of verses ending with the command, "Follow *their* guidance" with the preceding verses describing *whom* should be followed: "All of them were righteous... And all of them we preferred them above the worlds... And We chose them and guided them to a straight path. That is the guidance of Allah by which He guides whomever He wills of His servants. Those are the ones to whom We gave the Scripture and authority

---

[11] Ibid.

[12] The Arabic text of this passage reads:

أصحابي كالنجوم، بأيهم اقتديتم اهتديتهم

Al-Albani, *Silsilatu Al-Ahadeeth ad-Da'eefah wa al-Mawdhu'ah*, vol. 1, p. 78, Hadith 58.

and prophethood. But if the disbelievers deny it, then We have entrusted it to a people who are not therein disbelievers. Those are the ones whom Allah has guided, therefore follow their guidance" (6:85-90).

Ayatollah Ja'far Subhani affirms this, explaining, "The only criterion for destruction and success is the personality of the Prophet ﷺ. And as for his companions, it is not possible for them to be taken as the criterion for guidance and success except as far as their gestures and in following the Messenger of Allah ﷺ. Indeed the opinion of the *Sahabi* or *Taab'i* is proof between themselves, but not for other than themselves."[13]

The second is that some of the companions warred over interpretation and leadership, and therefore if they themselves did not adhere to such a narration in their practice, then it disproves its authenticity.

Sheikh Subhani further elaborates, "A group of companions and followers led a bitter campaign against (Caliph) 'Uthman (bin 'Affan) until the issue ended with his being overthrown and killed. So was the right and good on the side of the insurgents or on the side of 'Uthman?"[14]

Thirdly, the companions were of different levels in awareness and understanding so if one of them himself needed teaching, then how could he be a guide? As per the aforementioned verse, neither were the companions chosen by Allah ﷺ nor granted authority.

Fourthly, it contradicts a well-known narration in which Imam Ali b. Abi Talib ؏ said: "The example of the descendants of Muhammad is like that of the stars in the sky. When one star sets another one will rise."[15] Imam al-Sadiq ؏ and Imam al-Ridha ؏ said about the verse, "Through the signs and with the star people do find their way" (16:16), that "The star is the Messenger of Allah and the signs are the divinely appointed Imams."[16]

---

[13] Subhani, Ja'far, *Al-Milal wa al-Nahl*, Al-Madhahib al-Islamiyyah, pp. 36-37.

انّ المعيار الوحيد للهلاك و النجاة هو شخص النبي ص ، و اما أصحابه فلا يمكن أن يكونوا معيارا للهداية و النجاة الا بقدر اهتدائهم و اقتدائهم برسول الله ص ، ان قول الصحابي أو التابعي حجة لهما لا لغيرهما.

[14] Ibid, pg 38.

قاد جماعة من الصحابة و التابعين حملة شعواء ضد عثمان حتى انتهى الأمر الى الإطاحة به و قتله، فهل الخير كان الى جانب الثوار او الى جانب عثمان؟

[15] *Nahj al-Balaghah*, Sharif Radhi, Sermon 98.

[16] Al-Kulayni, *al-Kafi*, The Book about People with Divine Authority, Chapter 17, 'Imams are the signs of whom Allah has spoken in the Qur'an', Hadith 1-3, pp. 173-4.

Elsewhere, Imam al-Baqir 🕮 said, "We (the Ahl al-Bayt) only are like the stars in heaven. Whenever one star disappears another one will come into view."[17]

For those people who do accept the narration, Jabir is certainly amongst the greatest of companions. Therefore, just as this book is an invite to the Shi'i readership to explore their Prophet 🕮 and his companions to a greater extent - something that may be lacking in the Shi'a community, it is also an invitation to the Sunni readership to appreciate that companions, especially like Jabir, gave prominence to the Ahl al-Bayt 🕮.

The narration of: 'My companions are the like the stars' would therefore indicate that if following Jabir leads to correct guidance, then priority would be to appreciate from where Jabir took *his* guidance, and whom *he* promoted as the leaders and authorities of Islam. The title of this book is therefore purposeful in provoking reflection on who the stars of guidance are and from where these illuminated beings received their guidance.

To aid this goal of bringing a diverse readership, I attempted to collect narrations from a range of Islamic sources. This is also because I believe that all of the collections of *hadith* and historical literature are a shared Islamic inheritance, and not books belonging to a particular sect as is often quoted. Although I did my best to collect enough narrations reflecting the life and contributions of Jabir, it certainly by no means is a comprehensive collection. Indeed, considering my own historical and theological criterion there are many narrations attributed to Jabir that I found unacceptable, and thus chose not to include them, and to emphasise again, that is from all of the sources. Many others I may have simply missed by virtue of the limitations of my own research.

Jabir eventually died having been tortured at the hands of the then Umayyad king, Hajjaj b. Yusuf al-Thaqafi. His contributions to Islam are in my view, the most profound from all of the companions and deserves careful study and reflection. Truly if one wishes to know the religion of Islam by its adherents, then he is an ideal candidate in which to reflect upon for the aspirations of the religion.

---

[17] *Al-Kafi*, vol.1, Book 4, The Book about People with Divine Authority, Chapter 80, The Disappearance of the 12th Imam, Hadith 8, p. 308.

I am grateful to all of those who contributed to this work. Most notable of them is sister Marium Kaouri for her translations of the works from Sheikh Aal Fawzi and Sheikh al-Hakimi, Sheikh Kumail Rajani for his encouragement, and Sheikh Saleem Bhimji and his wife, sister Arifa Hudda for their editing and preparation of this work. Your true rewards are with Allah ﷻ.

Jabir has long since been my 'favourite' companion of study and reflection. This book is the culmination of a long desire to give something back to his efforts, insights and contributions - for without him, there would be a large gap in the true face of the Islamic tradition. We are forever grateful to you, dear companion of the Prophet ﷺ and the Ahl al-Bayt ﷺ.

All thanks belong to Allah for divine opportunity.

Was-Salaam Alaykum
Jaffer Ladak
Karbala al-Muqaddasa, 1438 AH

Chapter 1

Jabir's Background

The Name and Lineage of Jabir b. Abdullah al-Ansari

His full name is Jabir b. (son of) Abdullah al-Ansari al-Salmee al-Khazraji.[18]

Jabir hailed from the Medinan tribe Banu Salima, who became a committed group of the Ansar, the 'Helpers' of Prophet Muhammad ﷺ after his migration from the city of Mecca. Banu Salima were also part of the Khazraj group of tribes.

According to a narration of Jabir's, he states, "There were some plots of land vacant around the Masjid of the Prophet ﷺ. Banu Salima decided to move to this land and come nearer to this place. This news reached the Messenger of Allah ﷺ and he said to them, 'O Banu Salima, I have received news that you intend to shift nearer to the Masjid.' They replied, 'Yes, O Messenger of Allah, we have taken this decision.' Upon this the Prophet ﷺ said, 'O Banu Salima, live in your houses (where you are), for your (extra) steps (to the Masjid) are recorded (as reward)'; and then he repeated 'Live in your houses (where you are), for your (extra) steps are recorded (as reward)!'"[19] Jabir also reports the reaction to this advice saying that the tribes response was, "We could not be more delighted, even to shift closer

---

[18] The Arabic text of this passage reads:

جابر ابن عبد الله الأنصاري السلمي الخزرجي

[19] *Sahih Muslim*, The Book of Masajid and Places of Prayer, Chapter 50, The Virtue of Taking many Steps to the Masjid, Hadith 355.

to the Masjid than we were delighted upon hearing these words from the Prophet ﷺ."[20]

It is also narrated by Jabir that his tribe is referred to in the Holy Qur'an as having Allah ﷻ as their Guardian. He states that, "When the verse 'When two parties from among you were about to lose heart, but Allah was the Protector of both of them and in Allah should the believers trust.' (3:122) was revealed concerning us, the Banu Haritha and Banu Salima, we wished that it had not been revealed, or rather that is to say, I would not have been pleased about its revelation except for that Allah says "... And Allah was their Protector."[21] 'Allama Tabataba'i comments on this narration, "Jabir means that Allah then accepted their belief and confirmed that they were believers, because He counted Himself as their Guardian, and Allah is the Guardian of those who believe, and as for that this clause implies any praise, when it has been put in this contact of clear reprimand and censure."[22]

---

[20] Ibid., Hadith 356.

[21] *Sahih al-Bukhari*, Chapter of Qur'an Commentary, vol. 6, Book 60, Hadith 81.

[22] 'Allama Syed Muhammad Hussain al-Tabataba'i comments fully on this saying, "And Allah was the Guardian of them both" that this is a circumstantial clause, related to the verb, 'had determined.' It is meant as an admonition and reproof, as is the concluding sentence, 'and in Allah should the believers trust.' The connotation is as follows: The two parties had determined to show cowardice although Allah was their Guardian—and a believer should not show weakness and cowardice when one believes that Allah is one's Guardian, and when one is supposed to entrust all of one's affairs to Allah, and whoever trusts in Allah then He is sufficient for them. This explanation shows the weakness of an interpretation offered by an exegete who says: This intention of the two parties was merely a thought, a notion, and not a determination, because Allah has praised them and said that He was their Guardian. Had it been a firm determination and intention, then they should have been blamed rather than praised. But I do not understand what he means when he says that it was merely a thought, a notion. Does he mean merely a passing thought, a knowledge what cowardice means? If so, then everyone who was present there knew the meaning of cowardice, and it makes no sense to mention it in this context; nor is it called "determination" in Arabic language. Or, does he mean knowledge of cowardice coupled with some intention; a notion with determination to act upon it? (If so, then it was not merely a thought or a notion). Also, the verse shows that the condition of the two parties was obvious to the others; had it been merely a passing thought without showing any effect on their behaviour, then the others would not have known that they had determined to show weakness and cowardice. Moreover, the reminder that Allah was their Guardian and that the believers must put their trust in Allah, dovetails with firm

Biographers record three lineages from his father's side. The first is Jabir b. Abdullah b. 'Amru b. Huraam b. 'Amr b. Sawaad b. Salima al-Ansari al-Selmy of Banu Salima. The second is Jabir b. Abdullah b. 'Amr b. Huraam b. Ka'ab b. Ghanam b. Ka'ab b. Salima. As can be seen, both lineages reach his great grandfather, Huraam, but then separate from there. The third lineage is recorded as Jabir b. Abdullah b. Reyab- rejoining the lineage at Ghanam b. Ka'ab as above. It is said that the second lineage from the above is the most well-known and correct.

From his mother's side, Jabir is the son of Nasiba bint (daughter of) 'Akaba b. 'Abdi b. Sanaan b. Naabi b. Zaid b. Huraam b. Ka'ab b. Ghanam which means that both of his parent's lineage returns to Huraam b. Ka'ab b. Ghanam.

Different opinions exist regarding Jabir's kunya (honourable title) also. Some refer to him as Abu Abd al-Rahman or Aba Muhammad, however his most correct title is Abu Abdullah.[23] [24]

Jabir's father, as we will later detail, was amongst the seventy Ansar present at the second pledge of Aqabah with the Prophet ﷺ and he was considered as one of the leaders of the tribe. When the Prophet ﷺ migrated to Medina, Abdullah "sacrificed himself, his money and his family in the service of Islam. Jabir's father found utmost enjoyment in accompanying the Prophet ﷺ day and night, and his belief was strong. His love, or even

---

determination, not with a passing thought. In any case, we have explained that in the present context, the clause, "and Allah was the Guardian of them both", is not intended as a praise, but it is a reproof, an admonition. Perhaps this misunderstanding has sprung up from a tradition attributed to Jabir b. 'Abdillah al-Ansari in which he says: "(This verse) was revealed about us; and I would not prefer if it was not revealed, because Allah has said, and Allah is the Guardian of them both." The said exegete probably thought that Jabir had taken the clause as a praise. Even if the said tradition was accepted as correct, Jabir's theme is different from what that exegete has thought. Jabir meant that Allah then accepted their belief and confirmed that they were believers, because He counted Himself as their Guardian, and Allah is the Guardian of those who believe, and as for that this clause implies any praise, when it has been put in this contact of clear reprimand and censure." *Tafseer al-Mizan*, v. 7, pp. 7-9, World Organization for Islamic Services (WOFIS), 1990.

[23] For further information refer to the books *Al-Isti'aab* and *Usd al-Ghaba*.

[24] *Qasas al-Sahaba wa-Tabi'in*, Sheikh Muhammad Ridha al-Hakimi, p. 75.

eagerness, to die in the cause of Allah was his greatest ambition"[25] which he accomplished first by partaking in the Battle of Badr, and afterwards by being martyred in the Battle of Uhud.

Scholarly Opinions on Jabir

Jabir is a companion universally praised by the scholars of all of the sects and sciences in the Islamic tradition. In this section we will review what some of the scholars of Islam have noted about Jabir b. Abdullah.

Sheikh Muhammad Ridha al-Hakimi has gathered this scholarly praise and stated the following:

Abi al-Khayr in his *Tabaqaat al-Mufasireen* acknowledges Jabir as among the best interpreters of the Holy Qur'an, while Jalal al-Din al-Suyuti considers him to be among the most honoured Qur'anic commentators.

Al-Fadl b. Shadhan al-Nishapuri, a disciple of Imam Ali b. Musa al-Ridha 🕮 considers Jabir among the first supporters of the Commander of the Faithful, Ali b. Abi Talib and "He is one of the formers who referred back to Amir al-Mo'mineen Ali 🕮."

Ibn Abd al-Birr stated that after the Prophet 🕮, Jabir preferred Imam Ali b. Abi Talib 🕮 over all of the others.

Al-Kashy narrates about Jabir's embracing the Ahl at-Tashayyu' (being a Shi'a of Imam Ali). He also mentioned in his praise many narrations without saying anything that opposed it.

Sheikh al-Tusi ennobled Jabir in his *Rijal* counting him as among the companions of the Messenger of Allah 🕮 saying that, "Jabir b. Abdullah b. Haram lived in Al-Medina, witnessed Badr and eighteen other battles with the noble Prophet 🕮. He died in the year 78 AH." He also mentioned him among the devoted companions of Imams Ali, al-Hasan, al-Husayn, Ali b. al-Husayn and Muhammad al-Baqir 🕮.

'Allama al-Hilli in his work *Khulasa al-Aqwal fi Ilm al-Rijal* states that, "Jabir bin Abdullah was one of the companions of the Messenger of Allah 🕮 and he witnessed (the Battle of) Badr."

Muhammad al-Burqi in his *Khulasa* considers Jabir among the "true friends" (*asfiyaa'*) of the Ahl al-Bayt 🕮.

---

[25] *Men Around the Messenger*, Khalid Muhammad Khalid, Islamic Book Service, New Delhi, 2002, pp.g 416-7.

Ibn Uqdah described Jabir as "devoted to the Ahl al-Bayt" ﷺ.[26]

Imam Ahmed b. Hanbal considered Jabir as among the six most prolific reporters of narrations from the Prophetic companions.[27]

The Praises of Imam Muhammad al-Baqir ﷺ for Jabir b. Abdullah

While the scholars of Islamic history and exegesis have praised Jabir, the Ahl al-Bayt ﷺ themselves lauded Jabir for his knowledge and piety. Here we shall mention some of the narrations and comment upon them.

Zurara b. A'yun is narrated[28] to have said: "We asked Abu Ja'far ﷺ about some traditions." He ﷺ narrated [referenced] them from Jabir. In response we asked, "What do we need from Jabir (when we have asked the Imam ﷺ?" Imam al-Baqir ﷺ then said, "The belief (*imaan*) of Jabir has reached such a level to which he used to read the reality of this verse: 'Most surely He Who has made the Qur'an binding on you will bring you back to the destination' (28:85)."

Zurara b. A'yun is narrated[29] to have said: I said to Imam al-Baqir ﷺ, "What do we need from Jabir that you narrate from him?" Then he ﷺ said, "O Zurara, Jabir knew the real interpretation (*ta'weel*) of this verse 'Most surely He Who has made the Qur'an binding on you will bring you back to the destination" (28:85).[30]

---

[26] *Qasas al-Sahaba wa al-Tabi'in*, pp. 75-6.

[27] *Maqadimah b. al-Salah*, Ibn al-Salah, p. 492, Dar al-Ma'arif, Cairo.

[28] Chain of narrators: Ahmad b. Ali said: Idrees told me from al-Husayn b. Basheer who said: Hisham b. Salim told me from Mohammad b. Muslim and Zurara.

[29] Chain of narrators: Ahmad b. Ali al-Koummi Shakraan al-Salouly said: "Idrees told me from al-Husayn b. Saeed from Mohammad b. Ismaail from Mansour b. Uthayna from Zurara."

[30] *Qasas al-Sahaba wa al-Tabi'in*, p. 77.

Zurara also narrated[31] from Imam al-Baqir ﷺ who said: "Jabir knows[32] and truly upon him is goodness."[33] Then I said to him ﷺ "And he was one of Ali's ﷺ true companions." He ﷺ replied, "Jabir used to know the saying of Almighty Allah[34]: 'Most surely He Who has made the Qur'an binding on you will bring you back to the destination'" (28:85).[35]

What is fascinating is that according to Imam Muhammad al-Baqir ﷺ, Jabir knew the *ta'weel*, translated here as the real or inner meaning. According to the Holy Qur'an this real meaning is restricted *only* for those "firmly rooted in knowledge" or *Rasikhoona fi al-'Ilm*. This is explicitly mentioned where it says: "He it is Who has revealed the Book to you; some of its verses are decisive, they are the basis of the Book, and others are allegorical; then as for those in whose hearts there is perversity they follow the part of it which is allegorical, seeking to mislead and seeking to give it (their own) interpretation. But none knows its interpretation except Allah and those who are firmly rooted in knowledge. (They) say 'We believe in it, it is all from our Lord', and none do mind except those having understanding" (3:7).

According to the Shi'a interpretation of this verse, those being referred to as "firmly rooted in knowledge" are the divinely appointed Imams of the Ahl al-Bayt ﷺ, and therefore *ta'weel* or knowledge of the true meaning at a given point is restricted to them only. Yet in these narrations Imam al-Baqir ﷺ states that Jabir *also* has knowledge of the *ta'weel* of the Qur'an. In fact, elsewhere the companion Abdullah b. al-Abbas also claimed to have knowledge of the *ta'weel* of the Qur'an based on a narration in which the Prophet ﷺ supplicates for him, "O Allah, endow deep understanding of the

---

[31] Chain of narration: Ahmad b. Ali al-Qummi al-Salouly said: "Idrees b. Ayoub al-Koummi told me from al-Husayn b. Saeed from b. Mahboub from Abd al-Aziz al-Abdei from Zurara."

[32] This may indicate to 'know about divine Imamate or the Qur'an well'. Allah knows best.

[33] The Arabic text of this states:

قال: جابر يعلم: وأثنى (عليه) خيراً

[34] This statement from the Imam ﷺ means that 'not only was he a close companion of Imam Ali, but in addition to that he was also distinguished by his deep knowledge of the Qur'an.'

[35] *Qasas al-Sahaba wa al-Tabi'in*, p. 77.

religion to him (Ibn al-Abbas) and teach him the true meaning of the Qur'an."[36]

Is the restriction to knowledge of the *ta'weel* only for the Ahl al-Bayt ﷺ and Jabir or Ibn al-Abbas's reported knowledge of it contradictory? The response is that it is in the Hands of Allah whomever He may grant true knowledge of the Qur'an to, but in order to do so one *must* take their knowledge and learning through the Ahl al-Bayt ﷺ. Both Ibn al-Abbas and Jabir received knowledge of the Qur'an - not independently, nor directly from Allah ﷻ - but in both instances through the Ahl al-Bayt ﷺ. Abdullah b. al-Abbas received the prayer of the Prophet ﷺ and was a student of Imam Ali ﷺ. Similarly, Jabir was a student of the Ahl al-Bayt ﷺ who taught him.

Secondly, Imam al-Baqir ﷺ does not state that Jabir has the *ta'weel* of the entire Qur'an, but rather that he knew the realities of that particular verse. This demonstrates two additional important points. The first is that Jabir was an elderly man by the time Imam al-Baqir ﷺ stated that he knew the reality of this verse, showing the reward of a lifetime of dedication to the Qur'an and Prophetic household ﷺ. Secondly, if Jabir truly understood the *ta'weel* of this verse, it demonstrates how high his station was in the eyes of Allah ﷻ to have been granted such detailed and intimate knowledge.[37]

The Praises of Imam Ja'far al-Sadiq ﷺ for Jabir

Imam Ja'far al-Sadiq ﷺ has narrated on the authority of his grandfathers that when Allah ﷻ revealed the verse, 'Say: I demand not of you any reward for it (the toils of being the Prophet) except the love of my closest relations' (42:23), the Prophet ﷺ rose and said, 'A right for me has been imposed upon you. Will you pay it to me?' but no one responded and so he ﷺ went away. On the following day, the Prophet ﷺ again stood and asked the same question. Again no one answered, so he ﷺ left and went away. On the third day, he also asked the same question but this time addressed his companions

---

[36]The Arabic text of this states:

اللهم فقهه في الدين وعلمه التأويل

[37] For further reading refer to the book *Usul al-Tafseer wa al-Ta'weel* (*Principles of Commentary and Real Meanings*) by Ayatollah Syed Kamal al-Hayderi, published by Dar al-Faraaqid, Qum, Iran.

and explained, 'the right is not gold or silver, or food or drink.' The companions then queried, 'So what is right?' The Prophet ﷺ replied, 'Allah has revealed these Words of His, 'Say: I demand not of you any reward for it, except the love of my closest relations.' The companions responded, 'this is the best right.'

Imam al-Sadiq ؏ continued, "I swear by Allah that no one was loyal to this right except for seven people. They are: Salman, Abu Dharr, Ammar, Miqdad b. Aswad, Jabir b. Abdullah, the retainer of Allah's Messenger, and Zayd b. Arqam."[38]

Ayatollah Syed al-Khoei in his *Rijal* quotes al-Kishi, who narrates from Imam al-Sadiq ؏, "Indeed Jabir was the last remaining companion of the Messenger of Allah, blessings of Allah be upon him and his family. He was also a person partial and obedient towards us the Ahl al-Bayt. He would sit in the great Masjid of the Prophet ﷺ and would wear a black turban. He would call out 'O Baqir al-'Ilm! O Baqir al-'Ilm, to the extent that the people of Medina would say, 'Jabir has become crazy.' Jabir would reply, 'No, I swear by Allah that I have not, however I have heard from the Messenger of Allah, blessings be upon him and his family say, and 'You will meet a man from my family. His name is my name; his merits are my merits; and he will split open knowledge thoroughly.' It is for him that I call out what I call."[39]

Imam Ja'far al-Sadiq ؏ also specifically named Jabir as among those to be raised in the *raj'ah*[40] to participate in the movement of justice and victories with the Awaited Saviour of Humanity, Imam al-Mahdi ؏. It is narrated that he ؏ said, "When the Qa'im will rise from behind the Ka'bah, Allah will resurrect twenty-seven people for him. Fourteen of them are from

---

[38] *Tanqih al-Manqaal*, vol. 1, p. 200; *The Life of Imam Muhammad al-Baqir*, Ansariyan Publications, 2003, p. 490.

[39] *Mo'jam Rijal al-Hadith*, vol. 4, p. 331.

[40] A theological belief that at the end of times, both the 'best of the best companions' and the 'worst of the worst enemies of God' will be raised up from the graves to view and participate in the victory of God's justice on earth. This is because the 'best' strove hard for this in their lives and will be rewarded by seeing their efforts come to fruition. Similarly, the 'worst' who strove to deny God, created bloodshed and injustice will have to bear the sight of their efforts be defeated. For further information refer to '*180 Questions about Islam*,' vol. 2 by Ayatollah Makarim Shirazi or the online links below:

    a. https://bit.ly/33du29t
    b. https://bit.ly/337tiCN

the nation of Prophet Musa ﷺ who are described in the verse 'And of Musa's people there is a group who guide people with the truth and thereby do justice' (7:159). There are also the seven companions of the cave, (and the companions of Prophet Muhammad ﷺ) Miqdad b. Aswad al-Kindi, Jabir b. Abdullah al-Ansari, the believer of the nation of Firaun, and Yusha b. Noon - the successor of Prophet Musa ﷺ."[41]

---

[41] Al-Bahraani, Hashim, *The Qa'em in the Qur'an*, p. 66, www.shiabooks.ca.

Chapter 2

The Story of the Ansar

The Verses of the Qur'an Praising the Companions

In this section we will mention some of the verses generally praising the companions of the Prophet ﷺ and the verses specifically revealed in honour of or in regards to the conduct of the Ansar. Although there are times when the companions and the Ansar are critiqued by the Qur'an or shown guidance as to how to reform their actions, this does not necessarily mean that Jabir is included in those verses as well, since often history highlights particular individuals that rebelled or had forsaken their responsibilities, but the Qur'an spoke in general terms where necessary. Similarly, as mentioned above with regards to Banu Haritha and Banu Salima, in verse 3:122, Jabir felt the need to include himself or speak in general terms as to how the tribe was affected at the Battle of Uhud.

As Jabir was both a leading companion and a member of the Ansar, the purpose of this is to see generally how the Qur'an spoke about both classifications so as to appreciate Jabir's general role within these groups. Where appropriate, we will comment upon particulars that will relate to Jabir.

Verse 1: (7:157) "*Those who follow the Messenger*, the unlettered Prophet, whom they find written in what they have of the Torah and the Gospel, who enjoins upon them what is right and forbids them what is wrong, and makes lawful for them the good things and prohibits for them the evil and *relieves them of their burden and the shackles which were upon them. So, they who have believed in him, honoured him,* *supported him and followed the light which was sent down with him - it is those who will be the successful ones."*

Verse 2: (39:23) "Allah has sent down the best statement: a consistent Book wherein is reiteration. *The skins shiver therefrom of those who fear their Lord; then their skins and their hearts relax at the remembrance of Allah.* That is the guidance of Allah by which He guides whom He wills. And one whom Allah leaves astray - for him there is no guide."

Verse 3: (32:15-16) *"Only those believe in* Our verses who, when they are reminded of them, fall down in prostration and exalt (Allah) with praise of their Lord, and they are not arrogant. They arise from (their) beds; they supplicate their Lord in fear and aspiration, and from what We have provided them, they spend.

Verse 4: (42:36-39) "So whatever thing you have been given - it is but (for) enjoyment of this worldly life. But what is with Allah is better and more lasting for *those who have believed and upon their Lord rely. And those who avoid the major sins and immoralities, and when they are angry, they forgive. And those who have responded to their Lord* and established prayer and whose affair is (determined by) consultation among themselves, and from what We have provided them, they spend. And those who, when tyranny strikes them, they defend themselves."

The Verses of the Qur'an Revealed Specifically about the Ansar

Verse 1: (2:195) After the death of the Prophet ﷺ, the Muslims engaged in various expeditions against the empires surrounding its borders. Once a large Roman force marched from Constantinople and so the Muslim army gathered and formed their ranks. One of them broke the rank and attacked so ferociously penetrating the Roman ranks, thereafter returning back to the Muslim forces. The Muslims began shouting at him saying, "Glory be to Allah, he is throwing himself into destruction by his own hands" quoting the verse "Spend in the path of Allah and do not throw (lead yourselves) into destruction by (the doing of) your own hands."

Upon hearing this, Abu Ayyub al-Ansari stood up to correct them saying, "O people, you are interpreting this verse in this way, whereas it was actually revealed in regards to us the Ansar. For when Allah gave strength to Islam and there were many people to assist its cause, we said to each other without the Prophet ﷺ knowing that, 'Our fields have been destroyed. We should therefore stay in Medina to repair the damage done.' In response to what we had intended, Allah revealed the verse "...Do not throw yourselves into destruction..." The destruction referred to is our staying behind in Medina to tend to our fields."[42] The same incident is also narrated by Abu Ayyub saying, "We (the Ansar) know this verse best for it was revealed in reference to us. We remained in the company of the Prophet ﷺ, fought many battles with him, and were there to assist him. However, when Islam spread and became dominant, we the Ansar gathered together for the love of Islam and said, 'Allah has honoured us with the companionship of the Messenger of Allah and giving us the ability to assist him until Islam spread and its adherents have multiplied greatly. We had given preference to Islam over our own families, our wealth and our children, and now that the wars have stopped, we should return to our families and children and tend to them. It was with reference to this that the verse (2:195) was revealed. So, the destruction being referred to is staying with our families and properties and neglecting the struggle on the battlefield."[43] [44]

Verse 2: (9-100) "And the first forerunners (in the faith) among the Muhajireen and *the Ansar* and those who followed them with good conduct - *Allah is pleased with them and they are pleased with Him, and He*

---

[42] Bayhaqi, vol. 9, p. 45, and narrated similarly on p. 99; *Hayaat al-Sahaba*, vol.1, p. 460.

[43] *Tafseer ibn Katheer*, vol. 1, p. 228.

[44] Although Abu Ayyub al-Ansari disputed the application of this verse by trying to restrict it to just its purpose of revelation, commentators reject this approach. For example, Allama Tabataba'i, who also quotes the narration of Abu Ayyub says, "The order is anyhow general, and it prohibits any commission or omission which may cause perdition, whether it is on the side of excess or deficiency. For example, miserliness and avarice when preparing for war would weaken the fighters and make the army of Islam the target of the enemy; and many would be killed. On the other hand, extravagance in expenditure would bring poverty and misery to such a spender, degrade him in society and make life unbearable. Both of these actions arc prohibited by this verse." Also "The difference of the traditions in interpreting the meaning of this verse supports what we have said that this verse is general and covers both extremes (extravagance and miserliness) in spending, and that it is not confined to spending only, but covers other aspects also where 'casting oneself into perdition' can be applied." (*Tafseer al-Mizan*)

has prepared for them gardens beneath which rivers flow, wherein they will abide forever. That is the great attainment."

Verse 3: (9:117-119) "Allah has already forgiven the Prophet and the Muhajireen and the Ansar who followed him in the hour of difficulty after the hearts of a party of them had almost inclined (to doubt), and then He forgave them. Indeed, He was to them Kind and Merciful. And [He also forgave] the three who were left behind [and regretted their error] to the point that the earth closed in on them in spite of its vastness and their souls confined them and they were certain that there is no refuge from Allah except in Him. Then He turned to them so that they could repent. Indeed, Allah is the Accepting of Repentance, the Merciful. O you who have believed, fear Allah and be with those who are true."

Verse 4: (59:8-10) "For the poor emigrants who were expelled from their homes and their properties, seeking bounty from Allah and (His) approval and supporting Allah and His Messenger, (there is also a share). *Those are the truthful. And (also for) those who were settled in al-Medina and (adopted) the faith before them (the Ansar). They love those who emigrated to them and find not any want in their chests of what the emigrants were given, but gave (them) preference over themselves, even though they were in privation.* And whoever is protected from the stinginess of his soul - it is those who will be the successful ones. And [there is a share for] those who came after them, saying, "Our Lord, forgive us and our brothers who preceded us in faith and put not in our hearts (any) resentment toward those who have believed. Our Lord, indeed You are Kind and Merciful."

The Narrations Regarding the Ansar

Hadith 1: The Prophet ﷺ is narrated to have said, "O assembly of the Ansar, has Allah not favoured you by granting you strong faith, special virtues and the best of names, namely the Ansar (the Helpers) of the religion of Allah, and the Ansar of the Messenger of Allah. If everyone walks a valley and the Ansar walk in another valley, I shall walk in the valley of the Ansar."[45]

---

[45] Haythami, vol. 1, p. 31; *Hayaaat al-Sahaba*, vol.1, p. 396; *Al-Bidayah wa al-Nihayah*, vol. 4, p. 358; *Kanz al-Ummal*, vol. 7, p. 135; *Hayaat al-Sahaba*, vol.1, p. 395.

Hadith 2: The Prophet ﷺ is narrated to have said, "I will be waiting for you at the pond of Kawthar."[46]

Hadith 3: The Prophet ﷺ is narrated to have been on the pulpit and said, "Listen well! While all of the other people are like my outer garments, the Ansar are like my inner garments.[47] Had it not been for the virtue of migration (*Hijrah*) I would have wanted to be one of them! Whoever assumes authority over the Ansar should be good to the righteous of them and overlook the sinful of them. Whoever hurts the Ansar has hurt me."[48] "O assembly of the Muhajireen, while your numbers will continue to grow (as more people migrate), the population of the Ansar will not increase more than they are today. The Ansar are like my personal tree trunk with whom I have taken shelter. You should therefore honour the honourable ones among them and overlook the sinful ones."[49]

Hadith 4: Imam Ali ؓ is narrated to have said, "A person who does not like the Ansar and does not recognise the rights due to them cannot be a true believer. By Allah, they used their swords, their power of speech and the generosity of their hearts to nurture Islam, just like a mare nurtures her foal in a green pasture. They took the Messenger to their town, assisted him and sympathised with him. May Allah reward them with the best of rewards. Thereafter, we (the Muhajireen) came to them and took up residence in their homes. They preferred us above themselves to the extent that they would even draw lots to decide which of them would be host to us. Eventually, from the depths of their hearts they allowed us to have greater rights than them in their own wealth.[50] They even sacrificed their lives for the

---

[46] *Hayaat al-Sahaba*, vol. 1, p. 397.

[47] *Al-Bidayah wa al-Nihayah*, vol. 4, p. 356; *Hayaat al-Sahaba*, vol.1, p.397.

[48] Haythami, vol. 10, p. 35.

[49] Ibid, p. 26.

[50] This praise for the Ansar has many lessons for the current global refugee crisis. Many countries are deporting, detaining, processing or rehousing refugees. For those countries that have accepted a quota to rehouse refugees, depending on local laws, refugees may either be found government sponsored housing, or a family may offer to rehouse the refugees themselves. This may be done by either offering entry into their own houses or if they own a second house, by offering this as a place to the refugees. The greatest and well-known trait of the Ansar was to offer their own houses despite the difficulties placed on wealth or space. The praise of Imam Ali ؓ

protection of Allah's Prophet ﷺ. May the mercy and blessings of Allah be showered upon them."[51]

Hadith 5: The Prophet ﷺ said, "Had it not been for the great virtue of *Hijrah*, I would have been a man from the Ansar!"[52]

Hadith 6: The Prophet ﷺ said, "As far as I am concerned, you (the Ansar) turn out in large numbers when situations are hazardous and turn out in small numbers when the occasion arrives for receiving something (you care little for receiving things for yourselves)."[53]

Hadith 7: The Prophet ﷺ said to Abu Talha, "Convey my salutation to your people (the Ansar) and inform them that as far as I know, they are an extremely chaste and patient people."[54]

Hadith 8: The Prophet ﷺ said, "No harm can come to a woman whether she stays between two homes of the Ansar, or between her own parents (meaning that the Ansar would treat her as her own parents would treat her)."[55]

Hadith 9: The Prophet ﷺ gave food to a hungry and patient family of the Ansar and told them, "May Allah grant you the most sublime of rewards. O assembly of the Ansar! As far as I know you have always been the most chaste and patient people, however after I die, you shall soon see that others

---

is due to their love of the Prophet ﷺ, those who had struggled early with the Prophet ﷺ and recognised that they had lost almost everything, either in their time in the *she'b* of Abu Talib ؇ or through their migration, and having recognised this, they were not passive but offered so much in the way of helping the mission of Islam. The current refugee crisis allows Muslims around the world to emulate the practise of the Ansar and share in the great precedent set by them. When governments accept quotas for distribution, families may have in advance discussed the prospect of helping refugees becoming rehoused, providing for their early needs, creating a 'buddy system' whereby families join with refugee families in helping them learn the language, find friendship, work, understanding the local areas, customs and find a place in society. In this, we may also then be praised as Imam Ali ؇ praised the Ansar, God-Willing.

[51] Abu Nau'aym, *Al-Dalaa'il*, p. 105; *Hayaat al-Sahaba*, vol. 1, pp. 121-2.

[52] *Al-Bidayah wa al-Nihayah*, vol. 4, p. 358; *Kanz al-Ummal*, vol. 7, p. 135; *Hayaat al-Sahaba*, vol.1, p. 395.

[53] *Kanz al-Ummal*, vol. 7, p. 136; *Hayaat al-Sahaba*, vol.1, p. 397.

[54] Ibid.; *Al-Mustadrak* of al-Haakim, vol. 4, p. 79; *Hayaat al-Sahaba*, vol.1, p. 397.

[55] Haythami, vol. 7, p., 40.

will be given preference over you in leadership and in the distribution of wealth. I urge you to be patient until you meet me at the Pond of Kawthar."[56]

Hadith 10: Sa'ad b. Ubaadah al-Ansari once visited the Prophet ﷺ with his son. When he greeted him with the salutation, the Prophet ﷺ said, "Here and here" making Sa'ad and his son sit on his right hand side (a sign of respect and honour) saying, "Welcome to the Ansar, welcome to the Ansar!" Sa'ad then made his son stand in front of the Prophet ﷺ who bade him to sit closer to him. The youth came closer and began to kiss the hand of the Prophet ﷺ who responded by saying, "I am from the Ansar and from the children of the Ansar (meaning that there was no reason to elevate him when he felt as though he was truly one of them)." Sa'ad replied, "May Allah honour you as you have honoured us!" To which the Prophet ﷺ said, "Indeed Allah has honoured you before I could honour you. However, after I die, you shall soon see that others will be given preference over you. I urge you to remain patient until you meet me at the Pond of Kawthar."[57]

Hadith 11: Abdullah b. Abbas narrates that Hasan b. Thabit al-Ansari would compose poetry praising and in defence of the Prophet ﷺ whenever the pagans would compose poetry against the Prophet ﷺ.[58]

Hadith 12: When it became difficult for the Ansar to continuously use camels to draw and carry water, they gathered before the Prophet ﷺ to request that a flowing river be made for them (which required digging and heavy work). The Prophet ﷺ greeted them saying, "A warm welcome to the Ansar! I shall grant you anything that you ask me for today and anything that I ask from Allah for you will be granted." The Ansar consulted each other and said, "Let us make the most of this opportunity and ask the Prophet ﷺ to pray for our forgiveness" and they asked this from him. The Prophet ﷺ then supplicated asking, "O Allah, forgive the Ansar, the wives of the Ansar, the children of the Ansar, and the grandchildren of the Ansar."[59] Another narration states that the Prophet ﷺ also prayed for

---

[56] *Kanz al-Ummal*, vol. 7, p. 136; *Al-Mustadrak*, vol. 4, p. 79; *Hayaat al-Sahaba*, vol.1, p.398.
[57] *Kanz al-Ummal*, vol. 7, p. 134.
[58] *Al-Mustadrak*, vol. 3, p. 544.
[59] Ahmad, vol. 3, p. 139; *Hayaat al-Sahaba*, vol. 1, p. 403.

forgiveness for the "neighbours of the Ansar" and the "friends of the Ansar."[60]

The Prophet ﷺ also supplicated, "O Allah, give honour to the Ansar through whom Allah established the religion, who gave me shelter, who assisted me and who gave me their ardent support. They are my companions in this world, and will be my party in the hereafter, and the first of my nation to enter the paradise."[61]

Hadith 13: Waa'il b. Hujar narrates that the Prophet ﷺ said, "Whoever loves the Ansar loves them because of his love for me, and whoever hates the Ansar hates them because of his hatred for me."[62]

Hadith 14: Abdullah b. Abbas reports that the Prophet ﷺ said, "Harbouring enmity for Banu Hashim and for the Ansar will lead to disbelief (*kufr*) and harbouring enmity for the Arabs is a sign of hypocrisy."[63] [64]

---

[60] Haythami, vol. 10, pp. 40-1.

[61] Ibid.

[62] Haythami, vol. 9, p. 376.

[63] Ibid., vol. 10, p. 27.

[64] Harbouring enmity here means unwarranted or unjustified enmity for those who are righteous. Having enmity towards and disavowing the enemies of Allah ﷻ is an obligatory action, no matter which group they come from. For example, Allah ﷻ says in the Holy Qur'an that, "Stand firm in justice though it may be against your own selves, your parents or your relatives" (4:135). This is to ensure that no proximity of any nature is built between a person and the enemy of Allah ﷻ. For example, Allah ﷻ also says in the Holy Qur'an that, "And do not incline to those who are unjust whatsoever, lest the fire touch you" (11:113). In the branches of religion this action is called *Tabarra*, or disavowal of Allah's ﷻ enemies.

Chapter 3

The Story of Jabir and his Community, the Ansar's Conversion to Islam and the Early Period with the Prophet ﷺ

Introduction

Sheikh Fawzi Aal Sayf states, "Since the first day that he met the Messenger of Allah ﷺ at al-Aqaba while accompanying his father, Jabir felt a special care and blessings from the Prophet ﷺ towards him. This feeling used to overwhelm him with content and deep love towards the Messenger of God ﷺ."[65]

Confirmation of Jabir b. Abdullah being among those at the second pledge of allegiance, prior to the Prophet Muhammad's ﷺ migration to Medina, is given by Imam Muhammad al-Baqir ؏ himself. Zurara b. A'yun narrates[66] from Aba Ja'far al-Baqir ؏ who said: "Abdullah Abu Jabir (Jabir's

---

[65] *Rijal Hawl al-Rasool wa Ahl Baytihi*, p. 219.
[66] Chain of narrators: Mohammad b. Masoud said that Ali b. Mohammad b. Yazid al-Qummi told me that Ahmad b. Mohammad b. Isa al-Koummei told me from b. Fidaal from Abdullah b. Bakeer (Boukayr) from Zurara.

father) was one of the seventy,[67] as well as one of 'the twelve'. Jabir is one of 'the seventy,' but not one of 'the twelve'.[68]

Jabir learned from the earliest periods of Islam the difficulties that the Prophet ﷺ had to face, and the way in which he would call the people in Mecca, and those who visited the city to think about his message. He narrates that, "The Messenger of Allah ﷺ used to appear before the people during the *hajj* season and say, "Is there any man who can take me to his people, for the Quraysh have prevented me from conveying the speech (the Qur'an/Message) of my Lord?!'"[69] It was Jabir's tribe that would respond to this plea for a fair opportunity to present the Word of Allah.

In this chapter we will mention the history of Prophet Muhammad's ﷺ engagement with the Ansar until his migration to Medina. Since this is not intended to be a detailed review of the events, attention will be paid to build a picture of the Ansar's interactions and the narrations from or about Jabir.

Inviting the Aws and Khazraj

After the revelation, and the invitation to his own family and the people of Mecca, the Prophet ﷺ exerted all efforts to engage with as many tribes as possible. Al-Abbas, the uncle of the Prophet ﷺ narrates that the Messenger ﷺ once said to him, "I do not see any help forthcoming from you or your brother. Will you take me to the marketplace tomorrow so that we may stop at the places where the various tribes are staying?" This was during the time when all of the Arabs were gathered there for the *hajj* pilgrimage.[70] Hasan b. Thabit reports that he was performing *hajj* when the Prophet ﷺ was calling people to accept Islam and his companions were being tortured.[71]

Jabir narrates, "The Messenger of Allah ﷺ presented his case to the people as they stayed at their camps (during the *hajj* season). He would say,

---

[67] 'The twelve' is the number of those from the Medinan tribes who first paid allegiance to the Prophet ﷺ. After having disseminated this among their people, a second delegation was sent in the following year as confirmation and preparation for the invite of the Prophet ﷺ to migrate to Medina. This second group of people are known as 'the seventy' individuals who participated in that pledge. Details of this story will follow.

[68] *Qasas al-Sahaba wa al-Tabi'in*, p. 77.

[69] *Sunan b. Majah*, The Book of the Sunnah, Hadith 201.

[70] *Al-Bidayah wa al-Nihayah*, vol. 3, p. 140; p. *Hayaat al-Sahaba*, vol. 1, p.114.

[71] Waaqidi as quoted in *Al-Isaabah*, vol. 4, p. 312; *Hayaat al-Sahaba*, vol. 1, p. 117.

'Who will take me to his people because the Quraysh are preventing me from propagating the Word of Allah ﷻ?' Eventually a man from Hamdaan came to the Prophet ﷺ. After some discussions, the Prophet ﷺ enquired as to whether they had military might, (informing the man that their commitment would require military struggle) to which he replied that they do. However, the man feared that his people may not honour his commitment to the Prophet ﷺ and said, 'I shall first go to my people and inform them. Thereafter I will come back to you.' The Prophet ﷺ agreed and the man left. It was from this meeting that a delegation from the Ansar met the Prophet ﷺ in the month of Rajab."[72]

Imam Ali ؑ is narrated to have said, "During the seasons of *hajj*, the Messenger ﷺ used to go out and call the various tribes to Islam, however none of them were prepared to accept his message. He used to meet the various tribes at the market places of Majinna and Ukaaz, and at Mina until he would meet the same tribes returning year after year. The tribes used to say to him: 'When will the time come for you to give up hope on us because you have been meeting with us for such a long time?' Eventually the time came when the Most Powerful and Most Honoured Allah decided matters in favour of the tribes of the Ansar. The Messenger ﷺ presented Islam to them and they readily accepted it."[73] [74]

The Messenger ﷺ met a group of them at a place called 'Aqaba as they were busy shaving off their hair after performing *hajj*. Umm Sa'ad narrates, "There were six or seven people." The Prophet ﷺ sat down with them, conveyed the message of Islam and recited parts of the Qur'an to them. When they asked the Prophet ﷺ to present to them what Allah had revealed,

---

[72] *Fath al-Bari*, vol. 7, p. 156; *Hayaat al-Sahaba*, vol. 1, p. 375.

[73] Abu Nu'aym in *Al-Dalaai'l*, p. 105; *Hayaat al-Sahaba*, vol. 1, p.122.

[74] Jabir is quoted as having narrated that the first time the news about the Prophet's ﷺ Messengership reached Medina was by virtue of a jinn that belonged to a particular Medinan woman. It arrived in the form of a white bird and perched upon a wall and said, 'Will you not sit down so that we may converse and exchange stories?' The jinn then said to the woman, 'A Prophet has been sent to Mecca who forbids adultery and deprives the rest of us because we can no longer eavesdrop on the conversations of the angels.'" (Ibn Sa'ad, *Tabaqat al-Kubra*, vol. 1, p. 190). This is also attributed to Imam Zain al-Abideen ؑ who states that the jinn's name was under the control of a lady named Fatima (*Al-Bidayah wa al-Nihayah*, vol. 2, p. 338). The author does not accept these narrations as being correct, but has mentioned them as they are well-known.

he recited verses 35-52 of Surah Ibrahim.[75] Their hearts were moved by these words and they accepted Islam.

As they were engaged in conversation with the Prophet ﷺ, al-Abbas passed by. Recognising the voice of the Prophet ﷺ he said, "O my nephew, who are these people with you?" The Prophet ﷺ replied, "These are residents of Yathrib from the tribes of Aws and Khazraj. I gave them the same call that I had given to so many other tribes before them, and they accepted my message and believe in what I have said. They also said that they will take me back with them to their city."

---

[75] "And [mention, O Muhammad], when Abraham said, "My Lord, make this city [Makkah] secure and keep me and my sons away from worshipping idols. My Lord, indeed they have led astray many among the people. So whoever follows me - then he is of me; and whoever disobeys me - indeed, You are [yet] Forgiving and Merciful. Our Lord, I have settled some of my descendants in an uncultivated valley near Your sacred House, our Lord, that they may establish prayer. So make hearts among the people incline toward them and provide for them from the fruits that they might be grateful. Our Lord, indeed You know what we conceal and what we declare, and nothing is hidden from Allah on the earth or in the heaven. Praise to Allah, who has granted to me in old age Ishmael and Isaac. Indeed, my Lord is the Hearer of supplication. My Lord, make me an establisher of prayer, and [many] from my descendants. Our Lord, and accept my supplication. Our Lord, forgive me and my parents and the believers the Day the account is established." And never think that Allah is unaware of what the wrongdoers do. He only delays them for a Day when eyes will stare [in horror]. Racing ahead, their heads raised up, their glance does not come back to them, and their hearts are void. And, [O Muhammad], warn the people of a Day when the punishment will come to them and those who did wrong will say, "Our Lord, delay us for a short term; we will answer Your call and follow the messengers." [But it will be said], "Had you not sworn, before, that for you there would be no cessation? And you lived among the dwellings of those who wronged themselves, and it had become clear to you how We dealt with them. And We presented for you [many] examples." And they had planned their plan, but with Allah is [recorded] their plan, even if their plan had been [sufficient] to do away with the mountains. So never think that Allah will fail in His promise to His messengers. Indeed, Allah is Exalted in Might and Owner of Retribution. [It will be] on the Day the earth will be replaced by another earth, and the heavens [as well], and all creatures will come out before Allah, the One, the Prevailing. And you will see the criminals that Day bound together in shackles. Their garments of liquid pitch and their faces covered by the Fire. So that Allah will recompense every soul for what it earned. Indeed, Allah is swift in account. This [Qur'an] is notification for the people that they may be warned thereby and that they may know that He is but one God and that those of understanding will be reminded."

Al-Abbas descended from his ride, tied it up and then said, "O people of the Aws and Khazraj! This is my nephew and the person that I love the most. If you accept his message, believe in him, and intend to take him with you to your city, then I want you to make a promise so that my heart may be content. Promise me that you will never desert him nor ever betray him."

As'ad b. Zurara was the first to respond by saying, "O Messenger of Allah ﷺ! Permit me to answer him in a manner that will neither upset you, nor appear disrespectful to you. However, the reply will confirm that we have accepted your message and it will express our faith in you." The Prophet ﷺ, pleased with this permitted the response saying, "You may reply to him, for I have complete confidence in you."

Facing the Prophet ﷺ, As'ad stated, "O Messenger of Allah, there is a path to every call. While some paths are easy, others are difficult. Today you have called us to something that is both new and difficult for people to accept. You have asked us to forsake our religions, and follow you in your religion. This is not an easy task; however we have accepted your call. You have advised us to severe all (wrong) ties we have with both close and distant relatives (by following you and not them). This is not an easy thing to do, however we have accepted your call. You have invited us to Islam, even though we are a strong group living in a place that is powerful and mighty. No one could ever imagine that our leader would be someone who is not from among us, whose own people have ostracised him, and whose own uncles have deserted him. This is not an easy task, but we have accepted it.[76] These things appear difficult for everyone except those whose welfare Allah has decided upon and who foresee good in its results. We have accepted your call with our tongues, our hearts and our hands because we believe in what you have conveyed to us and we accept it with conviction that has settled deep within our hearts. We pledge our commitment to you in all of this, and we pledge it to our Lord and your Lord as well. Allah's

---

[76] The speech of As'ad regarding severing ties with their own practises and accepting a leader who was not seen as from among them should be reflected upon in regards to how people will need to see Imam al-Mahdi ﷺ. It may be argued that every community will feel equally as distanced to him for not having any apparent connection, but just like these were unimportant considerations to the Ansar, so too they should be to any adherent of Imam al-Mahdi ﷺ; and just like universal values and the truth were of great importance to the Ansar, so too these should be for the helpers of Imam al-Mahdi ﷺ.

Hand is above our hands (approving this pledge). We will spill our blood to protect yours and give our lives for yours. We safeguard you as we safeguard ourselves, our children and our wives. Should we fulfil this pledge, it shall be for Allah; and should we betray this pledge, it shall be betraying Allah to the cost of making us the most wretched of people. O Messenger of Allah, all that we have told you is the absolute truth and we seek Allah's assistance (to help us fulfil our pledges)."

As'ad then turned to al-Abbas and addressed him saying, "As for you who have used your words to be a barrier between the Messenger of Allah ﷺ and us, Allah knows best what you meant by your words; but you have mentioned that this is your nephew and a person whom you love most. However, we have cut ourselves from people who are near and distant, as well as from blood relatives. We testify that he is certainly the Messenger of Allah ﷺ whom Allah Himself has sent. He is certainly not a liar and what he has brought does not at all resemble the words of a man. As for your statement that you cannot be content with us until we make a promise to you, we shall certainly not refuse such a request made borne out of concern for the Messenger of Allah ﷺ. You may therefore take from us whatever promise you wish."

Turning again to the Prophet ﷺ, As'ad continued, "O Messenger of Allah ﷺ, take any promise you wish from us and make any conditions from the side of your Lord that you wish to make."[77]

They accepted Allah, his Messenger and religion, and pledged to meet him the following year at *hajj*. This monumental incident in the history of Islam is referred to as 'The first pledge of 'Aqaba'. Having returned to their home city of Yathrib, the Ansar sent a message to the Prophet ﷺ requesting him to send someone to them who could continue to teach them and call people towards Islam, as this would cause people to accept it more readily. The Prophet ﷺ sent Mus'ab b. Umayr who stayed with As'ad, and recited the Qur'an and taught them more about the religion. Mus'ab's mission was increasingly successful, until there was hardly a home from the tribes of the Aws and Khazraj that had not been guided by Allah ﷻ. The Ansar even gave Mus'ab the title of al-Muqri, meaning 'the mentor'.[78]

---

[77] *Al-Dalaa'il*, p. 105; *Hayaat al-Sahaba*, vol. 1, p. 126.
[78] *Al-Dalaa'il*, pp. 107-8; *Hayaat al-Sahaba*, vol. 1, (pp. 136-37).

As'ad took Mus'ab to various tribes, in particular Banu Abd al-Ash'hal and Banu Zafar, in order to convey the message of Islam. They entered one of the orchards of the Banu Zafar where there was a well called Bir Maraq. The two of them sat in the orchard and many Muslims gathered there with them. During that period, the leaders of the Banu Abd al-Ash'hal were Sa'ad b. Mu'aadh, and Usayd b. Hudhayr, who were steadfast on the practices of their forefathers. Sa'ad was also the cousin of As'ad.

When Sa'ad heard about this gathering he said to Usayd, "Have you no father (self-respect)?! Go to those two men who have come to our locality to make fools of our people. Admonish and reprimand them for coming to our area. I would have done this for you had it not been for my relationship with As'ad, for he is my cousin and so I cannot confront him. Usayd took his spear and went towards them. Seeing this, As'ad said to Mus'ab, "He is the leader of his people. He is coming to you, so be sincere to Allah when speaking with him." Mus'ab replied, "I will speak to him if he is willing to sit down."

When Usayd stood in front of them, he began to abuse and reprimand them saying, "Why have you come to us? Have you come to make fools of our people? If you want to preserve your lives you will leave us alone!" Mus'ab responded calmly, "Will you not be seated and listen for a while? If you like what you hear then you can accept it, otherwise we shall stop doing what you dislike."[79] Usayd agreed to this, struck his spear in the ground, and sat down. Mus'ab then spoke to him about Islam and recited the Qur'an to him. They saw on Usayd's face a glow and gentleness indicating his warmth and acceptance of the message. When they finished conveying the message

---

[79] This is a great example of the characteristics that we should adopt when calling people to Islam. In modern society, it is normal for representatives of various religions to have stalls on the streets, outside places of interest, or in universities. They will extend literature, free gifts and invite people to programs to know more about the religion or ideas being conveyed. It is sad however, and not uncommon to see individuals becoming overzealous with the presentation of their religion or ideas to others, and this includes Muslims too. The Qur'an advises, "Call to the way of your Lord with wisdom and good exhortation," and Mus'ab provided us with an excellent example of this. In doing so, it opens the door for discussion by leaving a kind and rational person no choice but to at least listen, and the choice that if he finds the discussion tedious, or of no benefit to freely depart from it. Much may be learned from the manners of this practise employed by Mus'ab, may Allah be pleased with him.

of Islam, Usayd spoke saying, "How excellent and beautiful this is! What do you do when you want to enter the fold of this religion?" They replied, "Take a bath to cleanse yourself, purify your clothes, recite the witness statement to bear the truth of Allah and His Messenger ﷺ and perform a prayer."[80] Usayd stood up and performed as he was informed. After having testified to his faith, he addressed Mus'ab and As'ad saying, "Behind me is a man who I will soon send to you. If he follows you, then not a soul from his people will fail to follow him. He is Sa'ad b. Mu'aadh."

Usayd then took his spear and went to where Sa'ad and his people had gathered. When he saw Usayd approaching he exclaimed, "I swear by Allah that Usayd is coming to you with a look that is very much different from the one that he left you with." Usayd stopped at the gathering and said, "I have spoken to the two men and see nothing wrong with what they say. I have also forbidden them from what they do, and they accepted to do as I tell them. I have also found out that Banu Haaritha tribe have left to kill As'ad b. Zurara because they found out that he is your cousin and thereby wish to insult you." Hearing the news, Sa'ad was filled with anger. He stood and grabbed his spear saying, "By Allah, you have done nothing!"

Sa'ad went straight to where As'ad and Mus'ab were and saw them sitting in peace, so he realised that Usayb had wanted him to go there to listen to them! He also stood in front of them and reprimanded them. Addressing As'ad he said, "O Abu Umamah, by Allah, if it was not for our relationship you would never have thought about doing this. You dare to introduce into our locality something that we detest?" Mus'ab followed exactly the same protocol, inviting Sa'ad to be seated and to give a chance for him to convey what he wanted to, and the promise of halting if Sa'ad disapproved. Mus'ab read from Surah al-Zukhruf and the same radiance and gentleness that had appeared on Usayb shone on Sa'ad. After some time

---

[80] The minimum requirement to enter into Islam is the *Shahadah* or witnessing which comprises of two testimonies: I bear witness there is no god but Allah, and I bear witness that Muhammad ﷺ is His servant and messenger. The practises instructed by Mus'ab are additional and assists in the purification process. Mus'ab may have suggested these as he wanted Usayd to purify his body and clothes as well so as to be acquainted to the rituals of self-purification. From the narration it appears that Usayd was very willing to learn and practise Islam, so Mus'ab may have sought to maximize this.

Sa'ad too asked about the way to enter into the religion and was instructed the same as Usayb, to which he obliged and also became a Muslim.

When Sa'ad's tribe saw him return they also exclaimed, "We swear by Allah that Sa'ad is returning with a look very different to the one that he left you with. When he stopped by them he addressed them saying, "O Banu Abd al-Ash'hal, how do you see my status among you?" They replied, "You are our leader, the one with the best opinions and most far sighted!" Sa'ad then conveyed the message of Islam to them, and by the evening, there was not a single person from the tribe who had not embraced Islam. Banu Abd al-Ash'hal was the first full family of the Ansar to accept Islam.

As'ad and Mus'ab returned to their house where Mus'ab continued his call towards Islam. Eventually there was not a single household that was devoid of a Muslim, making up the earliest conversion of what was to become the Ansar of Medina. Successful, Mus'ab then returned to Mecca to report the news about the fervour that was building up in the city of Yathrib.

Seventy Companions from the Ansar Pledge Assistance at the Valley of 'Aqaba

Jabir narrates that during the ten years that the Prophet ﷺ lived in Mecca after announcing his prophethood, he would visit different tribes when they came for *hajj*. This was at the market places of Ukaaz and Majinna. He would ask the people, "Who will give me asylum? Who will assist me so that I can propagate the message of my Lord? Whoever does this will receive paradise." However, he found very few people ready to grant him assistance. It reached such a low ebb that when tribes from across Arabia would leave for *hajj*, their family members would warn them and say, "Beware that man from the Quraysh does not beguile you." They would point out the Prophet ﷺ when he walked past the camps so that wherever he went people were wary. In fact, his uncle Abu Lahab would follow him and when he tried engaging in discussion, Abu Lahab would accuse the Prophet ﷺ of sorcery and try to falsify his message.

Jabir continues, "This situation prevailed until Allah sent us (the Ansar) from Yathrib to him. We offered him asylum and believed in him. Whenever a person from us left (to go to Mecca), he would end up believing in the Messenger ﷺ when he would recite the Qur'an to him. He would then return to his family and they would also accept Islam by virtue of his Islam. Eventually there was hardly a family from the Ansar that did not have a group of Muslims who made their Islam public." Jabir says that there grew a feeling of sadness at the plight of the Prophet ﷺ and the Ansar would ask each other, "For how long shall we leave the Messenger to invite the people, only to be kicked around in the mountains of Mecca and face the threats of others?"

Consequently, seventy men of the Ansar rode off and met the Prophet ﷺ during the *hajj* season, a year after their initial pledge. After agreeing to meet at the valley of 'Aqaba, they arrived in ones and twos until they were all present. They asked, "O Messenger of Allah ﷺ, to what should we pledge allegiance at your hands?" The Prophet ﷺ replied, "You should pledge that you will always listen and obey - whether your hearts are willing or not. You should also pledge that you will spend in the way of Allah, during times of hardship and ease; and that you will command others towards good and forbid evil. You should pledge that you will speak for the pleasure of Allah and will not fear the criticism of a critic when it concerns the religion of Allah. You should also pledge that you would assist me and when I come to you, you will protect me as you protect your own lives, wives and children. If you agree and comply, then you will have paradise."

The Ansar stood before the Prophet. As'ad b. Zurarah took hold of the Prophet's ﷺ hand and said, "O people of Yathrib, we have undertaken this journey only because we are convinced that he is the Prophet of Allah. Taking him (into asylum) will signal the enmity of all of the Arabs, the killing of the best of you, and their swords that shall make pieces of you. If you can endure this then take the Messenger ﷺ away (into asylum) and you will receive your reward from Allah. However, if you have some fears then leave him and make yourselves clear, for this will be a better way of excusing yourselves before Allah." The group responded, "Make way, O As'ad, by Allah, we will never forsake this pledge of allegiance and no one can ever make us do so." The seventy Ansar then pledged their allegiance to the Prophet ﷺ and this significant event is known as the second pledge of 'Aqaba.[81]

[81] *Al-Bidayah wa al-Nihayah*, vol. 3, p. 159, *Fath al-Bari*, vol. 7, p. 158; Haythami, vol. 6, p. 46; *Hayaat al-Sahaba*, vol. 1, pp.260-1.

Ka'ab b. Malik narrates that the Messenger addressed the Ansar saying, "Send to me twelve leaders from among you who will head their people in all matters." The Ansar then selected twelve leaders who comprised of nine from the Khazraj and three from the Aws.[82] After the pledge of allegiance had been taken, the Prophet told them, "You may leave for your camps."[83]

After the *hajj* season, the Prophet ﷺ stayed in Mecca during the remainder of the days of Dhul Hijjah, Muharram and Safar. The pagans of Mecca found out that the Ansar of Yathrib had pledged their allegiance and offered sanctuary to the Prophet ﷺ. They began conspiring against him and hatched a plot to murder him. Allah ﷻ revealed the verse, "And (remember, O Muhammad), when those who disbelieved plotted against you to restrain you or kill you or evict you (from Mecca). But they plan, and Allah plans. And Allah is the Best of Planners" (8:30) informing the Prophet ﷺ about their plots. Thereafter, the Prophet ﷺ prepared for his departure to migrate to Yathrib, soon to become Medina al-Nabi, the City of the Prophet, the capital of the Islamic nation.

Jabir states, "From the time that I accepted Islam, the Messenger of Allah ﷺ never prohibited me from attending any of his assemblies. Whenever he saw me he would smile."[84]

The Prophet ﷺ Chooses the Father of Jabir

Ahmad b. Ziyad b. Ja'far al-Hamadani, may Allah be pleased with him, narrated that Ali b. Ibrahim b. Hashim quoted his father, on the authority of Muhammad b. Abi Umayr and Ahmad b. Muhammad b. Abi Nasr al-Bazanty, on the authority of Aban b. Uthman al-Ahmar that a group of the elders said, "Allah's Messenger ﷺ chose twelve leaders or chiefs from amongst his nation just as many as the chiefs of Musa ﷺ did following an order delivered by Jibra'il. Nine of them were from the Khazraj clan and three of them were from the 'Aws clan. The ones from the Khazraj clan were as follows: As'ad b. Zurarah; al-Bara' b. Ma'rur; Abdullah b. Amr b. Haraml - the father of Jabir b. Abdullah; Rafe'a b. Malik; Sa'id b. Ibadat; al-Monzar b. Amr;

---

[82] Ibn Ishaq as quoted in *Al-Bidayah wa al-Nihayah*, vol. 3, p. 60.
[83] Ibid, p. 164.
[84] *Shamaa'il*, Chapter on the Laughing of the Prophet ﷺ; Tirmidhi, Hadith 4.

Abdullah b. Ravaheh; Sa'id b. al-Rabi'a; and Ibn al-Qawafil Ibadat al-Samit."[85]

The Prophet ﷺ Departs for Medina

When the Ansar in Yathrib heard that the Prophet ﷺ had departed from Mecca, they went out each morning to an area known as Harra to wait for him until the extreme heat of the afternoon forced them to return home. On one of those days, a Jewish man from that area spotted the Prophet ﷺ approaching and called out to the Ansar, "O Arabs, here comes the chief that you have been waiting for!" Excited, the Ansar rushed for their weapons (to ceremoniously receive the Prophet) and went out to meet him. Those Ansar who had never met the Prophet ﷺ but had pledged allegiance to him based on what they had been informed and inquired, were able to meet him for the first time. Among those who had not yet welcomed the Prophet ﷺ was Jabir b. Abdullah al-Ansari. Still outside of Medina, the Prophet ﷺ stayed with the tribe of Banu Amr b. Awf for more than twenty days, waiting for the arrival of Imam Ali b. Abi Talib ؏, the 'Fawaatim' (The three Fatima's of Mecca - Fatima al-Zahra ؏, Fatima bint Asad and Fatima bint Zubayr) and the Muhajireen of Mecca. While waiting, he established the first Masjid in Islam, called Masjid al-Quba, upon the revelation of the verse: "A Masjid founded on righteousness from the first day is worthier for you to stand in. Within it are men who love to purify themselves; and Allah loves those who purify themselves" (9:108).

When the Muhajireen reached the Prophet ﷺ, he welcomed them and prepared to formally enter Yathrib. The people walked with him and they sent word to announce to the Ansar about his arrival. Approximately five hundred of the Ansar came out to welcome the newly arrived Muslims. The Prophet and his companions walked among the people until the whole of Yathrib came out to greet them. Describing the scene of that day, Anas b. Malik says, "I saw the Prophet ﷺ the day that he arrived into Medina and the day that he passed away, and I have never seen any days like them."[86]

---

[85] *Al-Khisāl*, As-Sadooq, On 'twelve' numbered characteristics, Hadith 71.
[86] *Al-Bidayah wa al-Nihayah*, vol. 3, p. 197; *Hayaat al-Sahaba*, vol.1, p. 347.

Baraa b. Aazib narrates, "I have never seen the people of Medina happier on any day than on that occasion when they (the Migrants) arrived."[87]

The Prophet ﷺ walked until his camel sat at a location which was to later become the grand Masjid of Medina, Masjid al-Nabawi. It was where the males of the Ansar had been praying their obligatory prayers at the time. It was also a land where the dates were dried, and it belonged to two orphaned children named Sahl and Suhayl, who were under the guardianship of As'ad b. Zurara. These boys were called and offered to sell the land so that the Masjid could be built. They instead offered to gift the land to the Prophet ﷺ, however he refused. Once the land was bought, the Muslims began to work on building the Masjid. As the Prophet ﷺ would pick up and move the bricks he would recite couplets of supplication, including "O Allah, the true rewards are those of the hereafter. Do shower Your mercy on the Ansar and Muhajireen."[88]

Jabir narrates that from that time the Prophet ﷺ encouraged the building of Masaajid and he reports that the Messenger of Allah ﷺ said, "Whoever builds a Masjid for the sake of Allah, be it like a sparrow's nest or even smaller, Allah will build for him a house in paradise."[89]

Abu Ayyub al-Ansari reports that the Prophet ﷺ initially stayed in his house. Abu Ayyub and his family took the upper storey of the house, while the Prophet ﷺ took the ground floor. Throughout the day, the thought about being above the Prophet ﷺ plagued Abu Ayyub, or he thought that maybe his presence was an impediment for revelation. During the night, Abu Ayyub was unable to sleep for fear that moving too much might cause dust to fall upon the Prophet ﷺ or he would disturb him.

In the morning he told the Prophet ﷺ, "My eyes and those of my wife were unable to close all night" explaining his fears. The Prophet ﷺ put him at ease saying, "Do not worry in the future. Should I teach you some words that if you recite them ten times in the morning and ten times in the evening, you will be granted the reward of ten good deeds and have ten sins erased from your record, and that will elevate you ten stages in paradise, and on the Day of Judgement you will have the reward of freeing ten slaves? You

---

[87] *Kanz al-Ummal*, vol. 8, p. 331; *Hayaat al-Sahaba*, vol. 1, p. 348.
[88] *Al-Bidayah wa al-Nihayah*, vol. 3, p. 186; *Hayaat al-Sahaba*, vol. 1, p. 347.
[89] *Sunan b. Majah*, The Chapters on Building Masaajid and Encouraging Congregational Prayers, Hadith 738.

should recite 'There is no god but Allah, for Him is the Kingdom and for Him is the glorification, indeed He has no partner."[90] [91]

Abu Ayyub continues, "One of our jugs broke and the water spilled out. My wife and I immediately got up and with our blanket rushed to soak it up fearing that the water would leak below onto the Prophet ﷺ. We had nothing else to cover ourselves with and spent the night without anything else to use." Eventually Abu Ayyub insisted that it was not proper that they be above the Prophet ﷺ and that he ﷺ should move upstairs, and so the Prophet ﷺ took his belongings up, and Abu Ayyub and his wife moved downstairs."[92]

Ansar Pledge their Allegiance

Umm Atiyya narrates that when the Prophet ﷺ arrived in Medina, the women of Ansar gathered in a house to pledge their allegiance as well. At times the Prophet ﷺ met women individually; for example, on the road or in small groups. The pledge that he took from them was the same. They were asked to pledge "We will not ascribe any partner to Allah, will not steal, nor fornicate, nor kill our children, nor come forth with slander which we fabricate before our hands and legs (by claiming that another man's child is their husband's), and we will not disobey you (meaning the Prophet) in any deed (that you command us to do)"[93] - to this the Prophet ﷺ would add "To the best of your ability and according to your capacity." The women commented, "Allah and His Messenger ﷺ are more merciful towards us than we are to ourselves. Give us your hand that we may pledge allegiance to you." The Prophet ﷺ replied, "I cannot shake the hand of women. What I say to a hundred women is the same as I say to one woman." When Fatima bint 'Utba b. Rabee'ah came to pledge her allegiance, out of modesty she placed her hand upon her head, and act which greatly impressed the Prophet

---

[90] The Arabic text of this reads:

لا اله الا الله له الملك و له الحمد لا شريك له

Laa Ilaha Illallah, Lahu al-Mulk, wa Lahu al-Hamd, La Shareeka Lahu
[91] *Kanz al-Ummal*, vol. 1, p. 249.
[92] Ibid., vol. 8, p. 50.
[93] Qur'an 60:12.

🌸 [94] [95] So, the pledge of the women of the Ansar was accepted by their verbal commitment.[96]

Jabir narrates that the women of the community would often approach the Prophet 🌸 with their questions. For example, in one narration he states, "A woman came to the Messenger of Allah 🌸 and said, 'My mother has died, and she had made a vow to fast, but she died before she could fulfil it.' The Messenger of Allah 🌸 said, 'Let her guardian fast on her behalf.'"[97]

A'isha Praises the Ansariyyah Women for the Adjustment of their Practices

Safiyyah bint Shaybah reports that she was with A'isha discussing the women of the Quraysh and their virtues. A'isha remarked, "No doubt that the women of the Quraysh have great virtues, but I swear by Allah that I have not seen women better than the women of the Ansar. They were the strongest believers in the Qur'an and the revelation. When Allah revealed the verse, 'And they should wear (bring) their scarves over their chests' (24:31), their men went to them and recited the verse to them. Every man recited the verse to his wife, daughter, sister and every mahram[98] of his. Every one of these women took their decorated shawls and wrapped it around themselves because of their strong faith in what Allah had revealed. The following morning, they all performed prayers behind the Messenger of Allah with their shawls wrapped around them."[99]

---

[94] *Majma' al-Zawaa'id*, vol. 6, p. 37; *Hayaat al-Sahaba*, vol. 1, p. 268.

[95] This act signifies the saying 'May my head be sacrificed for you' or 'My head is at your service'. It is a gesture of pledging one's allegiance generally and ascribes the meaning mentioned specifically. It is with this meaning that the Shi'a Ithna'Asheri place their hands upon their heads when mentioning the name of Imam al-Mahdi b. Hasan al-Askari 🌸.

[96] *Al-Isaba*, vol. 4, p. 240; p. *Hayaat al-Sahaba*, vol. 1, p. 268.

[97] *Sunan b. Majah*, The Chapter on Expiations, Hadith 2133.

[98] A *mahram* is an unmarriageable kin with whom marriage or intercourse is prohibited.

[99] *Tafseer ibn Katheer*, vol. 3, p. 284.

The Ansar Youth Pledge their Support to the Prophet ﷺ

Anas b. Malik reports that there were twenty youth from among the Ansar who always stayed close to the Prophet ﷺ. The Prophet ﷺ would dispatch them when he needed something done for Islam.[100]

The Condition of the Muslims Early on in the Migration and them being hosted by the Ansar

During the immediate days after the migration, and the Ansar hosting the companions, the Arabs were showing their aggression towards the Muslims and threatening them with a war. Most of the Muhajireen's belongings had been left in Mecca and so everything including weapons had to be shared. Due to the tension, they were forced to carry their weapons day and night and be in a state of constant alert. They would ask each other, "When will the time come when we can spend a night in peace without having to fear anything besides Allah?" It was on this occasion that Allah ﷻ revealed the verse, "Allah has promised those who believe among you and do righteous deeds that He will surely grant them succession [to authority] upon the earth, just as He granted it to those before them; and that He will surely establish for them [therein] their religion which He has preferred for them, and He will surely substitute for them after their fear, security, [for] they worship Me, not associating anything with Me. But whoever disbelieves after that - then those are the defiantly disobedient" (24:55).[101]

One morning, some members of the Banu Mudhar tribe arrived. They were barefoot and practically naked, wearing just their shawls and carrying their swords. The Prophet ﷺ instructed Bilal to recite the *adhan* and *iqamah* and after the prayers, he addressed the community with the following verses, "O mankind, fear your Lord, who created you from a single soul and created its spouse from it. And spread great numbers of men and women from it. Fear Allah, whom you ask by, and (do not) break the relations and close ties. Indeed, Allah is ever watchful over you" (4:1); and "Fear Allah and let every soul consider what good deeds it has sent ahead for tomorrow" (59:18).

---

[100] Haythami, vol. 9, p. 22.
[101] *Kanz al-Ummal*, vol. 1, p. 259; *Hayaat al-Sahaba*, vol. 1, p. 314.

The Prophet ﷺ then called upon everyone to contribute something, regardless of how little it might be. Jabir narrates that one of the members of the Ansar then brought a bag of food as a donation so large, that he even struggled to carry it. He states, "The other Ansar followed suit until I saw two heaps of food and clothing. I saw the face of the Prophet ﷺ shining as if it was a piece of fine gold. The Prophet ﷺ then stated, 'Whosoever starts a good practice will receive the reward for it in addition to the rewards of all of those who do the same after him - without any of their rewards being diminished in the least; and whoever starts an evil practice will be burdened with the sin of it in addition to the sins of all of those who do the same after him, without the burden of any of their sins being lightened in the least.'"[102] This was to play a foundational role in the attitudes and practices of the Ansar towards the Muhajireen, as we shall see in the forthcoming narrations.

Jabir reports that someone came to ask the Prophet ﷺ for something and he gave it to him. Thereafter another person came to ask him for something, but because the Prophet ﷺ had nothing to give him, he promised to give him something later. 'Umar b. al-Khattab stood up and said, "O Messenger of Allah, when someone asked you for something, you gave it to him. Then when someone else asked you for something you promised to give it to him despite not having anything. Why do you burden yourself when you have nothing to give?" The Prophet ﷺ appeared to dislike this statement of 'Umar's. Abdullah b. Hudhaafa al-Sahmi stood up and said, "O Prophet, continue to spend without fearing any decrease from the Lord of the Throne!" The Prophet replied, "That is exactly what I have been commanded to do!"[103]

Jabir's Narration about Mu'aadh b. Jabal

Jabir reports that the companion Mu'aadh b. Jabal was amongst the most handsome of people, along with the best of characters and the most generous. In his eagerness to assist others he built up a large debt. When his creditors started to push him to pay, he hid away from them in his house for several days. The creditors eventually sought the Prophet's ﷺ intervention,

---

[102] *Targheeb wa Tarheeb*, vol. 1 p. 53.
[103] *Kanz al-Ummal*, vol. 3, p. 311.

and so he ﷺ sent for both parties. The creditors pleaded, "O Messenger of Allah, please claim our dues from him." The Prophet ﷺ responded to them, "Allah will shower His mercy on the person who is charitable towards him who writes off Mu'aadh's debt." Consequently, some of the creditors wrote off their debts, while others refused insisting that the Prophet ﷺ claim their rights from him.

The Prophet then turned to Mu'aadh and said, "O Mu'aadh, be patient and settle your remaining debts with them (even if you have to lose all of your wealth)." The Prophet ﷺ then took away all of Mu'aadh's wealth and handed it over to the creditors. After its distribution, it still only reached five-sevenths of what Mu'aadh owed. The creditors again turned to the Prophet ﷺ demanding that he sell Mu'aadh as a slave to them. The Prophet ﷺ refused stating, "Leave him alone now! You cannot lodge any further claim now."[104]

Having nothing left, Mu'aadh then went to live with Banu Salama. Someone there said to him, "O Abu Abd al-Rahman, why do you not ask the Prophet ﷺ for something now that you have become so poor?" Mu'aadh refused to ask, staying there for a few more days until the Prophet ﷺ called for him. The Prophet ﷺ then dispatched him to Yemen to act as a governor saying, "Perhaps Allah will redeem for you your losses." Mu'aadh remained there as governor until the Prophet died.[105] [106] Jabir also reports from Mu'aadh that he said, "The Messenger of Allah ﷺ settled my debts with my

---

[104] In the Shi'a jurisprudence it is compulsory for a loanee, if he is unable to pay back his loan or is declared bankrupt to sell all of his possessions in order to repay the debt - with the exception of his house, daily food, basic clothes and books of knowledge. This is based upon the narration of Imam Ja'far al-Sadiq ﷺ, "Do not remove a person from his house to pay off a debt." For further reading refer to *Fiqh al-Sadiq*, Mughniyya, Muhammad Jawad, vol. 4, p. 19, Mu'assasat al-Sibtain al-Aalamiyyah, Iran.

[105] *Al-Mustadrak*, vol. 3, pp. 123 and 272.

[106] In addition to demonstrating how the Prophet ﷺ dealt with the matter of creditors, bankruptcy and caring for his companions, it appears that the narration intends to make clear the reward of Mu'aadh's patience, like the Prophet ﷺ asked of him. Only a few days later was his patience rewarded by being made a governor over an entire country. In other narrations connected to this one narrated by Abdullah b. Mas'ood, it states that Mu'aadh regained all of his property and even more, such that when he returned for *hajj* in the year of Abu Bakr's reign, he had with him several servants. When asked about them, he explained that the people of Yemen had gifted them to him.

creditors using what wealth I had and then he appointed me as a governor."[107]

The Ansar Raise Funds to Beautify Masjid al-Nabawi

It is narrated that the Ansar spoke among themselves asking, "For how long will the Messenger of Allah ﷺ recite prayers beneath a roof made of palm branches?" The pillars of the Masjid were trunks of palm trees, while the roof was made of palm leaves seeping water and making the ground muddy when it rained. They collected gold coins which they presented to the Prophet ﷺ and said to him: "We wish to renovate and beautify this Masjid." The Prophet ﷺ replied, "I do not wish to veer from the example of my brother Prophet Musa ﷺ who had a shelter made of palm branches. The ceiling of the Masjid should remain like the shelter of Prophet Musa ﷺ."[108]

Jabir states, "When the wind blew fiercely at night, the Prophet ﷺ would hasten towards the Masjid and remain there until the wind subsided. He would also hasten to the place of prayer whenever the sun or moon eclipsed."[109]

Jabir also narrates that the Prophet ﷺ was a pioneer of health and safety in the Masjid, in a community that was famous for its roughness and valour. He narrates about companions drawing, viewing and exchanging unsheathed swords inside of the Masjid. The Prophet ﷺ said, "Allah curses the people who do this. Have I not forbidden you from this? When a person draws his sword and then intends on giving it to another, he should have it sheathed before handing it over."[110] Jabir himself narrates that he was asked about this issue by another companion, Sulaiman b. Musa, whom he told, "We have always disapproved of it (passing unsheathed weapons). In fact, when a person was giving an arrow away in charity in the Masjid, the Prophet ﷺ instructed him not to pass through the Masjid unless he held the head of the arrow firmly in his hand."[111]

---

[107] *Sunan b. Majah*, The Chapter on Rulings and Laws, Hadith 2357.
[108] Haythami, vol. 1, p. 16.
[109] *Kanz al-Ummal*, vol. 4, p. 289.
[110] Ibid., p. 262.
[111] Ibid.

The Prophet ﷺ has to Reconcile Between the Ansar

After the Prophet ﷺ had reconciled the longstanding feud between the Aws and Khazraj from the 'Period of Ignorance,' the enmity had not completely finished between the two tribes. One time when they were sitting in a gathering, someone from the Aws recited some couplets of poetry ridiculing the Khazraj. In response, someone from the Khazraj recited couplets mocking the Aws. This continued until it became so heated that some of the people got up ready to attack each other. They grabbed hold of their weapons and were ready for a skirmish that would have broken the unity between the Ansar.

When the news reached the Prophet ﷺ, he received revelation and hurried to them such that even his shins were exposed. When the Prophet ﷺ reached there, he recited to them the verse, "O you who believe, have the awe of Allah as He deserves to be respected, and do not die except as Muslims. Hold fast to the rope of Allah, all of you together, and do not separate. Recall Allah's favours upon you when you were once enemies and He created love between your hearts; then you became brothers by His grace. You were on the edge of an abyss of fire and He rescued you from it. In this way does Allah explain His signs to you that you may be guided" (3:102-103).

The Ansar immediately threw down their weapons and embraced one another, being conscious from what had happened.[112]

The Ansar begin to Shape their Practices of Generosity

As mentioned earlier, the Ansar showed great generosity towards the emigrants following the Prophet's ﷺ shaping of their attitude and encouragement. This continued in a number of ways. Anas narrates that Abu Talha was among the wealthiest of all of the Ansar due to the date plantations that he owned. From all of his plantations, the orchard of Bir Haa was his most beloved as it was situated adjacent to Masjid al-Nabawi and the Prophet ﷺ would visit there to drink water.

During that time the verse, "You shall by no means reach a state of righteousness until you spend out of that which you love (the most)" (3:92)

---

[112] Haythami, vol. 8, p. 80.

was revealed. Upon hearing this verse, Abu Talha visited the Prophet ﷺ saying, "The orchard of Bir Haa is certainly the possession that I love the most! So now I give it over in charity for the pleasure of Allah. I aspire for the good of this and that Allah will keep it as a treasure for me in the hereafter. O Messenger of Allah ﷺ, use it as Allah tells you." The Prophet ﷺ was overjoyed and repeatedly said, "This is an excellent investment!"[113]

In another incident, a person came to the Prophet ﷺ complaining of severe hunger. The Prophet ﷺ sent a message to one of his wives asking her to prepare some food and then send it but received the reply that, "I swear by the One who has sent you with the Truth that I have nothing but water with me." The Prophet ﷺ then sent the same message to another wife and received the same reply, until he asked all of his wives but received the same message.

The Prophet ﷺ then announced, "Who will host this man tonight and receive the abundant mercy of Allah?" Abu Talha from among the Ansar volunteered. He asked his wife, "Do you have any food?" She replied, "There is nothing but the children's food." He replied, "Pacify them with something and put them to sleep when they want their food. When our guest arrives, put out the lantern to suggest that we are also eating (and give him the children's food)." The guest ate while the family remained hungry.

The next morning, the Prophet ﷺ said to Abu Talha, "Allah was very pleased by what you did last night." A narration states that it was upon this incident that the verse, "They prefer others over themselves, even if they themselves are in need" (59:9) was revealed.[114]

The Extent of the Generosity of the Ansar towards the Muhajiroon and the Brotherhood Shared between Them

When the Muhajiroon arrived in Medina, due to their struggles in Mecca and having lost their property and wealth from the migration, the Ansar partnered with them by offering them whatever they could. The extent of the sharing is historically unprecedented, and it is evidence of the highest forms of bonding between, what previously were tribes who were alien to

---

[113] *Targheeb wa Tarheeb*, vol. 2, p. 140.
[114] *Targheeb wa Tarheeb*, vol. 4, p. 147; *Fath al-Bari*, vol. 8, p. 446.

each other or maybe even were enemies. Islam taught them to demolish the arbitrary barriers that their society had created between them and moulded their attitudes to think in terms of Islam, and to seek the pleasure and reward of Allah ﷻ first and foremost. In doing so, they no longer saw each other through the prism of tribes or members of a different city or skin colour, but rather through the lens of brotherhood in the way of Islam and for the sake of Allah ﷻ.

Verses of the Qur'an such as, "Most surely the believers are but brothers of each other" (47:7), and narrations from the Prophet ﷺ such as "A person is not complete in his faith until he wishes for his brother what he wishes for himself" will inspire this monumental shift in mentality. The acceptance of this practice by the early Muslims was a major contributing factor to their success. First of all, it was evidence that the true seeds of Islam had borne fruits in their hearts in two ways: That they were fully submitting to the command of the Prophet ﷺ, and through their own volition they were departing from the practices that had riddled the Arabian society in the Days of Ignorance. Through this they were understanding what Islam had intended for them all along.

The second factor was that in the early years following the migration, the Muslims had to undergo severe internal tests, some of which we shall narrate below. This included poverty, hunger, deprivation, war, siege, spying and internal strife. The bonds that were developed early on assisted the Ansar and Muhajireen through those struggles together, for it was in their unity and shared experience of overcoming those difficult times together that were able to yield the fruits of success and rewards that were to come, both in this world and the hereafter.

The Muhajireen had given up their own wealth in Mecca. In fact, this had been usurped by the pagans for themselves and the Migrants had little or no recourse to claim it back. Seeing this commitment to the Prophet ﷺ of Allah and Islam, the Ansar responded by offering their own sacrifices for the Muhajireen to ensure that whatever their needs were, they were fulfilled.

In order to encourage the Ansar, Jabir narrates an incident that occurred when the Prophet ﷺ visited Banu Amr b. Auf and addressed them saying, "O assembly of the Ansar!" The Ansar responded, "We are at your service, O Messenger of Allah!" The Prophet ﷺ continued his address saying, "During the Era of Ignorance when you were not serving Allah, you used to bear the burdens of others, engage your wealth in good deeds and care for the travellers. However, now that Allah has blessed you with Islam and His Prophet, you suddenly lock away your wealth (whereas you should be spending more now). Know that there are rewards for whatever a person eats from your wealth and there are also rewards for whatever even the birds get to eat from your wealth."[115] As a response, the Ansar went to their orchards and made thirty doors leading into them, signalling easy access to anyone who wanted to come in and take benefit. This address further laid the foundation for much of the Ansar's generosity towards the Muhajireen. Jabir narrates that the Prophet ﷺ encouraged access and usage of each other's unused properties so that nothing would go to waste, mentioning, "Once the Messenger of Allah ﷺ addressed us and said, 'Whoever has unused land, let him cultivate it or allow someone else to cultivate it, and not rent it out.'"[116]

When Abd al-Rahman b. Awf arrived in Medina, the Prophet ﷺ established the bond of brotherhood between him and Sa'ad b. Rabee' al-Ansari. Sa'ad addressed Abd al-Rahman saying, "Dear brother, I am the wealthiest person in Medina and you may have half of my wealth." Abd al-Rahman replied, "May Allah bless you in your family and wealth."[117]

The extent of this generosity was that for an interim period, the Ansar even forewent the rightful share of their own inheritances in order to create an equilibrium between them and the Muhajireen. That is to say that in addition to having given half of their wealth to the Muhajireen upon their arrival, after the deaths they again divided their remaining wealth in half and gave it as inheritance to the Muhajireen!

This practice demonstrated a great deal of patience and sincerity on behalf of the Ansar, and a desire to lift the Muhajireen out of poverty. In the mind of the Ansar there could not be true brotherhood or equity in their society if two distinct classes were created, known today as 'the wealth gap'. As a result of this vast socio-economic gap, this would have led to jealousy, envy and hatred between them, eroding the bonds of brotherhood that had been established. It also demonstrated that wealth was not the primary

---

[115] *Targheeb wa Tarheeb*, vol. 4, p. 156.
[116] *Sunan b. Majah*, The Chapters on Pawning, Hadith 2454.
[117] *Al-Bidayah wa al-Nihayah*, vol. 3, p. 228; *Hayaat al-Sahaba*, vol. 1, p. 377.

concern of the Ansar, but rather forging a just society and reiterating the evidence of their ascent towards a truer understanding of Islam.

Once this temporary transfer of wealth and realignment of social cohesion had fulfilled its goals, Allah revealed three verses abrogating the Ansar's practice by enforcing new laws of inheritance. The first was, "And for all, We have made heirs to what is left by parents and relatives. And to those whom your oaths have bound [to you] - give them their share. Indeed, Allah is ever, over all things, a Witness (4:33)." Thereafter was, "And those who believed after [the initial emigration] and emigrated and fought with you - they are of you. But those of [blood] relationship are more entitled [to inheritance] in the decree of Allah. Indeed, Allah is Knowing of all things" (8:75). The third verse was, "The Prophet is worthier of the believers than themselves, and his wives are [in the position of] their mothers. And those of [blood] relationship are more entitled [to inheritance] in the decree of Allah than the [other] believers and the emigrants, except that you may do to your close associates a kindness [through bequest]. That was in the Book inscribed" (33:6).

After these verses were revealed, if the Ansar wanted to gift wealth or property to a Muhajir it would have been out of goodwill, but could no longer be is the prescribed portions of inheritance.[118] Nevertheless, the fact that Allah ﷻ Himself had to legislate in order for the Ansar to understand their obligations and to halt their generosity, demonstrates the extent of their understanding of Islam. They showed complete faith in Allah ﷻ as the Giver of their wealth and their rewards, and they wanted to fulfil their responsibilities towards their fellow Muslim brothers in creating a balanced society.

Another example of this is mentioned when the Ansar once came to the Prophet ﷺ and said, "Divide our date plantations between us and our Muhajireen brothers." The Prophet ﷺ offered another suggestion. "Instead of giving up ownership of the land, why not absolve us of working on the plantations and share the dates with us?" The Ansar responded, "We hear and we obey."[119] The Prophet ﷺ also said, "Since the Muhajireen do not

---

[118] *Fath al-Bari*, vol. 7, p. 191; *Hayaat al-Sahaba*, vol. 1, p. 378.

[119] It appears here that the Prophet ﷺ intended to widen the economic potential of Medina by advising the Muhajireen to establish different trade or independence

know how to work on the plantations, will you rather not continue to do the work for them and share the dates with them?" to which the Ansar agreed.[120]

Anas b. Malik narrates that the Muhajireen came to the Prophet ﷺ and said, "O Messenger of Allah, we have never seen people better than those to whom we have come to (the Ansar). They are prepared to assist us even though they themselves have so little, and when they have plenty they spend it generously. They do all of the work on the plantations for us and then share the dates with us. They do so much for us that we fear that they should not take all of the rewards." The Prophet ﷺ replied, "This will not happen so long as you keep praising them and make supplication to Allah on their behalf."[121] [122]

Jabir narrates that when the Ansar harvested their crops, they would divide the crops into two - one part being smaller than the other. They would then place tree branches with the smaller portion (to make it look bigger) and then give the Muhajiroon the choice of which portion to take. The Muhajiroon would choose, what they conceived to be, the smaller portion without the branches aiming to return the generosity of the Ansar, thinking that they would be leaving the larger portion for them. The Ansar would then take the smaller portion for themselves. This practice continued until

---

from the Ansars' forms of trade. In this way, the Ansar could keep the land, which was the most valuable, but share part of their profits. It also encouraged the Muhajireen to seek the additional forms of work such as trade, which they were more used to doing from Mecca. This view is supported by the remainder of the tradition quoted.

[120] *Al-Bidayah wa al-Nihayah*, vol. 3, p. 228; *Hayaat al-Sahaba*, vol. 1, p. 379.

[121] *Al-Bidayah wa al-Nihayah*, vol. 3, p. 228; *Hayaat al-Sahaba*, vol. 1, p. 380.

[122] In hear lies great wisdom and a deep lesson from the Prophet ﷺ. As for the wisdom, the Prophet ﷺ understood human nature and the appreciation of recognition. The Ansar had demonstrated the extent of their generosity and were not in need of praise, however for the Muhajireen to express their gratitude would deepen the ties between the groups. In response it would continue to encourage the Ansar knowing that their sacrifices were being acknowledged and not overlooked. As for the lesson, people are often indebted to others in ways that cannot be rewarded through wealth, favour or gratitude. For example, parents or those who assist you beyond expectation - such as was case of the Ansar. For such people, when the extent of the favour cannot be returned, the best thing that one can offer is supplication on their behalf. One can seek from Allah ﷻ forgiveness and goodness in both realms for them.

the conquest of Khaybar. When the Khaybar was conquered, the Prophet ﷺ addressed the Ansar saying, "You have fulfilled your duty towards us. Now, if you please, you may hand over your shares in Khaybar to the Muhajiroon and have your date crops in Medina for yourselves without the need to share it." The Ansar accepted the proposal saying, "You have placed several responsibilities on us, and while you have taken the responsibility that in exchange for our sacrifices we shall attain paradise. We have now fulfilled what you had asked from us and require that your condition (of paradise) be met!" The Prophet ﷺ promised, "You have it!"[123]

This testament of fulfilment of the duties by the Ansar towards the Muhajireen was more than a symbolic gesture - it was in fact a drawing to conclusion the feeling of indebtedness. This would primarily bring about a psychological and sociological ease between the two groups. For the Ansar, it would foster a sense of accomplishment towards the pledges of assistance that they had promised, while for the Muhajireen they no longer needed to feel as though they had been a burden upon the Ansar. This demonstrated excellent leadership and management skills by the Prophet ﷺ. Later on, the Prophet ﷺ called the Ansar to gift them the land of Bahrain. Still maintaining their generosity, they refused to accept it unless the Muhajireen received an equal amount of land or its share. The Prophet refused, reminding them that their financial responsibilities had ended saying, "In this case we cannot distribute the land!"[124]

While towards the Muhajireen the Ansar were profoundly generous and understood the long term effects, in other times, this generosity and insight was not always present. During the battle of Ahzaab, the Muslims were suffering extreme hardships. The Prophet ﷺ sent for the leaders of Banu Ghitfaan - the tribe who was in the army against the Muslims. He offered them one third of the produce from Medina on the condition that they withdraw from fighting against the Muslims. The agreement was in place and ready to be ratified, however, the Prophet ﷺ asked Sa'ad b. Mu'aadh and Sa'ad b. Ubadah from the Ansar to agree to the document. The two men asked the Prophet ﷺ, "Is this something that you are doing because you wish to do it or something that Allah has commanded you to do, in which case

---

[123] Haythami, vol. 10, p. 40; *Hayaat al-Sahaba*, vol. 1, p. 380.
[124] *Sahih al-Bukhari*, vol. 1, p. 535.

we have no option but to carry it out? Or is it something that you are doing for our benefit?" The Prophet ﷺ replied, "I am doing this for your benefit because I see that the Arabs are attacking you from a united platform and are ravaging you from all sides. By engaging in this treaty, I wish to dilute their strength."[125] Sa'ad b. Mu'aadh considered this and responded, "Us and these people had been ascribing partners to Allah and worshiping idols. Neither did we worship Allah, nor did we recognise who He was. During those times, these people (Banu Ghitfaan) never entertained hopes of eating a single date from Medina unless it was offered to them as a token of hospitality or that they bought it. How can we now give them any portion of our wealth once Allah has honoured us with Islam, guided us to it, and accorded us tremendous respect because of it. By Allah, we have no need for this treaty." The Prophet ﷺ replied, "You know best what you want" and they did not complete the agreement.[126]

The Ansar Help Out in whatever the Others Struggled with

Asma' bint Umays narrates, "When I married Zubayr, he possessed neither property, money, slaves, and nothing else besides his horse and camel. I used

---

[125] This question suggests a lack of understanding from Sa'ad b. Mu'aadh. Referring to the Prophet ﷺ, the Qur'an states, "He does not speak of his own whim, it is not but inspiration." In this way there is no distance between the desire of Allah ﷻ and the practise of the Prophet ﷺ. Moreover, whatever Allah ﷻ desires for His creation and the Prophetic action is for the benefit of the people, therefore there is no separation between the three questions asked by Sa'ad, they are rather one and the same. Despite this being the case, when asked the Prophet ﷺ responded by stating that the treaty was for their benefit. This may have been because he wished to provide a logical reasoning to Sa'ad, which contained the theological assumptions of Allah ﷻ and the Prophet's ﷺ desires, or as Sa'ad had already questioned the theological authority and divine wisdom in the Prophet's ﷺ view, to convey the logical benefit to him. In either case, Sa'ad rejected the divine *and* conventional wisdom. The reaction of the Prophet ﷺ demonstrates his forbearance to allow his companions to reject his wisdom and efforts which he had already placed in constructing the treaty. It also demonstrates the lack of insight from the companions, as not only would the treaty have aided in the matters of the battle, but the produce of Medina was in the divine Hands of Allah ﷻ and such a practice may have drawn the Banu Ghiftaan closer to Islam.

[126] *Al-Bidayah wa al-Nihayah*, vol. 4, p. 104; *Hayaat al-Sahaaba*, vol. 2, p. 85.

to feed his horse for him, tend to it and care for it. I also used to crush the date stones to feed his camel that drew water from the well and fed it myself. I would also give it water to drink, sew the water bags and knead the dough. However, I was not good at making the bread so my Ansari neighbours would do it for me. They were extremely sincere and true friends!"[127]

The Ansar and Muhajireen Visit Each Other

Anas b. Malik narrates that the Prophet ﷺ established a bond of brotherhood between every two companions. The bonds became so strong that the day would be incomplete if one did not meet his brother. They would show great affection and enquire about what they have done for Islam since the last time that they met. As for those who did not have those formal bonds made, they did not like to allow even three days to pass without seeking news about the other companions.[128]

A Tribe Come to Visit the Prophet ﷺ and Stay with the Ansar

A delegation from the tribe of Banu Abd al-Qais visited the Prophet ﷺ and he greeted them and enquired about the various territories in their lands. The leader of the group, Mundhir b. Aa'idh exclaimed, "O Messenger of Allah, you know the names of our towns even better than us!" The Prophet ﷺ replied, "I have travelled extensively through your lands."

The Prophet ﷺ then turned to the Ansar and said, "O assembly of Ansar! Treat your brothers well because along with being Muslims like you, they also resemble you most closely in hair and complexion. Like you, they have accepted Islam willingly and were neither forced to accept it, nor was there any need to fight them for refusing to accept it."

The Ansar then hosted the delegation. Sometime later the Prophet ﷺ enquired from the delegation, "How did you find the hospitality that your brothers gave you?" They replied, "They are the best of brothers! They gave us soft beds to sleep on, lovely food to eat, and they spent their days and

---

[127] *Tabaqat al-Kubra*, Ibn Sa'ad, vol. 8, p. 250.
[128] Haythami, vol. 8, p. 174.

nights teaching us the Book of our Lord and the Prophetic practices of our Messenger ﷺ." This greatly impressed and pleased the Prophet ﷺ.[129]

The Ansar, Muhajireen and Banu Hashim Compete for the Closest Relationship with the Prophet ﷺ

Ka'ab b. Ujrah reports, "We were sitting in front of the Prophet's ﷺ room in the Masjid. There was a group from the Ansar, a group from the Muhajireen, and another group from the Banu Hashim. We started disputing about which group of us was the closest and more beloved to the Prophet ﷺ.

We said, 'It is us, the Ansar!' We believed in the Prophet (gave him refuge) and followed him, fought by his side and our army was always at the throats of the enemies. We are therefore closest. Our Muhajireen brothers said, 'It is us who migrated with Allah and the Prophet ﷺ, separating from our tribes, families and wealth. In addition, we were present where you were present, and fought the battles that you fought. We are therefore closest.' Our brothers from the tribe of Banu Hashim then spoke saying, 'We are the family of the Prophet. We were also present where you were present, and fought the battles that you fought.'

The Messenger of Allah then came out and enquired about what we were discussing. We the Ansar, repeated what we had said and the Prophet ﷺ remarked, 'You are right, who can deny this?' The Muhajireen then repeated their view to which the Prophet responded, 'They are right, who can deny this?' The members of Banu Hashim also repeated their argument and the Prophet ﷺ again replied, 'They are also right, who can deny this?'

The Prophet ﷺ then asked, 'Should I not pass a decision between you?' to which we all exclaimed, 'Please do!' The Prophet ﷺ stated, 'As for you, assembly of the Ansar, I am your brother.' The Ansar rejoiced saying, 'Allahu Akbar, by the Lord of the Ka'bah we are pleased with this.' 'As for you, assembly of the Muhajireen, I am one of you.' The Muhajireen rejoiced in the same way. 'And as for you, Banu Hashim, you are from me and I am from you.' The Banu Hashim members also rejoiced.

---

[129] *Targheeb wa al-Tarheeb*, vol. 4, p. 152; Haythami, vol. 8, p. 178.

We then all stood up, well pleased and coveting our relationships with the Prophet ﷺ."[130]

---

[130] Haythami, vol. 10, p. 14.

Chapter 4

Jabir's Participation in the Battles and Expeditions with Prophet Muhammad ﷺ

Introduction

Jabir participated in eighteen or nineteen battles with the Prophet ﷺ and has contributed many narrations regarding the events and personalities of people, providing a vivid picture of Islamic history. He is narrated to have said, "The Messenger of God ﷺ participated in twenty-one battles himself and I witnessed nineteen of those battles with him."[131] He is also narrated to have said, "After my father was killed in the battle of Uhud, I did not leave the Messenger of God ﷺ in any of the battles at all."[132] [133]

His father specifically requested him not to participate in the Battle of Badr, and historians are divided about his presence in the Battle of Uhud, where his father Abdullah was martyred. For example, Sheikh al-Tusi in his *Rijal* states that Jabir witnessed the Battle of Badr.[134] However, in *Al-Istia'ab* of Ibn Abd al-Barr it states 'that some people have mentioned Jabir as among

---

[131] The Arabic text of this passage reads:

غزا رسول الله بنفسه إحدى و عشرين غزوة، شهدت منها معه تسع عشرة غزوة.

[132] The Arabic text of this passage reads:

فلما قتل يوم أحد لم أتخلف عن رسول الله في غزوة قط.

[133] *Qasas al-Sahaaba wa al-Tabi'in*, p. 78.

[134] The Arabic text of this passage reads and is found at: https://bit.ly/2MxcDma

جابر بن عبد الله بن عمرو بن حرام، نزل المدينة، شهد بدرا وثماني عشرة غزوة مع النبي صلى الله عليه وآله، مات سنة ثمان وسبعين.

the Badreyeen (the people of Badr), but this is not correct due to the narration attributed to Jabir in which he said: "I neither witnessed Badr, nor Uhud as my father prevented me.'" [135] Al-Bukhari mentions that he witnessed Badr, but he used to transport the water to his companions on that day.[136] If this is correct, then this would likely include Uhud too and may also reconcile the above statement of Jabir referring to actual battlefield participation. Moreover, due to the many narrations and often unique narrations about the battle itself - without Jabir narrating these from another person - suggests that Jabir was present to some capacity. Allah knows best.

There are also many narrations generally regarding the attitude towards battle, or the ethos adopted by the Muslims from Jabir. He is narrated to have said, "The Messenger of Allah did not fight in the sacred months until he was fought against, and if ever he was in a fight and a sacred month began, he would desist (from fighting) until it came to an end."[137]

Other examples include that he is narrated to have said that once when the Prophet ﷺ was embarking on an expedition he said, "O assembly of the Muhajireen and Ansar, there are many of your brothers who have neither wealth, nor families to assist them. Therefore, each of you who is capable should attach yourselves to two or three of them." Jabir continues, "As a result, each one of us who had an animal would share turns to ride it, just like the others without an animal to ride shared their turns. I attached two or three people to myself and my turn to ride was just like the turns that they had."[138]

Jabir also describes what remembrance (*dhikr*) of Allah ﷻ the companions would recite when marching towards their destination, saying that whenever the companions ascended an incline they would recite Allahu Akbar (*takbir*), and whenever they descended from an incline they would recite Subhaan Allah (*tasbih*).[139]

In a famous narration, though narrated in different ways, Jabir is quoted as saying, "The Prophet ﷺ said, "I have been given five things which were

---

[135] The Arabic text of this passage reads:

لم اشهد بدرا ولا أحدا منعني ابي

[136] *Qasas al-Sahaaba wa al-Tabi'in*, p. 78.
[137] *Tafseer al-Mizan*, Commentary of the verse (2:194).
[138] Bayhaqi, vol. 9, p. 172; Hakim, vol. 2, p. 90.
[139] *Hayaat al-Sahaaba*, vol. 1, p. 474.

not given to anyone else before me. The first is that Allah made me victorious by awe (by His frightening my enemies)."[140] [141]

While Jabir did not participate in the battles of Badr and Uhud, I will mention some of the narrations regarding the Ansar in keeping with our goal to explore the role of the Ansar generally, and the events surrounding the life of Jabir specifically. This means that many of the narrations detailing the events of the battles will be excluded, since the battles themselves are not what we wish to explore, but rather the particulars of Jabir and the Ansar. For details of the battles please refer to the appropriate books.

The Battle of Badr

Narrations vary in regards to the initial response of the Ansar towards engaging in the Battle of Badr, the first battle in Islam. Abu Ayyub al-Ansari narrates that the Muslims were in Medina when the Prophet ﷺ said, "I have been informed that the trade caravan of Abu Sufyan is approaching. Do you want to march and capture the caravan so that Allah may give you plenty of spoils (and a return for the stolen properties when migrating from Mecca)?" When the companions agreed they marched out of Medina. After a day or two of marching, the Prophet ﷺ addressed the companions saying, "The Quryash have received intelligence about us and have prepared an army to fight against us, what do you say about fighting them?" Many from the companions were hesitant and replied: "By Allah, we do not have the strength (numbers) to fight them because we intended only on capturing the caravan." The Prophet, seeking a different answer, repeated, "What do you say about fighting them?" Again, the companions repeated their view. Miqdad b. Aswad al-Kindi, from among the Muhajireen, stood up and said, "O Messenger of Allah, we shall not say to you what the people of Musa ﷺ

---

[140] The rest of the narration continues as: "2. The earth has been made for me (and for my followers) a place for praying and a thing to perform *tayammum* on. Therefore, my followers can pray wherever when the time of a prayer sets in. 3. The booty has been made *halal* (lawful) for me (but it was not made so for anyone else). 4. Every Prophet used to be sent to his nation exclusively, but I have been sent to all of mankind. 5. I have been given the right of intercession (on the Day of Resurrection.)"

[141] *Sahih al-Bukhari*, The Book of Tayammum, Hadith 331, and The Book of Salaat, Hadith 429.

told him when they said 'Go, you and your Lord both, ahead and fight. We shall remain sitting here' (5:24)." Abu Ayyub continues, "We the Ansar wished that we had said what Miqdad said. This would have been more beloved to us than having an abundance of wealth."[142] [143]

Another narration suggests the indecisiveness to march to war was also in other members of the Muhajireen, while the Ansar were well prepared to engage in the battle. Anas b. Malik reports that when the Prophet ﷺ heard about the arrival of the caravan, he consulted his companions. When Abu Bakr voiced a negative opinion, the Prophet ﷺ turned away from him. Thereafter 'Umar b. Al-Khattab voiced a similar opinion and the Prophet ﷺ also turned away from him. Sa'ad b. 'Ubadah from the Ansar then stood up and said, "I swear by the One who controls my life! If you command us to ride our animals into the sea we shall readily do so, and if you command us to travel to (the distant city of) Bark al-Ghimaad (in Yemen) we would readily do so." It was then that the Prophet ﷺ commanded for the companions to march.[144] In another narration, Sa'ad b. Mu'aadh from the Ansar rose and offered the commitment of the Ansar saying, "We have believed in you, accepted you and testified that whatever you have brought to us is the truth. For this, we have pledged to you that we will always listen to and obey you. Therefore, O Messenger of Allah, you may proceed to do as you please for we are with you. I swear by the One who has sent you with the truth that even if you take us to the sea and then (ask us) to dive with you without any of us remaining behind we would do so. We are ready for you to lead us in battle against the enemy because we are unfaltering in battle and fearless when encountering the enemy. May Allah show you actions from us that will bring you great joy. (We say) proceed with the blessings of Allah!"[145]

Three hundred and thirteen Muslims participated in the battle. Among these, seventy-six were from the Muhajireen[146], while the Ansar numbered

---

[142] *Al-Bidayah wa al-Nihayah*, vol. 3, p. 263; *Hayaat al-Sahaaba*, vol. 1 p. 407.

[143] Another narration states that it was the Ansar who responded by citing the inaction of the Bani Israel towards Prophet Musa ﷺ, however it is more correctly attributed to Miqdad. See *Al-Bidayah wa al-Nihayah*, vol. 3, p. 263.

[144] Ibid.

[145] *Al-Bidayah wa al-Nihayah*, vol. 3, p. 262.

[146] Ibid., p. 269.

two hundred and thirty-six.[147] Women from the Ansar also took part in the expedition where they provided water for the ill and treat the wounded.[148]

Among the captives of the Battle of Badr was Abbas b. Abdul Muttalib. A man from the Ansar captured him and many of the Ansar wanted to kill him. When the news reached the Prophet ﷺ he is narrated to have said, "I was unable to sleep last night because the Ansar said they would kill my uncle Abbas. I will go to the Ansar and bring him with me."[149] The companions offered to get Abbas and wanted him to be released, but the Ansar responded, "We shall never release him." The companions asked, "Even if this pleases the Messenger of Allah ﷺ?" The Ansar immediately accepted saying, "If this pleases the Prophet ﷺ, then you may have him," whereby Abbas eventually formally accepted Islam.[150]

This was the only major battle that Jabir b. Abdullah al-Ansari did not participate in, owing to the fact that his father had obliged him to remain behind in Medina, however his father Abdullah did participate in the Battle of Badr and was victorious with the Muslims against the pagans. There are many narrations of the Prophet ﷺ commanding his companions to listen to their parents if they with a valid reason, refuse permission for them to participate in a war. For example, a woman came with her son and said to the Prophet ﷺ, "This son of mine wants to march in battle but I refuse to allow him to go", to which the Prophet ﷺ said to the son, "Remain with your mother until she permits you to fight, or until death claims her because this will earn you greater rewards."[151]

Abu Azeez b. Umayr narrates, "I was among the prisoners captured during the Battle of Badr. The Prophet ﷺ told his companions, 'I emphatically command you to treat the prisoners well.' I was with a group

---

[147] Haythami, vol. 6, p. 93.

[148] Ibid., vol. 5, p. 324.

[149] Abdullah b. Abbas narrates that during the Battle of Badr, the Prophet told the companions, "I know well that the men from Banu Hashim were forced to march in battle, but they have no desire to fight against us. Whoever confronts Abbas b. Abdul Muttalib should not kill him because he has been forced to fight." The narration also mentions that despite the Prophet's ﷺ command, some companions still wanted to kill Abbas anyways, thus he feared for his uncle. (*Al-Bidayah wa al-Nihayah*, vol. 3, p. 248; *Tabaqat al-Kubra*, Ibn Sa'ad, vol 4, p. 5.)

[150] *Al-Bidayah wa al-Nihayah*, vol. 3, p. 298.

[151] Haythami, vol. 5, p. 322.

of Ansar and whenever the morning and afternoon meals were served, they would eat only dates and would give me the wheat bread because of the Prophet's ※ instructions to treat us well."[152]

The Battle of Uhud

Jabir narrates about the moment that the Muslim army became overwhelmed during the Battle of Uhud, the second battle in Islamic history. Many of the Muslims dispersed from around the Prophet ※ and the only people left with him were eleven men from the Ansar and Talha b. Ubaydillah. The Prophet ※ had begun climbing the mountain when the pagans caught up with him. He ※ called out, "Is there no one to repel them?" "I am here O Messenger of Allah ※" responded Talha. "Stay where you are, O Talha" the Prophet ※ instructed him. One of the Ansar then responded, "I shall, O Messenger of Allah!" As the Ansari fought in defence, the Prophet ※ and the others with him continued climbing. The Ansari was eventually martyred and the pagans were again catching up with the Prophet ※.

The Prophet again had to call out, "Is there no one to repel them?" When Talha again volunteered for the task, the Prophet ※ gave the same instructions as before. One of the Ansar said, "I shall, O Messenger of Allah." As the Ansari fought in defence, the others continued climbing and again the Ansari was martyred, and the Prophet ※ continued to be attacked. This continued until each Ansari had been martyred and no one except Talha was left.

The Prophet ※ again called out, "Is there no one to repel them" to which Talha replied willingly and fought as hard as those before him. When his hands became injured he exclaimed, "*Hass!*" an Arabic expression roughly to the equivalent of "*Ah!*" The Prophet ※ said to him, "Had you exclaimed 'In the name of Allah' (*bismillah*), the angels would have lifted you to the heavens in full view of the people and entered you into the skies!" The Prophet ※ then climbed to the top of the mountain where he joined the other companions who had regrouped there.[153]

During the battle some people started saying that the Prophet ※ had been martyred. This news reached the people of Medina and the cries of the

---

[152] Ibid., vol. 6, p. 86.
[153] *Al-Bidayah wa al-Nihayah*, vol. 4, p. 26.

women could be heard in the furthest parts of the city. One of the Ansari women immediately left Medina and headed for the battlefield. When she arrived the corpses of her martyred father, husband, son and brother were brought before her. She asked who are these bodies of and was informed who lay there. Undaunted, each time she asked, "Where is the Messenger of Allah 🕮?!" until she was shown where the Prophet 🕮 was safe. When she reached him, she held on to the edge of his garment and said, "May my parents be sacrificed for you! When you are safe, I have no concern for all of those who have died![154] After seeing you, every calamity seems trivial to me."[155]

Jabir b. Abdullah al-Ansari reports that, "The Prophet 🕮 collected every two martyrs of Uhud in one piece of cloth, then he would ask, 'Which of them knew more of the Qur'an?' When one of them was pointed out for him, he would put that one first in the grave and say, 'I will be a witness for them on the Day of Resurrection.' He ordered them to be buried with the blood on their bodies, and they were neither washed, nor was a funeral prayer offered for them."[156]

It is also narrated that Jabir said, "The Prophet 🕮 said, 'Bury them (i.e. martyrs) with their blood.'" After the Battle of Uhud, he did not get them washed."[157] [158] Jabir added, "My father and my uncle were shrouded in one sheet."[159]

---

[154] Haythami, vol. 6, p. 115.

[155] *Al-Bidayah wa al-Nihayah*, vol. 4, p. 47.

[156] *Sahih al-Bukhari*, Kitab al-Jana'iz (Book on Funerals), Hadith 427; *Sunan b. Majah*, Chapter Regarding Funerals, Hadith 1514.

[157] Ibid., Hadith 430.

[158] The Chapter on Funerals has several narrations by Jabir affirming that the martyrs were not given a ceremonial bath (*ghusl*) and were buried in the clothes that they were martyred in, even with no ceremonial shroud (*kafan*). It is considered an honour (*karaama*) in the religion to meet Allah 🕮 in this state, and the jurisprudence requires that only the funeral prayer be recited over martyrs, however one's own personal ceremonial bath should be performed in anticipation of martyrdom. Al-Muhaqqiq al-Hilli (d. 676 AH) states in *Shara'i al-Islam*, p. 32, *Ahkam al-Amwaat* (Rules Regarding the Deceased).
The Arabic text of this passage reads:

و الشهيد الذي قتل بين يدي الامام و مات في المعركة لا يغسل و لا يكفن و يصلي عليه ، و كذا من وجب عليه قتل،

يؤمر بالاغتسال قبل قتله ثم لا يغسل بعد ذلك.

[159] Ibid., Hadith 431; *Sahih al-Bukhari*, Chapter on Funerals (al-Jana'iz), Hadith 431.

Jabir also states that, "When my father was martyred, I lifted the sheet from his face and wept and the people forbade me to do so, but the Prophet ﷺ did not forbid me. Then my aunt Fatima began weeping and the Prophet ﷺ said, 'It is all the same whether you weep or not. The angels are shading him continuously with their wings until you shift him from the field.'"[160] Jabir also mentioned, "During the Battle of Uhud, my father was brought after he had been martyred. He was placed in front of Allah's Apostle ﷺ and a sheet was over him. I went intending to uncover my father but my people forbade me; again, I wanted to uncover him but my people forbade me. The Messenger of Allah ﷺ gave his order and he was taken away. At that time, he ﷺ heard the voice of a woman crying and asked, 'Who is this?' The people replied, 'It is the daughter or the sister of Amr.' The Prophet ﷺ responded, 'Why does she weep, for the angels have been shading him with their wings until he was shifted away.'"[161] [162]

Jabir is narrated to have said, "When the time of the Battle of Uhud approached, my father called me at night and said, "I think that I will be the first amongst the companions of the Prophet ﷺ to be martyred. I do not leave anyone after me dearer to me than you, except Allah's Apostle's soul; I owe some debt and you should repay it and treat your sisters favourably

---

[160] *Sahih al-Bukhari*, Chapter on Funerals (al-Jana'iz), Hadith 336.

[161] Ibid., Hadith 381.

[162] Narrations are attributed to Jabir about Abdullah b. Ubay, the leader of the hypocrites in Medina. Due to their fame I will mention them here: "When Abdullah b. Ubay died, his son came to the Prophet ﷺ and said, 'Oh Messenger of Allah ﷺ, if you do not attend my father's funeral, people will always insult our family.' When the Prophet ﷺ arrived at the funeral he found the body already placed in the grave. The Prophet ﷺ asked, 'Why did you not call me before you lowered him into the grave?' The body was taken out and the Prophet ﷺ blew on it from head to toe." (*Tafseer ibn Katheer*, vol. 2, p. 378) In a separate narration attributed to Jabir it says: "Allah's Apostle ﷺ came to Abdullah b. Ubay after his death. He had been laid in his grave ready for burial. The Prophet ﷺ ordered that he be taken out of the grave and he was taken out. Then he placed him on his knees and placed some of his saliva on him and clothed him in his (the Prophet's ﷺ) own shirt. Abdullah b. Ubay had given his shirt to Abbas, the Prophets uncle, to wear. (Ibid., Hadith 433). These narrations depict the Prophet ﷺ as grieving and interceding at the death of Abdullah b. Ubay. However, according to many narrations, verses 1, 3, 7 and 8 of Surah al-Munafiqoon (Chapter of the Hypocrites) were revealed about Abdullah b. Ubay and his group. It is therefore unlikely that the Prophet ﷺ acted in such a manner upon Abdullah b. Ubay's death.

(honourably)." In the morning he was the first to be martyred and was buried along with another (martyr). I did not want to leave him with the other (martyr) so I took him out of the grave after six months of his burial and he was in the same condition that he was on the day of burial, except a slight change near his ear."[163] [164]

Jabir narrates that as they were returning from the battle, the Prophet ﷺ could not find his uncle Hamza ؑ. Someone told the Prophet ﷺ that he had seen him by a particular tree supplicating, "I am the Lion of Allah and the Lion of his Messenger ﷺ. O Allah, I absolve myself from what those people (the pagans) have done and I seek pardon from what these people (the hypocritical Muslims who disobeyed the Prophet's ﷺ command) have done (by causing their own defeat)." The Prophet ﷺ then went in that direction and started to cry when he saw Hamza's head cut open. However, when the Prophet ﷺ came closer and saw how the body of Hamza had been mutilated (by Hind) he wept uncontrollably. After a while the Prophet ﷺ asked, "Is there no burial shroud?" One of the Ansar stood up and threw a cloth over the body. Thereafter the Prophet ﷺ said, "In the sight of Allah, Hamza shall be the leader of all of the martyrs on the Day of Judgement."[165] Another narration states that when the news of Hamza's martyrdom reached his sister Safiyyah, she ran to the battlefield to see her brother and brought two sheets as his shroud, saying, "I want you to bury him in these." When the companions took the sheets to where Hamza was laying, they found a martyred Ansari man lying next to him just as mutilated as Hamza was. The

---

[163] Ibid., Hadith 434; *Tabaqat al-Kubra*, vol. 3, p. 563. Another narration mentions, "I noticed nothing different about his body except for a few strands of hair from his beard that had been touching the ground." *Al-Bidayah wa al-Nihayah*, vol. 4, p. 43.

[164] Although narrations mention that Jabir exhumed the body of his father six months after the Battle of Uhud, the author rejects these narrations for three reasons. First of all, it is impermissible to exhume the body of a buried person without just cause; the Prophet ﷺ would not have given permission for this and thus it is contrary to what is known about Jabir. Secondly, it was the Prophet ﷺ himself who buried Jabir's father in the same manner as the other martyrs and therefore there was no reason for Jabir to dislike this. Lastly, there are narrations which mention that Mu'awiyah b. Abi Sufyan forced some martyrs of Uhud to be exhumed (which will be mentioned in the Chapter of the Period of Imam al-Hasan ؑ); therefore, it is likely that these narrations of Jabir exhuming his father's body after six months became attributed to Jabir in order to cover Mu'awiyah's actions.

[165] *Mustadrak ala al-Sahihayn*, Hakim, vol. 3, p. 199.

companions felt it was wrong to use both of the sheets for Hamza while the Ansari man had none, so they decided to use one for each of them. After measuring the sheets, one was larger than the other so they drew lots to see who should receive the larger sheet."[166]

Jabir narrates that after the Battle of Uhud, Imam Ali ﷺ came home to Lady Fatima ﷺ and said the following lines of poetry:

O Fatima, take this flawless sword from me,

I am neither shaken with fear nor a worthless man.

By my life! I have truly exerted myself to assist Muhammed,

And for the pleasure of my Lord Who has complete knowledge about His bondsmen.

After this, the Arch Angel Jibra'il said, "O Muhammad, I swear by your father that this is certainly an occasion of grief." The Prophet ﷺ replied, "O Jibra'il, he (Ali) is from me." To this, Jibra'il said, "And I am from the two of you."[167]

Eight years after they had been martyred, the Prophet ﷺ returned to where the Battle of Uhud had taken place and again performed *Salaat al-Janazah* (the funeral prayers) for the martyrs. He appeared to be bidding farewell to those alive and those deceased. Thereafter he mounted the pulpit and said, "I will go ahead of you (to the hereafter) and will be your witness.[168] Our promised rendezvous shall be the Fountain of Kawthar and I can see it as I stand here. I have no fear that you will revert to polytheism after me, but I fear that you will vie with each other in acquiring this world."[169]

---

[166] Haythami, vol. 6, p. 118.

[167] Ibid., vol. 6, p. 122.

[168] "And thus We have made you a just community that you will be a witness over the people and the Messenger ﷺ will be a witness over you," (2:143); as well "And mention the Day when We will resurrect among every nation a witness over them from amongst themselves. And we will bring you (Oh Muhammad) as a witness over your nation." (16:89)

[169] *Hayaat al-Sahaaba*, vol. 2, p. 285.

The Revelation of Salaat al-Khawf

Salaat al-Khawf is a prayer which is recited during the state of fear or imminent danger from an enemy. Its initial practice was at the Battle of Asfaan when the pagan army was under the command of Khalid b. Walid. Jabir narrates, "We fought in the company of the Messenger of Allah ﷺ against the tribe of Juhaina. They fought with us terribly. When we had finished the *dhuhr* prayer, the polytheists said, 'Had we attacked them then, we would have killed them.' Angel Jibra'il informed the Messenger of Allah ﷺ about it (their plan). The Messenger of Allah ﷺ mentioned it to us, adding that they (the pagans) had also said 'Shortly there will be the time for the *'asr* prayer which is dearer to them (the Muslims) than even their own children.' It was then that the verse (4:102)[170] and *Salaat al-Khawf* was revealed."

Jabir continues: "When the time for 'Asr came, we formed two rows, and the pagans were between us and the Qiblah. The Messenger of Allah ﷺ said: Allah is Most Great, and we also repeated this. He bowed and we also bowed. He went down into prostration and the first row prostrated along with him. When they stood up, the second row went down into prostration. Then the first row went into the rear, and the second row came in the front and occupied the place of the first row. The Messenger of Allah ﷺ then said: Allah is Most Great, and we also repeated this. He then bowed, and we also bowed. He then went down into prostration and along with him the row also (went down into prostration), and the second row remained standing. When the second row had also prostrated, all of them sat down and then the Messenger of Allah ﷺ pronounced salutation to them."[171]

---

[170] "And when you are among them and lead them in prayer, let a group of them stand [in prayer] with you and let them carry their arms. And when they have prostrated, let them be [in position] behind you and have the other group come forward which has not [yet] prayed and let them pray with you, taking precaution and carrying their arms. Those who disbelieve wish that you would neglect your weapons and your baggage so they could come down upon you in one [single] attack. But there is no blame upon you, if you are troubled by rain or are ill, for putting down your arms, but take precaution. Indeed, Allah has prepared for the disbelievers a humiliating punishment."

[171] *Sahih Muslim*, The Book of Prayer, Chapter 57, The Prayer of Fear, Hadith 840; *Al-Bidayah wa al-Nihayah*, vol. 4, p. 81.

The Battle of Khaybar

Jabir reports that during the Battle of Khaybar, Imam Ali ﴾ lifted up the door of the fortress which the Muslims used to climb over the walls. This led to their victory. When the companions tried to lift the door, forty of them were unable to do so.[172]

Jabir also narrates, "When Imam Ali ﴾ proceeded to the Messenger of Allah ﷺ upon the victory, the Prophet ﷺ said to him ﴾, 'I swear by Allah! Had it not been that a section from my community would say about you what the Christians say about the Messiah, Isa son of Mariam, I would have said today regarding you such words that you would not pass by an assembly except that they would have taken the dust from under your feet and would seek to be healed by it.'

'But it suffices for you that you are from me and I am from you. You give preference to me and I give preference to you. You are in the status with me like Haroun was to Musa, except that there is no Prophet after me; and you shall uphold my responsibilities and you will fight for (upholding) my Sunnah.'

'And tomorrow you will be at the Fountain being my successor. You will be the first one to return to me at the Fountain, and you will be the first one to be robed (in a divine outfit from Paradise) with me. You will be the first one from my community to enter Paradise with me, and your Shi'a will be upon pulpits of Light, their faces radiating around me. I shall intercede for them and they will be in Paradise tomorrow as my neighbours.'

'Your war is my war and your peace is my peace. Your righteous actions are like my righteous actions. Your public actions are like public my public actions, and the secret in your chest is like the secret in my chest. Your children are my children, and you will be accomplishing my promises. The truth is with you and upon your tongue, your heart and in front of your eyes.'

'Faith is blended in your flesh and blood just like it is blended to my flesh and blood, and it will be such that no one will ever return to me- the one who is hateful to you; and he will never be absent from me, the one who loves you - until he returns to the Fountain along with you.'"

---

[172] *Al-Bidayah wa al-Nihayah*, vol. 4, p. 189.

Jabir then says, "Ali fell into prostration and said, 'All Praise is for Allah Who favoured me with al-Islam and endeared me to the best of all of the creation, the seal of the Prophet ﷺ and chief of the Messengers, a favour and a grace from Him upon me!' So the Prophet said, 'Had it not been for you, the believers would not have been recognized after me.'"[173]

Jabir reports that after the battle, a Jewish woman from Khaybar poisoned some roasted goat meat and presented it to the Prophet ﷺ. The Prophet ﷺ took hold of a foreleg of the goat and was about to start eating it, while a group of companions also began to eat. The Prophet ﷺ stopped his companions saying, "Take your hands off of the food!" He then sent for the woman. When she arrived he asked, "Did you poison the food?" The woman replied, "Who told you about this?" The Prophet ﷺ responded, "The same foreleg here in my hand informed me about it."

When she admitted that she had indeed poisoned the meat, the Prophet ﷺ asked her why she did it. She replied, "I wanted to see if you are really a Prophet. I said to myself that if you are a Prophet, then it will do you no harm and if you are not a Prophet, then we can get rid of you." The Prophet ﷺ forgave her and did not punish her.[174] [175]

After the conquest the Prophet ﷺ addressed the Ansar, "You have fulfilled your duty towards us (the Muhajireen). Now, if you please, you may hand over your shares of plantations in Khaybar to the Muhajireen and have your date crops in Medina for yourselves without having to continue sharing it, as the others will now receive from Khaybar." The Ansar accepted the proposal and said, "You have placed several responsibilities on us, while you have taken the responsibility that in exchange for this we shall have Paradise. We have now fulfilled what you had asked of us and request that

---

[173] *Bashaaratu al-Mustafa li Shi'ati Murtaza*, Ibn Abi Qasim al-Tabari, Section 4, pp. 21-2, Hadith 35.

[174] *Hayaat al-Sahaaba*, vol. 2, pp. 561-2.

[175] Other narrations suggest that this meat came to harm the Prophet ﷺ and that some companions died from their eating it, to which the Prophet ﷺ had the lady executed as a punishment. Other narrations claim that this meat was a cause of the Prophet's ﷺ martyrdom, however the battle took place four years earlier and so this explanation appears weak. In any event, it is generally accepted that the Prophet ﷺ was poisoned at this battle, however I have quoted the narration of Jabir.

our condition is also met!" to which the Prophet ﷺ replied, "You will have it!"[176]

The Battle of Khandaq

Jabir narrates, "As we were digging the trench for the Battle of Khandaq, a very hard and large boulder got in our way. We went to the Messenger ﷺ and said, 'This large boulder in the trench has come in the way.' The Prophet ﷺ replied, 'I shall come to see it.' As he stood up we saw that he had a stone tied to his stomach and we had not as much as tasted food for three days.[177] The Prophet ﷺ then picked up a pickaxe and with one strike he reduced it to a heap of dust.

During the dig, the Prophet ﷺ went to the trench one morning. He found the Ansar and Muhajireen digging in the cold, preparing for the battle. When he saw their fatigue and hunger he supplicated, 'O Allah, there is no life but the life of the hereafter. Please forgive the Ansar and the Muhajireen (their faults).' In response to this, the companions said, 'We are those who have pledged allegiance to Muhammad ﷺ to struggle hard so long as we live.' Upon hearing this, the Prophet ﷺ, was impressed and appreciative and again he supplicated saying, 'O Allah, there is no good but the good of the hereafter, so bless the Ansar and the Muhajireen.'"[178]

Jabir was a catalyst for and privy to one of the miracles of the Prophet ﷺ during the preparation of the trench. He narrates, "We worked with the Messenger of Allah ﷺ in the trench and I had a small fleshy sheep with me. I said to myself 'I swear by Allah, that I would like to make it for the Messenger of Allah ﷺ.' I asked my wife about this and so she ground some barely making bread from it for us. She slaughtered that small sheep and we prepared it for the Messenger of Allah ﷺ. When we retired in the evening - and we used to work digging it all day except at the end of the day when we would go back to our families - the Messenger of Allah ﷺ wanted to leave the trench. I said, 'O Messenger of Allah ﷺ, I have made for you a small sheep and some bread from what we had so I would love if you come with me to my house to eat.' I wanted the Messenger of Allah ﷺ only to come

---

[176] *Hayaat al-Sahaaba*, vol. 3, pp. 94-5.
[177] *Al-Bidayah wa al-Nihayah*, vol. 4 p. 97; *p. Hayaat al-Sahaaba*, vol. 1, p. 328.
[178] Ibid., p. 95.

with me, but upon my invitation, he called out loudly to everyone, 'Come with the Messenger of Allah ﷺ to the house of Jabir b. Abdullah for food!'[179]

I gasped saying, 'Surely we are all from God and to Him we shall surely return.' When we all arrived my wife said, 'O dear! The Prophet ﷺ has come with the Muhajireen and the Ansar! Did the Prophet ask you about this?' When Jabir confirmed that he had she became content that the Prophet ﷺ would make arrangements for the extra people. The Prophet ﷺ then told Jabir, 'Tell your wife not to take the pot off of the fire and not to take the bread out of the oven until I arrive.'

When they arrived, the Prophet ﷺ told the companions, 'Enter the house but do not crowd it.' Then he sat and we brought the food out to him. The Prophet ﷺ then took the food and started to break the bread into pieces, placing the meat onto the pieces of bread and serving it to the companions. He knelt down and said 'Bismillah' and then he ate. The Prophet ﷺ continued to take from the pot, breaking the bread and serving it. The people started to come in one after the other, and whenever a group of people finished eating from the plate they would get up and another group would come until it sufficed *all* of the people of the trench."[180]

Jabir also narrates that once when the Prophet ﷺ came to visit him in his house, they slaughtered a goat in his honour. The Prophet ﷺ commented appreciatively, "It seems like they know we like meat!"[181]

The Patience of Jabir's Wife and the Miracle of Bringing their Children Back to Life

Jabir narrates that when he hosted the Prophet ﷺ and his friend on the Day of the Battle of the Trench, he had a ram which he slaughtered for them. Jabir also had two sons, the youngest of whom was absent when Jabir slaughtered the ram, so when that son returned and did not see the ram, he asked his brother about it. He replied, "Your father has slaughtered it to host the Messenger of God ﷺ."

He asked, "How did he slaughter it?" The brother replied, "Come and I will show you how," and taking his hand he took him to the roof where his

---

[179] As quoted in *Rijal Hawl al-Rasool wa Ahl Baytihi*, Aal Sayf, Fawzi, pp.g 219-20.
[180] *Sahih Muslim*, vol. 2, p. 180.
[181] *Shamaa'il*, Chapter of the Food of the Prophet, Tirmidhi, Hadith 28.

father had slaughtered the ram. He tied his hands and his feet (and took a knife) and said to him: "That is how he slaughtered it, (and while playing accidentally) he cut his (brother's) head off."

When the blood started to flow, startled, he became intensely scared and wanted to flee so that his mom would not see what he had done. He attempted to escape but in his hurried state, he fell from the high roof to the passageway (and also died).

During that time Jabir's wife, their mother, was busy cooking the bread. She heard a sound and went out to see what it was and what had happened. It was then that she saw the blood flowing in the gutter. Gasping, she ran to the roof and saw that her youngest son's head had been cut off.

Then she went to the edge of the roof to check for her eldest son where she saw that he had fallen and also died. She went down from the roof and got the help of her maid and said: "A disastrous incident has happened and we must hide it." She rushed to the two bodies, brought them into the house and hid them, and then carried on in performing her work.

When the Messenger of Allah ﷺ approached with several hundred people of Medina to partake in the meal, the angel Jibra'il descended and said, "Do not eat until Jabir's sons join in the meal."

The Prophet ﷺ told Jabir, "Allah has instructed me not to eat until your two sons are present so please bring them." Jabir asked his wife about them, but all she could say was, "They went out of the house." Jabir went out and looked for them for a while but could not find them so he came back and said to the Prophet ﷺ, "I tried to find them but I could not see them." Jibra'il again descended and informed the Prophet ﷺ about what had transpired and the patience of their mother and said to him ﷺ, "Give her the glad tidings of Paradise and ask them to bring the two children. Pray to God to bring them back to life so that they can also join in eating the food with you."

Then the Prophet ﷺ asked Jabir to bring them, and when he ﷺ prayed for them they became alive and engaged in eating the food with them."[182]

---

[182] *Layali al-Akhbar*, Muhammad Nabi al-Tawseerkani, vol. 1, p. 306; *Qasas al-Sahaaba wa al-Tabi'in*, pp. 88-9.

An Ansari Husband and Wife in the Battle

During one of the battles, a man from the Ansar by the name of Khallaad was martyred. Some of the Muslims went to inform his wife that he had been slain. She wore a veil and went out to receive the body. One of the Muslims remarked, "Khallaad has been killed and you are wearing your veil?" She replied, "I may have lost my Khallaad but I have not lost my modesty!" When the Prophet ﷺ was informed about this he said, "Take note that Khallaad will receive the rewards of two martyrs!"[183]

The Battle of Dhaat al-Riqaa' and the Prophet ﷺ builds a Special Bond with Jabir

Jabir narrates that the companions were accompanying the Prophet ﷺ to a place called Nakhl during the expedition of Dhaat al-Riqaa'. It so happened that a man from the pagans had sworn revenge upon the Muslims and took an oath that he would not rest until he killed the companions of the Prophet ﷺ. He was following the tracks of the group in the hope of an ambush or an opportunity to attack.

When the Prophet ﷺ set up camp he asked, "Who shall stand guard over us tonight?" Ammar b. Yasir volunteered from among the Muhajireen and Abbaad b. Bishr from among the Ansar stood up and offered to do so. The Prophet ﷺ gave them instructions to stand guard at the mouth of the valley that they were camping in. When they reached the mouth, Abbaad said to Ammar, "For which part of the night would you like me to relieve you, the first part or the second part of the night?" Ammar replied, "Relieve me for the first part of the night."

Ammar lay down to rest as Abbaad stood up to perform his night prayers. The man who had sworn revenge upon the Muslims arrived quietly and saw the silhouette of Abbaad in prayer. He took the opportunity and immediately fired an arrow which struck Abbaad. Abbaad removed the arrow from his body, threw it aside and continued his prayer. The pagan fired a second arrow and it again struck Abbaad, who removed the arrow and remained in his prayer. When the man fired a third arrow, Abbaad went

---

[183] *Tabaqat al-Kubra*, vol. 3, p. 83.

into prostration and completed his prayer. He then woke Ammar up and said, "Sit up because I have been incapacitated." As soon as Ammar got up, the man saw two of them and fled.

When Ammar saw the blood on Abbaad he exclaimed, "Glory be to Allah, why did you not wake me up when he shot at you the first time?" Abbaad replied, "I had started reciting a chapter of the Qur'an in my prayer and did not like to cut it short before completing it. However, when the firing persisted I went into prostration to complete my prayer and inform you. I swear by Allah, that had it not been for fear of jeopardizing the mouth of the pass that the Prophet ﷺ had instructed me to guard, I would have given my life rather than cut short the chapter that I was reciting."[184]

Jabir narrates, "I went out with the Messenger of Allah ﷺ to the Battle of Dhaat al-Riqaa' on my camel which was very weak. When the Messenger of Allah ﷺ returned back, I let my friends go ahead and delayed myself to stay at the back until the Prophet ﷺ reached me.

He said, 'O Jabir, what is wrong?'

'O the Messenger of Allah ﷺ, my camel has slowed me down.' He ﷺ said, 'kneel it down.' I knelt it down and the Prophet ﷺ knelt down as well. He ﷺ said, 'Give me the stick that is in your hand or cut for me a stick from a tree.' I did so and the Prophet ﷺ took it. He ﷺ prickled the camel with it a few times and then said to me, 'Now ride it!' So I rode it out and I swear by He Who sent him ﷺ with the truth, it competed with his ﷺ camel (like in a race)!"

Later on the Prophet ﷺ asked me, "Will you sell me your camel?" I replied, "Rather, I will give it to you, O Messenger of Allah ﷺ." He refused saying, "Not at all, sell it to me." Agreeing, I said "Estimate its worth, O Messenger of Allah ﷺ." He said, "Okay then, I will take it for one dirham."

I said, "No, you are being unfair to me, O Messenger of Allah ﷺ." He ﷺ responded, "Two dirhams then!" I again refused the offer, so he ﷺ continued to raise its price for me until it reached to forty dirhams. Then I asked, "Are you pleased, O Messenger of Allah ﷺ?" "Yes" he said. "It is yours then", I told him ﷺ.[185]

---

[184] *Al-Bidayah wa al-Nihayah*, vol. 4, p. 85.

[185] The Prophet ﷺ was being very astute with his negotiation. Jabir may have accepted any reasonable offer even if it was slightly less than the camel was worth.

A separate narration says that the Prophet ﷺ then inquired, "O Jabir, you will shortly arrive into Medina. Will you sleep on your bed (mattress)?" Jabir narrates, I replied, "O Messenger of God ﷺ, no. I swear by He Who sent you with the truth, we do not have beds (mattresses) to sleep on. Our floor is sandy so we spray it with water to soften it and then we sleep on it."[186]

Returning to the main narration, the Prophet ﷺ then asked, "O Jabir, are you married?" I replied, "Yes, O Messenger of Allah ﷺ." He asked, "Was she a virgin or a widow (previously married)?" I replied, "She was a widow."

He ﷺ continued: "Is there not a bondmaid where you can be joyful to her and she can be joyful to you?"

I replied, "My father died in the Battle of Uhud and he left seven daughters, so I married a caring woman who would keep them together and look after them." He ﷺ said, "You did well, God-Willing."[187]

In another separate narration Jabir is narrated to have said that he was advised to go home and try to conceive a child. He mentions, "The Prophet ﷺ said, 'You will reach home soon, so when you have arrived, I advise you to have relations with your wife (that you may have an intelligent son).'"[188]

In the next part of the main narration, the Prophet ﷺ decided to do something nice for Jabir and his wife. Having enquired about their difficult lifestyle and financial state and hearing about their extensive responsibilities toward Jabir's sisters, the Prophet ﷺ wanted to aid Jabir financially, create a warm reception for him upon his return home and ensure that he would

---

The Prophet ﷺ knowing this did not want Jabir to under sell the camel, nor did he want to pay too much for it; so he started the offer at one dirham, giving Jabir the comfort of being able to reasonably say "no" to the Prophet ﷺ without feeling bad. Once the Prophet reached a fair amount, Jabir could then say yes to whatever price he was satisfied with. We can also see the tone of the entire chain is one of friendship. It is likely that the offer of one dirham was evidently not serious by the Prophet ﷺ nor was he trying to heavily undervalue the camel, but rather it conveyed a comical starting point to allow for the comfort of negotiations to take place. In this there is a great lesson of how friends or family can negotiate with each other where necessary.

186 *Qasas al-Sahaaba wa-Tabi'in*, p. 79.

187 In another tradition it says that Jabir said: "I have sisters and did not want her to create trouble between them and me." The Prophet ﷺ said: "That is better then." (*Sunan b. Majah*, The Chapter on Marriage, Hadith 1860).

188 *Sahih al-Bukhari*, The Book of Sales and Trade, Hadith 310.

do something romantic for his wife, which until then, would have been out of his financial capacity.

Jabir continues in the main narration, "When we reached Suraaran[189] the Prophet ﷺ said 'We will ask for a camel suitable for slaughtering. Once it is slaughtered, we will eat it today and Jabir's wife will hear about us so she will dust off the cushions (to make the house ready for Jabir).'[190]

I said, 'O Messenger of Allah, we do not have any cushions (cannot afford those items for the house).' The Prophet ﷺ replied, 'You will have them. So when you arrive, do something very kind for your wife.'"

The next day they left Suraaran for Medina and the Prophet ﷺ asked Jabir, "Would you like to sell me your camel?" Jabir replied in the affirmative and they agreed on a price. He mentions, "Allah's Apostle reached before me and I reached later on in the morning. When I went to the Masjid, I found the Prophet ﷺ at the door of it. He asked me, 'Have you arrived just now?' I replied in the affirmative. He said, 'Leave your camel and come into the Masjid and pray two units of prayer.' I entered and offered the prayer."[191]

After Jabir finished his prayer of arriving back (safely) into Medina, the Prophet ﷺ said, "O the son of my brother, grab the head of your camel" and then he ﷺ called Bilal and told him: "Take Jabir and give him forty dirhams." Jabir continued: "So I went with him and he gave me even more than that for the camel, and I swear by God that it grew with me, and it had its place in our house until he was afflicted with what happened on the day of Hurra."[192] [193]

Bilal then weighed (the camel) for me and I went away, then the Prophet sent for me and I thought that he would return to me my camel which I

---

[189] A place three miles from Medina.

[190] Meaning if the companions entered into Medina without warning, Jabir's wife would not be able to prepare the house for him. If they waited until the evening, then the news would reach Medina that the Prophet ﷺ is camped closely outside of the city so Jabir's wife would prepare the house.

[191] *Sahih al-Bukhari*, The Book of Sales and Trade, Hadith 310.

[192] *Al-Seera al-Nabawiyyah*, Ibn Hisham, vol. 3, p. 218.

[193] A battle fought at al-Harrah on 26 Dhu al-Hijjah 63 AH lying to the northeast of Medina, led by Yazid b. Mu'awiyah. Following their victory, the Syrian army looted the city of Medina for three consecutive days, killing scores and raping women of the Quraysh and Ansar. When Medina was stabilised, Yazid's forces then attacked the city of Mecca.

hated more than anything else. But the Prophet said to me, 'Take your camel as well as its price' leaving Jabir with the money, a gift and the camel."[194] [195]

Jabir also narrates, "When we returned - I mean from the Battle of Dhaat al-Riqaa' - while we were travelling, the Messenger of God ﷺ asked me: 'O Jabir, what did you do with your father's debt?'

I replied, 'O Messenger of God ﷺ, it is still the same... (I am) waiting until we harvest his palm trees (and are able to collect the dates).'"

Jabir asked the Messenger of Allah ﷺ to intercede for him with the creditor, to which he ﷺ asked, 'To whom is your father's debt?' I replied, 'The Jewish man, Abu al-Shahm has upon my father the arrears of dates.' The Messenger of Allah ﷺ went and spoke to that Jew, asking him to accept dates in lieu of what was owed, but he refused to give respite. Then the Messenger of Allah ﷺ went to area of the date-palm trees and walked among them. Then he ﷺ said to Jabir: 'Pick (dates) for him and pay off what is owed to him in full.'[196] The Prophet ﷺ continued: 'When you reap them, separate al-Ajwa[197] to one side, and keep aside the other types of dates and bring them to me.'

I put al-Sayhani (type of date) to one side, Amhat al-Haddadeen (another type of date) to another side, and I kept al-Ajwa separately. Then I went back to a pile of the dates which contained different types of dates and it was the least amount of all of the dates and I put it into one pile.

When the Messenger of God ﷺ looked at the assorted dates, he ﷺ said: 'May God bless it for him (Jabir's father).'[198] He ﷺ then stopped before the

---

[194] *Sahih al-Bukhari*, The Book of Sales and Trade, Hadith 310.

[195] It is probable that the slow camel mentioned in the first narration and the second camel exchanged at the Prophet's Masjid are the same camel. This is because Jabir is narrated to have said, "I sold a camel to the Prophet ﷺ on one of the journeys. When we reached Medina, he ordered me to go to the Masjid and offer two *rak'at salat*. Then he weighed for me (the price of the camel in gold) and gave an extra amount over it." (*Sahih al-Bukhari*, The Chapter of Gifts and the Superiority of Giving, Hadith 788; and in this only one camel is mentioned.) Also the prices of both of them were the same and it was unlikely that Jabir had any additional camels considering his financial state. Therefore, the second narration where the Prophet ﷺ enquires about Jabir's circumstances is an expansion of the first narration.

[196] *Sunan b. Majah*, The Chapter on Charity, Hadith 2434.

[197] A type of date that is compressed and mixed together. Al-Ajwa are considered one of the finest types of dates, and it was also the Prophet's ﷺ favourite kind.

[198] *Allahumma Baarik Lahu*: اللهم بارك له

al-Ajwa pile, touched it and then touched the different types of dates. He then told me, 'Call your creditor.'

When Abu al-Shahm came, he weighed all of that what he was owed which came to one pile, being that of al-Ajwa. The Prophet ﷺ asked me, 'O Jabir, is there any debt left upon your father?' I replied, 'No.'

The rest of the dates were left so we ate from part of it which lasted us a long time, and we sold the other part of it until the dates ripened the following year. I used to say that if I would have sold its source [the palm trees], then I would not have been able to pay off what debt was upon my father.

You (companions) have seen me, that when the Prophet ﷺ said to me: 'What have you done with your father's debt?' I said: 'God has paid it off!' Responding to this, the Prophet ﷺ said: 'O Allah, forgive Jabir!' such that he ﷺ prayed for my forgiveness (istighfaar) twenty-five times in one night."[199] [200]

Jabir mentions in another narration, "I swear by Allah that I was prepared to have all of my father's debts settled from him, even if it meant that I would not have a single date to take back to my sisters, however Allah kept the heap of dates intact for us."[201]

Event of a Miracle During an Expedition

The Ansar were on an expedition with the Prophet ﷺ when they informed him, "O Messenger of Allah, the enemy is here. They have eaten well while we are hungry." The Ansar offered "Let us slaughter our camels and feed everyone." The Prophet appreciating this gesture of sacrifice responded,

---

[199] *A'yaan al-Shi'a*, vol. 4, p. 84.

[200] Sheikh Fawzi Aal Sayf, a compiler of the biography of Jabir mentions the following comments upon this story: "He, the Prophet ﷺ, checked upon the situation of his companions and inquired about their circumstances so that he could help them as much as he ﷺ could afford. How beloved he was, that leader, who gave importance to the situations of his companions and asked about their personal issues! But how great it would be if that person checking was the Messenger of God, the greatest of the prophets, inquiring about Jabir. And how great would be the feeling of Jabir's contentment even if he ﷺ didn't do anything for him, so imagine how satisfying it would be if the enquiry was added to by the fulfilment of the need by the Messenger!" (*Rijaal Hawl al-Rasool wa Ahli Baytihi*, pp. 221-2)

[201] *Dalaa'il al-Nubuwwa*, p. 156.

"Whoever has any leftover food should bring it here." Everyone brought whatever little food that they had. The Prophet ﷺ then sat on the side and prayed to Allah ﷻ to bless the food. Having finished he said to the companions, "Take but do not loot" and so the group started taking. When everyone had finished taking, the food was the same amount as had been gathered in the beginning. The Prophet ﷺ said, "I bear witness that there is none worthy of worship but Allah, and that I am His Messenger. Whosoever says this with sincerity, Allah will save him from the heat of the fire of hell."[202]

The Expedition of Khabat (Leaves)

In the year 8 A.H. the Prophet ﷺ dispatched towards the sea shore an expedition of 300 men. Their mission was to watch the caravan of the Quraysh tribe of Juhaynah at al Khabat near the Red Sea. He ﷺ gave them a bag full of dates as part of their rations.

Jabir reports, "The Prophet ﷺ sent us on an expedition. We stayed at the coast for two weeks and were so much afflicted by extreme hunger that we were obliged to eat leaves. That is why it was called the Expedition of the Leaves." He continues, "The Prophet ﷺ appointed Abu 'Ubaydah as our commander and sent us to intercept a caravan of the Quraysh. Unable to find anything else to eat, we took a bag of dates with us for our provisions. From there, Abu 'Ubaydah used to give us a single date each." When asked what they would do with a single date each, Jabir replied, "We would suck on it as a child suckles and then drink some water. This would have to suffice us for the entire day until the night. We also used our staffs to bring down leaves from the trees which we soaked in water to eat." Jabir was asked, "What use was that one date (during the day?)", to which he replied, "When all of the dates were finished, we would miss that one date!"[203]

When the army suffered extreme hunger, the commander, Qays b. Sa'ad b. Abi 'Ubaydah slaughtered nine riding animals for us to eat. 'Umar b. al-Khattab implored him not to as it would deprive the army of their transport, however he went ahead and did that. After the expedition this was

---

[202] Haythami, vol. 8, p. 304; *Hayaat al-Sahaaba*, vol.1 p. 330.
[203] *Al-Bidayah wa al-Nihayah*, vol. 4, p. 276; *Hayaat al-Sahaaba*, vol.1, p. 329

mentioned to the Prophet ﷺ, and he responded, "Indeed generosity is the hallmark of his family."[204]

Jabir continues, "When we set up camp by the shore, the sea cast out for us a giant fish. We lived off of it for three days and took with us as much of it as we could in our satchels. When our expedition finished we travelled back until we came to the Prophet ﷺ and informed him about what happened saying, "If we thought the fish would not rot before we reached you, we would have loved to bring some of it back for you."[205]

The Incident on the Expedition of Muraysee

Jabir b. Abdullah narrates that the companions were once on an expedition when someone from the Muhajireen punched another companion from the Ansar in the back. The Ansari man called for help and so too did the Muhajir. A fight was about to break out between the Ansar and Muhajireen, but they were stopped. When the Prophet ﷺ heard about this he exclaimed, "What are these calls from the Period of Ignorance (Jahiliyyah)? Forget these kinds of talks for they are foul-smelling."

Among the chief hypocritical companions was Abdullah b. Ubay b. Salool. When news reached him about the incident he wanted to continue the episode so he made a provocative comment saying, "We used to entertain hopes in you that you would defend us, however you have proven that you can no longer cause any harm nor any benefit. These '*jalaabeeb*'[206] have assisted each other against us. Are the Muhajireen doing this? By Allah if we return to Medina, the honourable among us (the Ansar) shall certainly exile the humiliated."

Another prominent hypocrite, Malik b. Dukhshun also tried to stoke the flames of hatred towards the Muhajireen by saying, "Did I not tell you people not to spend on those who are with the Prophet ﷺ?" When these comments reached the Prophet ﷺ, 'Umar b. al-Khattab stood up and said, "O Messenger of Allah ﷺ, permit me to cut off the neck of this hypocrite!", referring to Abdullah b. Ubay. The Prophet ﷺ seeking to calm the situation

---

[204] *Jaami'ul Fawa'id*, vol. 1, p. 147; *Kanz al-Ummal*, vol. 5, p. 260.
[205] Haythami, vol. 5, p. 37; *Sahih Muslim*, book 21, Ahadith 4757-4762.
[206] A derogatory term meaning 'new muhajireen', *Hayaat al-Sahaba*, vol. 1, p. 463.

responded, "Leave him. We do not want people to say that Muhammad kills his companions."[207]

In order to maintain the calm, the Prophet ﷺ travelled with the companions the entire day. He demanded that they continue the expedition throughout the day and night allowing for rest the following day. By the time they set up camp, the companions were so exhausted that they fell asleep immediately. The Prophet ﷺ did this so the companions would not have an opportunity to continue to argue when settled in the camp![208]

After the expedition, the Prophet ﷺ called for 'Umar and asked him, "Would you have killed him if I had issued the command?" to which he replied in the affirmative. The Prophet ﷺ chided 'Umar for his recklessness saying, "Had you killed him on that day, many of the Ansar would have felt insulted (because by then the Ansar were outnumbered by the many Muhajireen from Medina and thus in a weaker position). However, if I was to issue the command today, even they would have been prepared to execute him. (But had you killed him then) people would have said that I attack my own companions, take them out of their homes and then kill them having them bound."

It was with reference to this incident that Allah revealed verses 7 and 8 of the Chapter of the Hypocrites (63), "They are the ones who say, "Do not spend on those who are with the Messenger of Allah until they disband." And to Allah belongs the depositories of the heavens and the earth, but the hypocrites do not understand. They say, "If we return to Medina, the more honored [for power] will surely expel therefrom the more humble." And to Allah belongs [all] honor, and to His Messenger, and to the believers, but the hypocrites do not know. [209] [210]

---

[207] *Tafseer Ibn Katheer*, vol. 4, p. 370.

[208] *Hayaat al-Sahabah*, vol. 1, p. 464.

[209] *Tafseer Ibn Katheer* vol. 4, p. 372.

[210] This narration highlights a number of issues. First of all, while many narrations indicate the bonds of brotherhood between the Ansar and the Muhajireen, there were naturally tensions that arose between them just like in any walk of life this may occur. The Prophet ﷺ tried to downplay this aiming to extinguish its impact, while individuals like Abdullah b. Ubay tried to keep the wounds open. This often happens when individuals seek to cause discord between people. While Umar b. al-Khattab may have intended good, but his shortsightedness would have caused

The Incident on the Return from the Expedition to Najd

Jabir narrates that he accompanied the Prophet 🕊 on an expedition to fight the Muharib and Ghatfaan tribes in Najd. On the way back they decided to rest at a valley with lots of trees. As the companions dispersed to take shade, the Prophet 🕊 too found shade and put aside his sword. Jabir continues, "We had only slept for a short while when the Prophet 🕊 called for us. When we responded to his call we found a bedouin sitting with him.

The Prophet 🕊 explained, 'This person drew my sword while I was asleep. I woke up to find it in his hand and he was asking me, 'Who will save you from me?!' I replied to him, 'Allah!' He asked me the same question again and I replied the same. The sword then fell from his hand and so I took it and asked him, 'Who will save you from me?' The Bedouin begged him, 'Be a good captor.' The Prophet asked him to testify to Allah 🕊 but he would not, and instead said, 'I pledge that I will never fight against you, nor join forces with anyone who fights against you.'"

Jabir concludes that the Prophet 🕊 did not punish him and in fact forgave him.[211]

The Battle of Hunayn

When the Battle of Hunayn took place, the tribes came to the battlefield with their livestock, as well as their families indicating that they intended to fight until the end. The Prophet 🕊 arrived with 10,000 companions along with many people who had been granted amnesty in the liberation of Mecca, now fighting for Islam for the first time. Despite their overwhelming numbers, the Muslims were caught by surprise and many fled the battlefield leaving the Prophet 🕊 all alone. The Prophet 🕊 made two distinct calls to the Ansar,

---

greater discord by taking a life, adding to the issue between the Muslims and causing harm to Islam externally by ruining the reputation of the Prophet 🕊. The Prophet 🕊 however again demonstrating his wisdom and management presented the various techniques that he applied to neutralize the matter. This narration not only has practical lessons for similar incidents in common life, but it also demonstrates the care that the Prophet 🕊 had for the unity of the Muslims, and his reputation among non-Muslims for it is all too easy for them to receive wrong information.

[211] *Al-Bidayah wa al-Nihayah*, vol. 4, p. 85.

turning to his right and his left calling out, "O assembly of the Ansar!" The Ansar, hearing their name being called, responded "We are at your service, O Messenger of Allah ﷺ! Accept glad tidings that we are with you!" This turn around in attitude saw a second surge by the Muslim army and eventually the enemy suffered a resounding defeat, leaving a vast amount of spoils.

Jabir narrates, "During the battle, the Prophet ﷺ saw the companions dispersing when they were caught by surprise. He instructed Abbas to call for the Ansar and those who pledged allegiance beneath the tree at Hudaybiyyah. The Ansar responded, 'We are at your service!'[212] (The extent of the service was such that) those unable to quickly turn their camels, threw on their armour, grabbed their swords and shields and hurried on foot towards the call. Soon hundreds of companions had gathered around the Prophet ﷺ. The enemy attacked and the battle started. While the first call had been for all of the Ansar, the second call was specifically for the Banu Khazraj because they were known to be unwavering in battle. The Prophet ﷺ looked to see his cavalry and when he saw them fighting in earnest he said an expression, 'Now is the time to heat up the pebbles.'"

Jabir continues, "I swear by Allah, that the companions had hardly returned to the battlefield, when the prisoners were being brought to the Prophet ﷺ.[213] Allah destroyed those enemies who were destined to be defeated. Allah then gave the spoils to the Prophet ﷺ."[214]

The Prophet ﷺ distributed the spoils among the Muhajireen and those who had been granted amnesty, but gave nothing to the Ansar. The Ansar, disappointed, commented "We are called upon when times are difficult, but the spoils of war are given to others?" Some of the Ansar viewed it as favouritism toward the Meccan's whom the Prophet ﷺ was related to and grew up with saying, "By Allah, the Messenger ﷺ has rejoined his people." Sa'ad b. Ubadah al-Ansari approach the Prophet ﷺ and said, "O Messenger of Allah ﷺ, the Ansar feel hurt by your actions."[215] The Prophet ﷺ

---

[212] Yaa Labbayka.

[213] Meaning, how quick the battle was finished by their eagerness and service.

[214] *Al-Bidayah wa al-Nihayah*, vol. 4, p. 329.

[215] Allah ﷺ says in the Holy Qur'an, "And of them, there are those who lay blame upon you with respect to alms; thus if they are given from it they are pleased and if

instructed, "Gather your people (the Ansar) and call me once they have gathered." Once they gathered the Prophet ﷺ stood to address the concerns of the Ansar saying, "O Assembly of the Ansar, when I came to you were you not all astray, after which Allah ﷻ guided you? Were you not poverty stricken after which Allah ﷻ enriched you? Were you not enemies (of one another) after which Allah ﷻ bonded your hearts?" The Ansar agreed. The Prophet ﷺ continued, "(In the same way) By Allah, you would be speaking the truth and people would believe you if you were to say '(O Muhammad ﷺ) You came to us as an outcast and we granted you shelter. You came to us as a destitute person and we granted you financial assistance. You came to us in fear and we granted you security. You came to us without any helpers and we granted you the assistance that you needed." The Ansar humbly replied, "The favour is upon us from Allah ﷻ and His Messenger ﷺ."

The Prophet ﷺ then sought to comfort them by saying, "O Assembly of Ansar, do you feel hurt because of some short-lived sprouts of this world that I have given to some of the new Muslims whose hearts I intend on winning over, whereas I have left you to the bounty of Islam that Allah has granted you? O assembly of Ansar, does it not please you to know that while other people return to their homes with goats and camels, you will return to your homes with the Messenger of Allah ﷺ? I swear by the One who controls my life that if everyone walks through a valley, and the Ansar walk through another valley, I shall walk with the Ansar. Had it not been for the great virtue of the migration, I would have been a man from the Ansar! O Allah, shower your mercy on the Ansar, on the children of the Ansar, and on the grandchildren of the Ansar."

---

they are not given from it, then lo! they are full of rage. And if only they were to be content with what Allah and His Apostle gave them and had said: Allah is sufficient for us, Allah will soon give us more out of His grace and His Apostle too. Surely to Allah do we make our petition." (9:58-59)

The Ansar then wept until their beards were soaked (with the tears) and they said, "We are pleased with Allah as our Lord and with the distribution of the Messenger of Allah ﷺ."[216] [217] [218]

---

[216] *Al-Bidayah wa al-Nihayah*, vol. 4, p. 358, *Kanz al-Ummal*, vol. 7, p. 135; *Hayaat al-Sahaaba*, vol. 1, p. 395.

[217] This narration provides great insight into the aspirations and management of the Prophet ﷺ. Initially one may question the management skills of the Prophet ﷺ by enquiring why he had not informed the Ansar that they were not going to receive any of the spoils of war, thereby avoiding any negative sentiment. As the narration progresses, one may wonder whether the Prophet ﷺ was using a form of emotional blackmail by asking, "When I came to you were you not all astray, after which Allah guided you" indicating that the Ansar had no right to feel hurt as they 'owed' the Prophet ﷺ. However, the Prophet ﷺ wanted to teach a number of lessons by purposely not informing them prior to the distribution. The first one was to remove any thoughts that the Ansar had that the Prophet felt the Ansar owed him, and so addressed this by admitting his need towards their asylum and generosity saying, "In the same way that By Allah, you would be speaking the truth and people would believe if you were to say '(Oh Muhammad) You came to us as an outcast and we granted you shelter.'" By this the Prophet ﷺ intended to demonstrate the mutual reliance between himself and the Ansar and that both of their successes were mutually intertwined. This would remove any potential for accusation towards the Prophet ﷺ by either side. Thereafter the Prophet ﷺ wanted to address the issue of understanding matters through the lens of the Prophet ﷺ. Just like the Ansar had a perspective, so did the Prophet ﷺ and importantly, the newly initiated Muslims. The equal division of the spoils would have resulted in the new Muslims receiving less and this may have had its own ramifications. The Ansar were not in need of financial rewards, favours or persuasions, while the Meccans who only recently before were staunch enemies of the Prophet ﷺ needed a different approach. In this way the Prophet ﷺ was conveying the lesson of empathy by understanding a more holistic approach to the Muslim dynamics. Had the Ansar so quickly forgotten when they had become new Muslims and the importance of receiving the spoils to strengthen their faith and community? Why then deny this to a new batch of Muslims? This demonstrated the gap between Prophetic wisdom and conventional wisdom. Lastly, the Prophet ﷺ wanted to inquire from the Ansar that to which extent they were fighting for Allah's pleasure, and/or for the rewards or worldly gain. It may have been that he noticed this attitude creeping into the Ansar and so he needed to address it. While a newly converted Muslim may have had alternative goals, the Ansar were expected to demonstrate a loftier attitude; and win or loss, or the spoils of war were not to be central to their aspirations. Moreover, rewards may be directly linked to intentions, so while the new Muslims returned with goats and camels, the Ansar returned with the Prophet ﷺ, thereby subtly questioning which they preferred. Their history and commitment had demonstrated the purest of

The Battle of Ta'if

Jabir narrates that during the Battle of Ta'if, the Prophet ﷺ sent Handhala b. Rabee to the people of Ta'if. However, after Handhala spoke to them, they captured him and were taking him up to their fortress. The Prophet ﷺ called out, "Who will take care of them (and rescue Handhala)? Such a person will receive the reward of this entire expedition (from Allah ﷻ)." Only Abbas rose to the occasion. He intercepted the enemy as they were taking Handhala into the fortress. Abbas was a powerful man and he rescued Handhala from them and was able to snatch him away from their hands. The Prophet ﷺ prayed for him all of the time and he brought Handhala to the Prophet ﷺ despite the rocks that the army in the fortress were raining down upon him.[219]

The Extent of the Contribution by an Ansari before the Battle of Tabuk

The period surrounding the Battle of Tabuk had been a great strain on the Muslims. Poverty had struck, hypocrisy was widespread, dependence on the state and charity had greatly increased, and the battle was to take place in the intense heat of the summer. When a military expedition was about to occur, the Muslims would contribute by aiding those preparing for battle by feeding and equipping them for battle. In this way, they anticipated rewards and spoils for assisting the army.[220] Umm Sinan Aslamiyya narrates that she saw a cloth spread out in the house of the Prophet ﷺ filled with bangles, bracelets, anklets, earrings, rings and other jewellery that the women had

---

intentions and any shift in this, whether owing to forgetfulness, weakness or a new influence creeping in from the new Meccan Muslims required the Prophet ﷺ to address it. In this way, great leadership and lessons were imparted by the Prophet ﷺ.

[218] Sheikh Hamza Yusuf narrates a fuller version of this incident in this video. I have not quoted it all as the focus of this book are the narrations from Jabir. The video is available at: https://www.youtube.com/watch?v=x97FriDU2gk.

[219] *Kanz al-Ummal*, vol. 5, p. 307.

[220] *Hayaat al-Sahaaba*, vol. 1, p. 410.

sent to assist the Muslim army in its preparations.[221] [222] However, there were others from amongst the hypocrites who abstained from contributing, and even discouraged others from donating towards the battle. Abu 'Aqeel from the Ansari brought a mere saa'[223] of dates as his contribution. When the hypocrites saw this donation they started mocking what they considered to be an insignificant amount. Abu 'Aqeel responded saying, "I spent the entire night pulling a rope up and down to draw water from a well in exchange (as paid work) for two saa' of dates. I brought one saa' and left the other one for my family. By Allah, I have nothing else to give besides this."[224]

Jabir narrates that during the expedition to Tabuk, the Prophet ﷺ stopped at a place called Hijr, where the community of Prophet Salih ﷺ were destroyed, and addressed the companions saying, "O people, do not ask your Prophet for miracles because here lies the nation of Salih who asked their Prophet to raise a pregnant camel for them; he complied and she would arrive by the road to drink water. However, they hamstrung her and Allah gave them only three days to repent. The promise of Allah is always true and a terrible cry came which destroyed all of them."[225]

The Expedition against Banu Hurqah

Usama b. Zayd reports, "The Prophet ﷺ sent us on a military expedition against a branch from the tribe of Banu Hurqah. We launched a surprise attack at dawn against them, and among them was a man who was the fiercest of warriors who defended their tribe. One of the members of the Ansar, and me managed to corner him, and as we overpowered him, he recited the *shahadah* – the testimony bearing witness to the Oneness of God and the *prophethood* of Muhammad ﷺ – thus bringing him into the fold of

---

[221] Ibn Asakir, vol. 1, p. 110.

[222] This is a practice that remains until today, for example the women of Yemen have been recorded as donating their jewellery to raise funds in fighting the invasion from Aal Saud (Saudi Arabia). See:
http://www.vocativ.com/189513/yemen-women-donating-gold/

[223] A *saa'* was a measurement of weight. It would be the equivalent of between 2.8 and 3.2 grams depending on the city one hailed from.

[224] Ibn Asakir, vol. 1, p. 105; *Kanz al-Ummal*, vol. 1, p. 249; *Hayaat al-Sahaaba*, vol. 1 p. 412.

[225] Haythami, vol. 7, p. 38.

Islam. The Ansari man backed off (in fighting against him), however I proceeded to kill him.

When the news reached the Prophet ﷺ he said to me, 'Usama! Did you kill a man who had recited 'There is no god but Allah?!'' I argued, 'But O Messenger of Allah ﷺ, he said it only to save himself from being killed! The Prophet ﷺ responded, 'Did you tear open his heart to know whether he said it for that reason or not?!' The Prophet ﷺ continued to repeat his question until I wished that I had become a Muslim that very day so as to have become cleansed of all of my previous sins, including this one.[226] From that day forward, I took a pledge with Allah that I would never kill anyone who professes the *shahadah*. The Prophet ﷺ asked, 'Even after me?' to which I affirmed, 'Even after you.'"[227]

The Companions of Al-Qurra

It is narrated that the Prophet ﷺ gathered seventy youth from the Ansar with the purpose of sending them to different communities for propagation of the faith, teaching the Qur'an and to build bridges among the people. In addition to these duties, during the day they would fetch water to place in the Masjid and gather firewood to sell, the profits of which would be used to fund the care and feeding of the extremely poor who would seek shelter at the Masjid of the Prophet ﷺ.[228]

These people were called al-Qurra. Anas b. Malik narrates, "The Prophet ﷺ sent seventy men, called al-Qurra for a purpose. The two groups of Banu Sulaym called Ri'l and Dhakwan surrounded them near a well called Bir Ma'una. The group (al-Qurra) said, 'By Allah, we have not come to harm you, but we are passing by you on our way to do something for the Prophet ﷺ.' But the tribe killed them all. The Prophet ﷺ therefore invoked Allah's curse upon them for a month during the morning prayers."[229]

Anas also narrates that their last supplication was, "O Allah, convey our message to Your Prophet on our behalf that we are going to meet You, that we are pleased with You, and You are pleased with us."[230]

---

[226] *Kanz al-Ummal*, vol. 1, p. 78; *Sunan Bayhaqi*, vol. 8, p. 192.
[227] *Al-Bidayah wa al-Nihayah*, vol. 4, p. 222.
[228] *Tabaqat al-Kubra*, vol. 3, p. 514.
[229] *Sahih al-Bukhari*, vol. 5, The Book on Military Expeditions, book 59, Hadith 414.
[230] *Tabaqat al-Kubra*, vol. 3, p. 514.

Conquest of Mecca

Jabir narrates that the Prophet ﷺ was wearing a black turban on the day he entered Mecca and freed it from idolatry.[231]

Assassination of Ka'ab b. al-Ashraf

Ka'ab b. al-Ashraf was a Medinan Jew who would visit the Quraysh in Mecca in order to provoke their hatred for the Muslims and ignite war between them.

Jabir narrates that the Prophet ﷺ once said, "Who is there to see Ka'ab b. al-Ashraf because he has caused great harm to the religion of Allah and His Messenger?"

A companion by the name of Muhammad b. Maslama stood up and said, "Do you want me to kill him?" to which the Prophet ﷺ said, "Yes."

Muhammad b. Maslama requested, "Permit me to say something to him as well" to which the Prophet ﷺ agreed.

Muhammad b. Maslama took some companions with him and went to go see Ka'ab and said, "That man (the Prophet ﷺ) has asked us for charity and has tired us with the extent of his requests. We have therefore come to you for a loan." Ka'ab replied, "By Allah, (even if you give him this amount of charity) he will again tire you out (with more requests) afterwards." Muhammad b. Maslama said, "We have started following him and do not like to leave him until we see what happens to him in the end. We want you to lend us some grain." Ka'ab agreed saying, "Fine but I require some collateral first."

Muhammad b. Maslama and the companions asked, "What collateral would you like?" to which Ka'ab replied, "Give me your women as collateral." They responded, "How can we give you our women as collateral when you are the most handsome of the Arabs?" Ka'ab replied, "Then give me your children." They replied, "How can we give you our children when people will taunt us by saying that these children were given as collateral for a mere amount of grain. This is too embarrassing. We will give you our weapons as collateral."

---

[231] *Shamaa'il*, Chapter on the Prophet's Turban, Tirmidhi, Hadith 1.

Ka'ab agreed and so they arranged to meet again at night. Ka'ab arrived wearing a belt studded with jewels and exuded the fragrance of perfume. Muhammad b. Maslama praised Ka'ab saying, "To this day I have never smelt anything so good! Do you allow me to smell your head?" Ka'ab agreed and the companions smelt the perfume. Muhammad b. Maslama asked again, "May I smell a second time?" When Ka'ab allowed him, Muhammad b. Maslama grabbed Ka'ab's head and immediately killed him.

When the companions reached the graveyard of al-Baqi' in Medina, they shouted "Allahu Akbar!" The Prophet ﷺ who was praying also shouted "Allahu Akbar" understanding that they had killed Ka'ab. When they reached the Prophet ﷺ he said, "You have the faces of successful people." They replied, "Your face is too, O Messenger" and then threw Ka'ab's head before the Prophet who proceeded to praise Allah for Ka'ab's death.[232]

---

[232] As quoted in *Fath al-Baari*, vol. 7, p. 239; *Hayaat al-Sahaaba*, vol. 1, p. 382.

Chapter 5

Jabir's Narrations about Prophet Muhammad's ﷺ Activities

Introduction

Jabir spent more than a decade with the Prophet ﷺ and being among the closest and most trusted companions, he had an abundance of exposure to him ﷺ and the Ahl al-Bayt ﷺ in that period. Many of his narrations are wonderful descriptions of the Prophet's ﷺ activities, personal interactions and private conversations. In fact, Jabir was blessed with having a deep insight into the Prophetic character, which he often narrated.

For example, Jabir quotes from the Prophet ﷺ that, "From the noble characteristics of the Prophets and the truthful people is that when they see one another, cheerfulness is on their faces and they shake hands when they meet."[233] As well he said: "When the Prophet walked, his companions would walk in front of him and he would leave his back free for the angels to follow behind."[234]

In this chapter we will explore Jabir's direct experiences with the Prophet ﷺ, and narrations that he reported about the prophetic activities, particularly with the Ansar. What we will find is the extent of the proximity that Jabir enjoyed by virtue of his efforts toward the Prophet ﷺ, but also how much the Prophet ﷺ reciprocated that joy from his company. As a

---

[233] *Ethics of the Prophets*, Langroodi, Taaj, Ansariyan, p. 9.
[234] *Sunan Ibn Majah*, The Book of the Sunnah, Hadith 246.

result, Jabir was in a position to describe the Prophet's ﷺ character and movement in detail, arguably unrivalled by any other companion. We will also appreciate the Prophet's ﷺ ongoing care and interaction with the Ansar and the impact that this continued to have on their development.

Eating with Jabir

Jabir narrates, "I was once sitting at home when the Prophet passed by and motioned at me to come with him, so I stood up and went to him. He took me by the hand and led me to the home of one of his wives and he entered. He then allowed me to enter[235] the secluded area of the house, where he asked for some food.[236] We were served three pieces of bread that were placed on the fronds of a date palm. The Prophet then placed the bread in front of me, another before himself and tore the third into two pieces, halves for each of us. He then asked, 'Is there any gravy?' to which he was informed that there was nothing but vinegar. He said, 'Bring it because it is an excellent gravy!'"[237]

Abdul Wahid b. Ayman reports from his father that once some guests came to Jabir. He brought them some bread and vinegar and told them, "Eat this because I have heard the Prophet say that vinegar is an excellent gravy. Destroyed are those people who look down on what is offered to them and destroyed is the person who feels ashamed to offer his companions whatever is in his house."[238] [239]

---

[235] This demonstrates the excellent morals of the Prophet ﷺ to check that the household was in the proper attire to welcome a guest. After he inquired this, he allowed Jabir to enter.

[236] Imam Ali ؓ is narrated to have said, "To gather a few of my friends to share a Saa' of food is more beloved to me than going to the marketplace to purchase a slave and set him free." (*Kanz al-Ummal*, vol. 5, p. 12)

[237] This narration suggests that the Prophet ﷺ enjoyed the company of Jabir to the extent that he would seek out his company and invite him to his home. This kind of thing was reserved for only a few of his companions. One can only imagine what discussions and lessons transpired between them.

[238] *Kanz al-Ummal*, vol. 5, p. 64.

[239] Given the two narrations, it appears that Jabir was told by the Prophet ﷺ about the destruction of the ungrateful individual and the destruction of the one embarrassed to share the food even if it be simple, when he was invited to his house. Above, the commentator wondered what kind of discussions and lessons transpired at their lunches, and the subsequent narration appears to explain that!

Trusting in the Gift of the Prophet ﷺ

Jabir narrates that once a man approached the Prophet ﷺ to ask him for some food. The Prophet ﷺ gave him a sufficient amount of barley from which the man, his wife and his servant were able to eat for a long period of time. After some time they decided to weigh it (to see how much it was), to which the barley began to deplete and came to an end. The Prophet ﷺ said, "Had you not weighed it (to see how much it was and just trusted in it) it would have lasted as long as you continued to eat from it."[240] [241]

Jabir Describes the Sermons of the Prophet ﷺ

Jabir states, "When the Messenger of Allah delivered a sermon, his eyes would turn red, he would raise his voice, and he would speak with intensity, as if he was warning of an enemy army saying, 'They will surely attack you in the morning, or they will surely attack you in the evening!'

He would say, 'I and the Hour have been sent like these two' and he would hold up his index and middle finger (meaning I the Prophet, and the Day of Judgement are inextricably close together). Then he would continue, 'The best of matters is the Book of Allah, and the best of guidance is the guidance of Muhammad ﷺ. The most evil matters are those which are newly-invented, and every innovation (bid'ah) leads to going astray.'

He also used to say, 'Whoever dies and leaves behind some wealth, it is for his family, and whoever leaves behind a debt or dependent children, then they are both my responsibility (meaning the Prophet ﷺ would take it upon himself to see that they are cared for).'"[242]

Jabir is also narrated to have said, "When revelation would come to the Prophet or when he was delivering a sermon, he would appear like a person warning his people about an impending punishment. However, when this

---

[240] *Al-Bidayah wa al-Nihayah*, vol. 6, p. 104.
[241] Jabir is narrated to have mentioned a similar incident with a lady by the name of Umm Maalik Bahziyyah to whom the Prophet ﷺ gave a bag with some butter to make gravy for her son to eat. He ﷺ is narrated to have said, "Had you left it alone, it would have given you enough butter forever." (*Al-Bidayah wa al-Nihayah*, vol. 6, p. 104)
[242] *Sunan Ibn Majah*, The Book of the Sunnah, Hadith 45.

was not happening, you would see that he was smiling constantly, was the most jovial of people, and the most handsome of them."[243]

Jabir mentions elsewhere, "The Messenger of Allah used to stand by the root of a tree, or by a tree trunk, and then later he started to use a pulpit. This is because an Ansari woman said to Allah's Apostle, 'O Allah's Messenger! Shall I make something for you to sit on, as I have a slave who is a carpenter?' He replied, 'If you wish.' So she got a pulpit made for him.[244] When it was Friday, the Prophet sat on that pulpit. When he left using the tree, it made an audible grieving sound (complaining of the absence of the Prophet from it, while before being blessed with his proximity) such that the people in the Masjid could even hear it."

Jabir is also narrated to have said that the trunk "Cried like a pregnant she-camel."[245] He narrates that the Prophet ﷺ explained, "It has cried because of (missing) what it used to hear of religious knowledge."[246] This was until the Messenger of Allah ﷺ returned to it and rubbed it, then it calmed down. Jabir states, "Some people said, 'If he ﷺ had not come to it, then it would have grieved until the Day of Resurrection.'"[247]

People considered the pulpit of the Prophet ﷺ to be a sacred place as this was often the site of revelation, and the place where the blessed guidance came from the Messenger ﷺ. Sadly though, some people used the pulpit for their own gains and so the Prophet ﷺ had to correct this behaviour. Jabir narrates that the Prophet ﷺ said, "Whoever swears a false oath near this pulpit of mine, let him take his place in hell, even if it is for a green twig."[248]

Jabir mentions one of the Prophet's ﷺ sermons forewarning about the *Dajjal*. He states that the Prophet ﷺ stood on the pulpit and said, "O people, I have not gathered you for news coming from the heavens (revelation) (but to tell you about *Dajjal*). He is a false messiah for whom the earth will be folded in forty days and he will travel everywhere except for Taybah

---

[243] Hayhtami, vol. 9, p. 17.

[244] *Sahih al-Bukhari*, The Book of Sales and Trade, Hadith 308.

[245] Ibid., The Book of the Friday Prayer, Hadith 41.

[246] Ibid., The Book of Sales and Trade, Hadith 308.

[247] *Sunan Ibn Majah*, The Chapter of Establishing the Prayers and the Sunnah Regarding them, Hadith 1417.

[248] *Sunan Ibn Majah*, The Chapter on Rulings and Laws, Hadith 2325.

(Medina) which will have an angel at its entrance with a drawn sword to prevent its entry, and the same will be the case for Mecca."[249]

The Prophet ﷺ would Regularly Visit the Ansar

Abdullah b. Qays reports that the Prophet ﷺ visited the Ansar often, both on an individual and collective basis. When he visited someone on an individual basis, he would go to the person's house, and when he wanted to visit the Ansar collectively he would go to the Masjid.[250] Anas b. Malik adds that once the Prophet ﷺ visited the house of an Ansari, where he joined him for a meal. Before he ﷺ left, he sprinkled some water on a certain spot where a mat was spread out for him to sit on. He ﷺ then performed a prayer there and supplicated for the people of that house."[251]

The Prophet ﷺ Visits Jabir when He was Ill

Jabir narrates, "I once fell ill and the Prophet came with Abu Bakr to visit me. They both arrived on foot and found me unconscious. The Prophet performed his wudhu and sprinkled the wudhu water on me. When I recovered consciousness I saw the Prophet (and fearing that death may come to me) I asked him, 'O Messenger of Allah, what should I do with my wealth? How should I wrap up my estate?' The Prophet gave no reply and waited until the verses of inheritance were revealed to him."[252] [253]

In another narration, it specifies the following, that initially the verse "Allah enjoins you concerning your children: The male shall have the equal of the portion of two females" was revealed. Jabir then said, "O Messenger of God. No one would inherent me except those who are neither my parents (as they

---

[249] Haythami, vol. 7, p. 346.
[250] Ibid., vol. 8, p. 173.
[251] *Hayaat al-Sahaaba*, vol. 2, pp. 454-5.
[252] *Sahih al-Bukhari*, vol. 2, p. 843, Hadith 554.
[253] Imam Ali ﷺ is narrated to have said that when the Prophet ﷺ would visit a sick person, he would place his right hand on the person's right cheek and say, "O Lord of the People, remove the difficulty. Do grant cure, for only You can cure. There is no one who can remove the ailments except for you."
The Arabic text of this passage reads:
لاَ بَأْسَ أَذْهَبِ الْبَأْسَ رَبَّ النَّاسِ إِشْفِ أَنْتَ الشَّافِي لاَ يَكْشِفُ الضُّرَّ إِلاَّ أَنْتَ

have died), nor my children (as I do not have any yet)." Then the verses of requisites and ordinances which are known as Ayaat al-Fara'ed were revealed."[254]

Narrating about the Prophet's ﷺ humility, Jabir is reported to have said, "The Prophet came to visit me when I was sick and he was riding neither a mule, nor a thoroughbred horse" (meaning that the Prophet ﷺ rode neither something below his station, nor was he excessive).[255]

Jabir's Narrations Regarding the Friday (Jum'ah) and Other Prayers

Jabir reports that the Prophet ﷺ encouraged people to participate in, and also warned them not to abandon or belittle the Friday prayers. He states that the Prophet ﷺ addressed them saying, "O people, repent to Allah before you die and hasten to do good deeds before you become too busy to do so. Join the ties between yourselves and your Lord by engaging in the abundant remembrance of Allah (*dhikr*), and by giving plenty of charity. You will then be given sustenance, assistance and you will be compensated for your losses. Take note that Allah has made the Friday prayers compulsory for you in this place, on this day, in this month and on this year until the Day of Judgement. Whoever regards it as trivial, rejects or neglects it during my lifetime, or after my death in the presence of a just or unjust leader, may Allah not set his affairs in order, and may Allah not bless him in anything. No prayer, *zakaat, hajj*, fast, or good deed of his will be accepted until he repents and Allah will certainly forgive anyone who repents to Him.

Take note that no woman can lead a man in prayer, no Bedouin can lead a Muhajir, and no sinner can lead a righteous person - unless forced to do so by a tyrannical ruler whose sword is feared."[256]

Jabir also narrates that one Friday the Prophet ﷺ addressed them saying, "When a person lives a mile away from Medina and does not attend the Friday prayers, Allah will seal his heart." The following Friday, the Prophet ﷺ said, "When a person lives two miles away from Medina and does not attend the Friday prayers, Allah will seal his heart." The next Friday the

---

[254] Hakimi, Muhammad Ridha al-, *Qasas al-Sahaba wa al-Tabi'in*, p. 80.
[255] *Sahih al-Bukhari*, vol. 7, Book 70 on Patients, Hadith 568.
[256] *Targheeb wa al-Tarheeb*, vol. 2, p. 31.

Prophet ﷺ said, "When a person lives three miles away from Medina and does not attend the Friday prayers, Allah will seal his heart."[257]

He mentions elsewhere that, "The Messenger of Allah ﷺ said, 'Whoever abandons the Friday prayers three times in a row for no valid reason, Allah will place a seal over his heart.'"[258]

Jabir also reports that a man entered the Masjid one Friday when the Messenger of Allah ﷺ was delivering the sermon. He started stepping over the peoples' shoulders and interrupting people unnecessarily, and the Messenger of Allah ﷺ said: 'Sit down, for you have annoyed people and you are late!'"[259]

Jabir also describes how one time, nearly all of the companions walked out of the Friday prayer to meet with a trade caravan. He states, "While we were praying the Friday prayer with the Prophet, some camels loaded with food, arrived (from Syria). The people diverted their attention towards the camels and left the Masjid. Only twelve people remained with the Prophet. So this verse was revealed, *'But when they see some bargain or some amusement, they disperse headlong to it, and leave you (the Prophet) standing'* (62:11)."[260]

Since a majority of the people had deserted the Friday prayer for the promise of little more than first access to and choice from a trade caravan, the Prophet ﷺ wanted to teach them better understanding of their business principles, and to comprehend the relationship between Allah's sustenance and destiny. Jabir reports that the Prophet ﷺ said, "O people, fear Allah and be moderate in seeking a living, for no soul will die until it has received all of its provision, even if it is slow in coming. So fear Allah and be moderate in seeking provision - take that which is permissible and leave that which is forbidden."[261]

Jabir also narrates that the Prophet ﷺ would encourage staying in the Masjid and to wait for the next prayer whenever it was possible. He ﷺ asked, "Shall I not point you towards something that wipes out your sins and is an

---

[257] Ibid.
[258] *Sunan Ibn Majah*, The Chapter on Establishing the Prayers and the Sunnah Regarding it, Hadith 1126.
[259] Ibid., Hadith 1115.
[260] *Sahih al-Bukhari*, The Book on the Friday Prayer, Hadith 58.
[261] *Sunan Ibn Majah*, The Chapter on Business Transactions, Hadith 2144.

expiation for misdeeds?" "Yes Oh Messenger of Allah", the companions responded. The Prophet ﷺ informed them, "Making proper ablution in adverse conditions, taking many steps to the Masjid, and waiting for one prayer after another. This is in an act that will earn you rewards equal to guarding the borders (of the nation)."[262]

Jabir narrates that after performing his prayers, the Prophet ﷺ would recite the following supplication, "There is none worthy of worship but the One Allah Who has no partner. To Him belongs the whole kingdom and to Him belongs all praise. He gives life and death, and has power over everything. O Allah, there is none to prevent what You give, and none to give what You prevent. No one can overturn what You decree, and the wealth of the wealthy cannot help against You."[263]

The Prophet's ﷺ Business Ethics

Jabir narrates, "The Messenger of Allah bought a load of fodder from a Bedouin man. When the transaction was concluded, the Messenger of Allah said: 'Choose (either to go ahead with or to cancel the transaction).' The Bedouin said: 'May Allah grant you a long life of good transaction!'"[264]

Jabir also mentioned that the Messenger of Allah ﷺ said: "May Allah have mercy on a person who is lenient when he sells, lenient when he buys, and lenient when he asks for payment"[265]; and also that he ﷺ said, "When you weigh, allow more (of the buyer's merchandise) to be on the scale."[266]

The Forbearance of the Prophet ﷺ and His Forgiving a Companion

Imam Ali ؓ narrates that the Prophet ﷺ dispatched him, Zubayr and Miqdaad with instructions to ride until they reach Rawda Khaak, which was

---

[262] *Targheeb al-Tarheeb*, vol. 1, p. 247.
[263] Haythami, vol. 10, p. 108.
The Arabic text of this passage reads:

لَا إِلَهَ إِلَّا اللهُ وَحْدَهُ لَا شَرِيكَ لَهُ لَهُ الْمُلْكُ وَلَهُ الْحَمْدُ وَهُوَ عَلَى كُلِّ شَيْءٍ قَدِيرٌ. أَللَّهُمَّ لَا مَانِعَ لِمَا أَعْطَيْتَ وَلَا مُعْطِيَ لِمَا مَنَعْتَ وَلَا يَنْفَعُ ذَا الْجَدِّ مِنْكَ الْجَدُّ

[264] *Sunan Ibn Majah*, The Chapter on Business Transactions, Hadith 2184.
[265] Ibid., Hadith 2203.
[266] Ibid., Hadith 2222.

approximately twelve miles outside of Medina. There they would find a woman in her carriage with a hidden note that they should confiscate from her.

When they reached her, she denied having the note until they threatened to have it removed from her hair, to which she gave up the note. When they brought it back to the Prophet ﷺ, they discovered that it was written from a companion named Hatib b. Abi Balta'ah and it was addressed to the polytheists of Mecca, passing on some information about the Prophet ﷺ.

Hatib was brought to the Prophet ﷺ to explain his actions. He asked the Prophet ﷺ not to be hasty. Jabir b. Abdullah narrates that Hatib said, "O Messenger of Allah, I did not write the note because I am a hypocrite nor because I wished to betray the Messenger of Allah. I knew that Allah would grant victory to His Prophet ﷺ and complete His religion irrespective of whether I wrote it or not. However, I was always an outsider in Mecca, and my mother still lives there. So I wished to gain favour with the people of Mecca so that they would be indebted to me and care for her on account of this."

'Umar b. al-Khattab interrupted exclaiming, "Permit me to behead this hypocrite!" The Prophet ﷺ replied, "Do you want to kill a veteran of the Battle of Badr? Allah has looked kindly upon the veterans of Badr with forgiveness."

It was with reference to this event that Allah ﷺ revealed the opening verse of Surah al-Mumtahina which reads, *"O you who believe, do not take My enemy and your enemy as friends, offering your friendship to them when they reject the Truth which has come to you. They have driven out the Messenger and yourselves simply because you believe in Allah as your Lord. If you emerge to strive hard in My path and earnestly seek My pleasure (then you would not befriend the enemy). You secretly show friendship to them while I am most aware of what you conceal and what you reveal. The one who does this from among you has certainly strayed away from the straight path."*[267]

---

[267] *Al-Bidayah wa al-Nihayah*, vol. 4, p. 248; *Kanz al-Ummal*, vol. 7, p. 137.

The Prophet ﷺ Laments Over an Ansari Person's Punishment

Abdullah b. Mas'ood narrates, "The first Muslim whose fingers were cut off for theft was a man from the Ansar. When he was brought before the Prophet ﷺ it grieved him ﷺ so much that it looked as if dust had been thrown over his face. Some people asked, "O Messenger of Allah ﷺ, it appears as if this is very hard for you?" The Prophet ﷺ replied, "What is there to prevent me from being so aggrieved when you people are aiding Satan against your brother by not forgiving him, but rather demanding him that he be punished? Allah is indeed Most Forgiving and loves to forgive. It is unfit for a leader not to enforce the law when a case is brought before him; but it is you who should pardon one another for the crimes committed between each other."

The Prophet ﷺ then revealed the verse, *"They should rather forgive and pardon. Do you not like that Allah should forgive you? Allah is Most Forgiving, Merciful."* (24:22)[268]

The Prophet ﷺ Teaches a Supplication for Forgiveness

Jabir narrates that a person came to the Prophet ﷺ and said, "Woe unto me! How many are my sins!" and he repeated this three times. The Prophet ﷺ addressed him and said, "Rather you should say, 'O Allah, Your forgiveness is greater than my sins and I have more hope in Your mercy than I do in my deeds.'"

When the man recited the supplication, the Prophet ﷺ asked him to repeat it three times after which he ﷺ told the man, "You may now leave as Allah has forgiven you all of your sins."[269]

---

[268] *Kanz al-Ummal*, vol. 3, pp. 83, 89 & 117.
[269] Ibid., p. 132.
The Arabic text of this passage reads:

اللَّهُمَّ مَغْفِرَتُكَ أَوْسَعُ مِنْ ذُنُوبِي وَرَحْمَتَكَ أَرْجَى عِنْدِي مِنْ عَمَلِي

The Prophet ﷺ with His Grandchildren ﷺ

Jabir narrates, "I once went to the Prophet ﷺ and he was on his hands and knees playing with Imams Hasan and Husayn on his back. He was telling them, 'You two have an excellent camel and are both excellent loads!'"[270]

Jabir also reports, "We were with the Messenger of Allah when we were invited for a meal. We came across Imam Husayn playing with some other children in the street. The Prophet ran ahead of us and stretched out his arms to pick up Husayn. The Imam started running to and fro playing 'catch me if you can' and the Prophet laughed playing along. The Prophet stretched out his arms, held him and while hugging and kissing his grandson said, 'Husayn is from me and I am from Husayn. May Allah love those who love him. Hasan and Husayn are two distinguished grandsons from among (all) grandsons.'"[271]

The Prophet ﷺ Gives a Sermon

Jabir reports that the Prophet ﷺ stood on the pulpit and asked everyone to be seated. Abdullah b. Mas'ood was about to enter the Masjid and upon hearing the instruction immediately sat down outside of the door! When the Prophet saw this he said, "Come in, O Abdullah!"[272]

An Ansari Lady's Gift to the Prophet ﷺ

A'isha bint Abu Bakr narrates, "A woman from the Ansar once visited me and noticed that the bedding of the Prophet was merely a double folded sheet. She then sent me a bedding filled with wool. When the Prophet ﷺ saw it he asked, "What is this, O A'isha?" to which I informed him that an Ansari lady had given it. The Prophet ﷺ told me, "Return it. By Allah, if I wanted Allah would make mountains of gold and silver travel with me."[273]

---

[270] Haythami, vol. 9, p. 182.
[271] *Kanz al-Ummal*, vol. 7, p. 107.
[272] Ibid., p. 55.
[273] *Targheeb wa Tarheeb*, vol. 5, p. 163.

The Prophet ﷺ Mentions the Good and Negative Qualities in Women and Men

Jabir reports, "We were sitting with the Messenger of Allah and we mentioned the topic of women, and the virtues that some of them have over others. So the Prophet ﷺ asked, 'Shall I not inform you about this?' and we responded 'Yes, O Messenger of Allah, do inform us.'

He ﷺ said: 'Surely, from the best of women are: the fertile, loving, secret-keeping, cherished among her family, humble with her husband, one who looks good for her spouse, and is aloof with other than him, who listens to his words and obeys his commands; and if he is alone with her, she makes an effort to do whatever he wants from her, and does not behave with him the way that a man would behave.'

Then, he ﷺ said: 'Shall I not inform you about the worst of your women?' We said: 'Yes.'

He ﷺ said: 'Surely, from the worst of your women are the low-standing ones among her family, the mighty with her husband, the infertile, the spiteful one who does not refrain from obscenity, who looks good when her husband is not there, and is aloof when he is present, who does not listen to his words and does not obey his commands, and when her husband is alone with her, she is resistant to him with arduous resistance when he wants to have intercourse with her; she does not accept his excuses and does not forgive his mistakes.'

Then, he ﷺ continued: 'Shall I not inform you about the best of your men?' So, we said: 'Yes.'

He ﷺ said: 'Surely, from the best men of your men are the possessors of piety, the pure, the generous [with his] two hands (gives charity), the peaceful ones, kind to both of his parents, and he does not force his family [in seeking help] from others.'

Then, he ﷺ said: 'Shall I inform you about the worst of your men?' We said: 'Yes.'

He ﷺ said: 'Surely, from the worst of your men are the slanderers, the obscene, those who eat by themselves (not sharing with others and not restraining himself), the one refusing assistance, the one who beats his family and his slaves, the stingy one who causes his family to seek assistance from others, and the disobedient with their fathers.'"[274]

The Ansar are Given Glad Tidings of Paradise

Anas b. Malik reports that the companions were sitting with the Prophet ﷺ when he said, "A man from among the people of Paradise will now appear before you." A man from the Ansar then arrived with his beard wet from his ablution. The next day the Prophet ﷺ said the same thing and the same man appeared as he did the first time. On the third day, the Prophet ﷺ again repeated this and the same thing happened again.

After the Prophet ﷺ left, Abdullah b. Amr went to the man and said, "I have had an argument with my father and have sworn not to go home for three days. May I stay with you until my oath expires?" The Ansari man agreed.

Abdullah b. Amr narrates that he did not see the man perform any night prayers, however, he engaged in a lot of *dhikr* reciting "Allahu Akbar" whenever he woke up at night or would turn over, and he would sleep until the morning prayers. He states that after the three days, he thought these deeds were not worth the accolade that the Prophet ﷺ had paid to him and so he decided to enquire. He went to that man and said to him: "O servant of Allah, there was never any argument nor a severed tie with my father, rather I just wanted to stay with you, because on three occasions the Prophet stated 'A man from Paradise will appear' and on each occasion you appeared. I therefore wanted to stay with you to observe your actions so that I may follow suit. What is it that you do which makes you so respected in the eyes of the Prophet?"

The Ansari man replied, "There is nothing besides what you have observed. However, another thing is that I harbour no ill-feelings towards any Muslim, nor do I resent anyone for the good that Allah has granted them."[275]

---

[274] *Tahdheeb al-Ahkam*, Ibn Hasan at-Tusi, Hadith 1597.
[275] *Targheeb wa Tarheeb*, vol. 4, p. 328; Haythami, vol. 8, p. 79.

Rain Falls on the Graves of the Ansar

It is narrated that a particular tribe of the Ansar were blessed with a supplication that the Prophet ﷺ had taught them. As a result a cloud would rain upon the grave of any one of them when they passed away. When one of their freed servants died, they said, "Today we shall see the truth of the Prophet's statement that a freed slave of a tribe is considered as one of the tribe." After they buried the man a cloud appeared and rained upon his grave as well.[276]

The Ansar and People of Quba Patiently Bear Fever

Jabir narrates that fever came in a human form and sought permission to speak to the Prophet ﷺ.[277] The Prophet ﷺ enquired who had come to visit to which Umm Mildam[278] was the reply. The Prophet ﷺ then instructed it to go the people of Quba afflicting many people with illness. When the people of Quba came to the Prophet ﷺ to complain, the Prophet ﷺ responded, "You have a choice. If you prefer I will pray to Allah ﷻ to remove your fever or it can remain among you longer as means of purification of your sins." They enquired further, "Can this really be?" Then they agreed for the fever to remain after the Prophet ﷺ confirmed that their sins will be expiated for the illness.[279]

In a similar narration, when fever approached, it asked the Prophet ﷺ, "Send me to those people or your companions who are the most beloved to you!" The Prophet ﷺ replied, "Go to the Ansar!" When the Ansar came to him and asked for his prayers to end the illness, the Prophet ﷺ prayed and the fever subsided. A woman from the Ansar came and also asked for a prayer to end her illness. The Prophet ﷺ said to her, "Which do you prefer? For me to pray to end the illness or for you to exercise patience in which case Paradise will be incumbent upon you?" The Ansari lady repeated three

---

[276] *Kanz al-Ummal*, vol. 7, p. 136.

[277] The Prophet a was often visited by the Arch-Angel Jibra'il ﷺ in human form so that people could benefit from this experience and the questions asked of the Prophet ﷺ. It is therefore possible for an angel responsible for fever or the manifestation of fever to visit the Prophet ﷺ too. Allah knows best.

[278] A title that the Arabs gave to fever.

[279] *Targheeb wa Tarheeb*, vol. 5, p. 260.

times, "I swear by Allah, I prefer to exercise patience during this illness!" She added, "I swear by Allah, I will never jeopardize Paradise for anything!"[280]

The Prophet ﷺ Admonishes 'Umar b. al-Khattab

Jabir narrates that once 'Umar b. al-Khattab brought a scripture to the Prophet ﷺ that he had received from some people from the Ahl al-Kitab (Jews and Christians). 'Umar was pleased at his new found knowledge and told the Prophet ﷺ, "I just got an excellent scripture from the Ahl al-Kitab." The Prophet ﷺ became angry and said, "Are you in doubt, Oh son of Khattab? I swear by the One Who controls my life! What I have brought to you is pure and clear. You have no need to ask them (for guidance). The danger is that they might tell you some truth that you may reject, or tell you some false that you may believe. I swear by the One Who controls my life that even if Prophet Musa ﷺ was alive, he would have had no option but to follow me."[281]

---

[280] Haythami, vol. 2, p. 306.
[281] Birr, Ibn Abd al-, *Jaami' al-Bayan al-Ilm*, vol. 2, p. 42; Haythami, vol. 1, p. 174.

Chapter 6

Jabir's Narrations on the Rank and Leadership of Imam Ali b. Abi Talib 🖼 and the Ahl al-Bayt 🖼

Among the most famous aspects of Jabir's life was his conveying the salutations of the Prophet 🖼 to Imam Muhammad al-Baqir 🖼 more than half a century after the Messenger's 🖼 death. This came from a question that Jabir raised about who are those 'vested with authority from among the Muslims' by Allah 🖼. This answer first lead to Jabir's certainty in the lofty status and authority of Imam Ali 🖼 and also the Ahl al-Bayt 🖼. Second, it began a consistent enquiry from Jabir about their station in the eyes of Allah 🖼, something that he would regularly seek and then relay to others.

In this chapter we will survey the narrations of Jabir regarding those ranks and unique features of the Ahl al-Bayt 🖼. This chapter is central to the reasoning of the title of this book in that if Jabir is a source of guidance, then we will appreciate the extent of the authority and rank of the Ahl al-Bayt 🖼 to whom Jabir would obey and turn to for his guidance. We will also appreciate wondrous narrations regarding the Ahl al-Bayt 🖼 that demonstrate Jabir's theological positioning.

Hadith 1: The Successor of the Prophet 🖼

Jabir narrates, "I came to the Prophet 🖼 and said to him "O Messenger of Allah, who is your guardian (or successor) after you?" He kept quiet and did not answer me until after I asked him ten times, then he 🖼 said, "O Jabir, shall I tell you about what you have asked me?!" I replied, "May my mother and my father be sacrificed for you. I swear by Allah that when you kept quiet, I thought that you had become angry with me."

Then he ﷺ replied, "I did not get angry at you O Jabir, but I was waiting for what was coming to me from the sky. Then Jibra'il ﷺ came to me and said, "O Muhammad, your Lord sends His *salam* upon you and says, 'Indeed Ali b. Abi Talib is your guardian, your successor upon your family and your nation, the defender of your heavenly pond (*hawdh*) and he is the holder of your banner before you leading (the people) to Paradise."

Then I said, "O Prophet of Allah ... Do you see the ones who do not believe in this, shall I fight them?"

He ﷺ replied, "Yes O Jabir, this situation was not placed except to be followed, so whoever follows it will be with me tomorrow (on the Day of Judgement); and whoever transgresses it, will not ever reach me at the pond (*hawdh*)."[282]

Hadith 2: The Miraculous Journey of Imam Ali b. Abi Talib ﷺ

Jabir b. Abdullah al-Ansari narrates that,[283] "Amir al-Mu'mineen ﷺ used to go out of the city of Medina every Thursday night (*laylat al-jum'ah*) without telling anyone where he goes." Jabir explains, "He kept doing so for a while and one night, when he ﷺ was out, 'Umar b. al-Khattab said, 'I must go out to see where Ali b. Abi Talib goes.'"

Jabir says, "So one night 'Umar sat waiting for him at the gate of the city until he ﷺ went out as usual. 'Umar followed him and wherever Ali ﷺ was placing his foot he was placing his foot on the same place [following his footsteps]. After a short while, he ﷺ reached a great town filled with date palms, trees and an abundance of water.

Then Amir al-Mu'mineen ﷺ entered a garden in which there was running water. He ﷺ performed ablution (*wudhu*) and stood among the date palms praying until the majority of the night had passed. As for 'Umar, he fell asleep and when Amir al-Mo'mineen ﷺ had finished praying, he went

---

[282] *Al-Amaali*, Sheikh Mufid, p. 168.
[283] *Al-Muhtadhar* of Sheikh al-Saleh al-Hasan b. Sulaiman says: "Some of the scholars mention this in a book on Jabir."

back to the city of Medina and prayed the *fajr* prayer with the Messenger of God 🖏.

When 'Umar woke up, he did not find Amir al-Mo'mineen 🖏 in his place. When he got up, he saw a place that he had not seen before and people he did not recognize, nor did they recognize him. He approached someone, whereby that man said to him, "Who are you and where did you come from?" 'Umar replied, "From Yathrib, the city of the Messenger 🖏."

The man replied, "Think, consider and watch carefully what you are saying." 'Umar said, "This is what I am saying." The man said, "When did you leave the city? 'Umar responded, "Yesterday." The man said to him, "Keep quiet so people will not hear this from you, or you will be killed, or they will say that you are mad." 'Umar insisted, "But what I am saying is the truth."

Then the man said: "Tell me about yourself and why you came here." 'Umar said, "Ali b. Abi Talib 🖏 goes out of the city every Thursday night and we did not know where he goes. When it was this night [this *laylat al-jumu'ah*], I followed him. So we arrived here, then he stood up to pray and I slept and I do not know what he did afterwards."

The man said: "Enter this city and see the people, and spend your days here until the coming Thursday night as there is no one to take you back to your place in which you came from except the man who brought you here - for between us and Medina is more than the journey of two years. When we see those who have seen Medina and the Messenger of God 🖏, we seek blessings from them and visit them. Sometimes we also see the one who brought you so we can say that you were brought here in less than a night from Medina.

'Umar entered the city and saw all of the people cursing whoever (will) tyrannize and oppress the household of Muhammad 🖏 and calling them with their names one by one to the extent that even every trader was cursing those oppressors while he was working. When 'Umar heard this, he felt as if the earth, spacious as it is, had become constrained and tight, and as if the days have become very long, until he went back on the following Thursday night to that place where Amir al-Mo'mineen 🖏 arrived every week. Then 'Umar sat watching him until most of the night has passed and when Ali b. Abi Talib 🖏 had finished his prayers and began to return back, then 'Umar followed him until they arrived at *fajr* [time] back to Medina. Amir al-

Mo'mineen ☸ entered the masjid and prayed behind the Messenger of God ☸ and so did 'Umar. Afterwards, the Prophet ☸ looked back at 'Umar and said, "Where have you been, we did not see you for a week with us?" 'Umar explained, "O the Messenger of God, such and such happened to me" and he told him what he had witnessed. Then the Prophet ☸ said to him, "Do not forget what you have seen with your own eyes." Whenever the Prophet ☸ was asked about that event, he ☸ would reply, "He has experienced the miracle of the Banu Hashim."[284]

Hadith 3: The Brother of the Prophet ☸

Jabir narrates from the Prophet ☸, "On the door of Paradise it is written, 'There is no God except Allah, Muhammad ☸ is the Messenger of Allah, and Ali is the Brother of the Messenger of Allah.' Allah wrote this two thousand years before the creation of the heavens and the earth."[285]

Hadith 4: Commentary of the Verse: "And Those in Authority from Among You" (4:59)

Jabir b. Abdullah al-Ansari narrates, "When Almighty Allah revealed the following verse His Prophet ☸, 'O you who believe, obey Allah and obey the Messenger and those possessing authority among you' (4:59), I asked him, 'O Messenger of Allah! We know Allah and His Messenger. But who are the possessors of authority whose obedience Allah has accompanied with your obedience?'

He ☸ explained, 'They are my caliphs, O Jabir, and the Imams of the Muslims after me. The first one of them is Ali b. Abi Talib, then Hasan and Husayn, then Ali b. Husayn, then Muhammad b. Ali - the one who is famous as al-Baqir in the Old Testament. Soon, you will meet him, O Jabir, so when you face him, convey my salutations to him.

He will be followed by Sadiq, Ja'far b. Muhammad, then Musa b. Ja'far, then Ali b. Musa, then Muhammad b. Ali, then Ali b. Muhammad, then al-Hasan b. Ali, then the one who will have my name and bear my patronymic,

---

[284] *Saheefa al-Abrar, Li-Hujjati al-Islam*, p. 22; *Qasas al-Sahaaba wa al-Tabi'in*, al-Hakimi, pp. 86-8.
[285] *Al-Khisal*, Chapter on the Number 2000, p. 638.

the proof of Allah on His earth and His remainder among His servants, the son of Hasan b. Ali. He ﷺ is the one from whose hands Allah, High be His remembrance, will open the east and the west of the earth. He ﷺ is the one who will be concealed from his Shias and his friends, an occultation in which no one will be steadfast on the belief of his Imamate except the one whose heart has been tested by Allah for faith.'

Jabir says that he asked, "'O Messenger of Allah! Will the Shias benefit from him during the occultation?' He ﷺ replied, 'Yes, by the One Who sent me with prophethood! Surely they will benefit with his light and gain from his mastership in his occultation just like people derive benefit from the sun when the clouds hide it. O Jabir! This is from the hidden secrets of Allah and the treasures of His knowledge, so hide it except from the ones worthy of it.'"[286]

Hadith 5: Qualities of Ali b. Abi Talib ﷺ

Jabir says, "I heard the Messenger of Allah ﷺ saying such qualities about Ali ﷺ that if even one of these was to be said regarding the entirety of the people, it would have sufficed as enough of a merit.

From these merits the Prophet ﷺ said: 'The one whose Master I am, so Ali is his Master; Ali is from me like Haroun was from Musa; Ali is from me and I am from him; Ali is from me like my own self. Obedience to him is obedience to me and disobedience to him is disobedience to me.'

Further he ﷺ said: 'The war of Ali is the war of Allah and peace of Ali is the peace of Allah; A friend of Ali is a friend of Allah's and an enemy of Ali is an enemy of Allah; Ali is the Divine Authority of Allah and His Caliph upon His servants. Loving Ali is faith and hating him is disbelief.'

Continuing on he ﷺ said: 'The party of Ali is the party of Allah and the party of his enemies is the party of Satan; Ali is with the Truth and the Truth is with Ali. They will not separate until they return to me at the Fountain (in paradise); Ali is the distributor of paradise and hell. The one who separates from Ali has separated from me and the one who separates from me has separated from Allah, the Mighty and Majestic; the Shi'a of Ali will be the successful ones on the Day of Judgement.'"[287]

---

[286] *Tafseer al-Burhan*, Hashim al-Bahrani, vol. 1, p. 381.
[287] *Bashaaratu al-Mustafa li Shi'ati Murtadha*, Section 1, pp. 32-3.

Hadith 6: The Position of Ali ☺ to the Prophet ☺

Jabir is narrated to have said, "I heard the Messenger of Allah ☺ say to Ali b. Abi Talib ☺: 'O Ali! You are my brother, my successor, my inheritor, my caliph during my lifetime and after my passing away. The one who loves you also loves me, and the one who hates you also hates me; and your enemy is my enemy, and your friend is my friend."[288]

Hadith 7: The Prophet ☺ Lauds Imam Ali ☺ by the Ka'bah

Jabir narrates, "We were in the presence of the Prophet ☺ and Ali b. Abi Talib ☺ walked over. So the Prophet said, 'My brother has come to you all.' Then he ☺ turned towards the Ka'bah and struck it with his hand and said, 'I swear by the One in Whose Hand is the soul of Muhammad! This one and his Shias, will be the successful ones on the Day of Judgement.'

Then he ☺ continued, 'He is the first one among all of you in faith along with me, and is the most fulfilling among all of you with regards to the Covenant of Allah; the strongest one of you all with the Commands of Allah, the Mighty and Majestic; and the most just of you among all of the citizens; the most equitable among you all with matters; and the one with the greatest privileges in the Presence of Allah.'"

Then Jabir says, "And the verse descended '(As for) those who believe and do good, surely they are the best of the created beings' (98:7)."[289]

Hadith 8: Jabir Inquires about the Position of Ali b. Abi Talib ☺

Jabir narrates that he said, "O Messenger of Allah ☺, what do you say about Ali b. Abi Talib ☺?' He ☺ replied, 'O Jabir, I and Ali were created from one Light 2000 years before Allah created Adam. We were placed in his loins and did not cease to travel in the purified loins and pure wombs until we separated in the loins of Abdul Muttalib.'

So the prophethood was placed in me, and the caliphate in him (Ali) with the Divine Authority. O Jabir! Ali has neither worshipped an idol nor an

---

[288] Ibid., Section 1, p. 40.
[289] Ibid., Section 2b, p. 30, Hadith 99.

image, he did not drink wine, nor indulge in any disobedient act at all, nor has a mistake been performed by him, nor a sin! So a person who intends to be free from hypocrisy, let him love the People of my Household, for they are from my origin and the inheritors of my knowledge. The example of them in paradise is like the Garden of Firdaus among the Gardens. Indeed the archangel Jibra'il informed me with what I just said, O Jabir.'"290

Hadith 9: Looking at the Face of Ali 🖼️ is worship

Jabir narrates, "Ali b. Abi Talib 🖼️ went over to the Prophet 🖼️ and the Messenger 🖼️ said to him 🖼️, 'O Ali, console Imraan b. Husayn for he is ill.' So Ali consoled him with Mu'aadh b. Jabal and Abu Hurayra. It happened that Imraan went on continuously looking at the face of Ali. Mu'aadh said to him, 'What is the matter with you, O Imraan that you are staring at Ali?' He replied, 'I am doing so because I heard the Messenger of Allah 🖼️ say that, 'Looking at Ali is worship.' Mu'aadh said to him, 'I too have heard this from the Prophet.' Abu Hurayra also said, 'I also heard this from the Prophet.'"291

Hadith 10: The Rank of Lady Fatima 🖼️

Jabir narrates that once the Prophet 🖼️ had not had anything to eat for several days. When the hunger became unbearable, he went to the rooms of his wives but found no food with any one of them. He then went to his daughter Lady Fatima 🖼️ and said, "Dear daughter, do you have anything for me to eat as I am very hungry?" She replied that she had nothing. However, when the Prophet 🖼️ left, a neighbour of Lady Fatima's 🖼️ sent her two pieces of bread and a piece of meat. After receiving it she placed it on a platter and said, "I swear by Allah, I will give this to the Messenger of Allah rather than keeping it for myself and my family." She said despite the fact that her and her family were also hungry and were without any food. Lady Fatima 🖼️ then sent Imam Hasan 🖼️ and Imam Husayn 🖼️ to call back the Prophet 🖼️. When he 🖼️ returned, she said, "Allah has sent something that I have reserved for you."

---

290 Ibid., Section 5, p. 17, Hadith no. 21.
291 Ibid., p. 21, Hadith no. 27.

Lady Fatima 🕮 states, "When I brought the platter and uncovered it, I found it filled with bread and meat. I immediately knew that it was the blessings of Allah. I praised Allah and then placed it before the Prophet 🕮 nd when he saw it, he also praised Allah. He 🕮 asked me, 'Where did you get this from, dear daughter?' 'It is from Allah because Allah provides for whomever He wills without counting' I replied.

The Prophet 🕮 responded, 'Dearest daughter, all praise belongs to Allah who has made you like the Leader of all of the Women from the Banu Isra'el (Lady Mary), because whenever she was asked about the sustenance provided for her, she would respond in the same way that, 'It is from Allah because Allah provides for whomever He wills without counting."

The Prophet 🕮 then sent for Imam Ali 🕮, Hasan 🕮, Husayn 🕮 and the wives of the household of the Prophet to partake in the food. The platter remained as full as it had been and so the Prophet 🕮 told me to give it to the neighbours. Allah indeed placed blessings and abundant goodness in the food."[292]

Hadith 11: Allah Presents the Authority of Imam Ali 🕮 to the Heavens and the Earth

Jabir narrates that the Prophet 🕮 said, "When Allah created the heavens and the earth, He called on them and they responded. He presented my prophethood, and the authority (*wilayat*) of Ali b. Abi Talib to them, which they both accepted. Then Allah created the creatures and entrusted the religious affairs to us. Therefore pleased are those who are pleased with us, and unhappy are those who are unhappy with us. We permit that which Allah has made permissible, and prohibit that which Allah has made unlawful."[293]

---

[292] *Tafseer ibn Katheer*, vol. 1, p. 360.
[293] *Bihar al-Anwar*, Al-Majlisi, vol. 17, p. 13, Hadith 25.

Hadith 12: The Narration of the Event of the Cloak (Hadith al-Kisaa)

Jabir narrates[294] that he heard from her eminence Lady Fatima al-Zahra ﷺ the following event surrounding the revelation of the verse, "Indeed Allah wishes only to remove all of the impurities from you Ahl al-Bayt, and purify you a most thorough purification" (33:33).

"My father, the Prophet of Allah, came to my house one day and said to me: 'Peace be upon you, O Fatima.' I replied: 'And upon you be peace.' Then he ﷺ said: 'I feel weakness in my body.' I said: 'May Allah protect you from weakness, father.'

He ﷺ said: 'O Fatima, please bring the Yemeni cloak and cover me with it.' So, I brought the Yemeni cloak and covered him with it. Then, I looked at him and saw that his face was shining like a full moon with its glory and splendour.

After a while, my son Hasan came in and said: 'Peace be upon you, O mother.' I replied: 'And upon you be peace, O light of my eyes, and the delight of my heart.' He then said: 'O Mother! I smell a fragrance so sweet and so pure as that of my grandfather, the Prophet of Allah ﷺ.' I replied:

---

[294] The chain of narrators of this as is as follows: Sheikh Abdullah al-Bahrani in his book *al-Awaalim,* and he saw it written by the pen of Sheikh Jaleel Sayyid Hashim al-Bahrani – He from Sheikh al-Hadeeth Sayyid Majid al-Bahrani ﷺ, he from Sheikh Hasan b. Zayn al-Din, he from Sheikh Muqaddas al-Ardbaili ﷺ, he from Sheikh Ali b. Abdul A'laa al-Karki ﷺ, he from Ali b. Hilal al-Jazaaeri, he from Ahmad b. Fahd al-Hilli ﷺ , he from Ali b. Khazan al-Haaeri ﷺ, he from Sheikh Zia al-Din Ali b. Shaheed al-Awwal ﷺ, he from Shaheed al-Awwal ﷺ, he from Fakhr al-Muttaqeen ﷺ, he from his revered father Allamah al-Hilli ﷺ, he from his elder Mohaqqiq al-Hilli ﷺ, he from his elder Ibn Numma al-Hilli ﷺ, he from Sheikh Mohammad b. Idris al-Hilli ﷺ, he from Ibn Hamza al-Toosi ﷺ author of *Thaqib al-Manaaqib,* he from Allamah Mohammad b. Shahr Ashoob ﷺ, he from Allamah al-Tabrasi ﷺ author of al-*Ihtejaaj,* he from Sheikh Jaleel Hasan b. Mohammad b. Hasan al-Toosi, he from his revered father Sheikh al-Taaif ﷺ, he from his teacher Sheikh al-Mufid ﷺ, he from Sheikh b. Qawliya al-Qummi ﷺ, he from Sheikh al-Kulayni ﷺ, he from Ali b. Ibrahim ﷺ, he from Ibrahim b. Hashim ﷺ, he from Ahmad b. Mohammad b. Abi Nasr al-Bazanti ﷺ, he from Qasim b. Yahya al-Jila al-Kufi ﷺ, he from Abu Baseer ﷺ, he from Aabaan b. Taghlab ﷺ, he from Jabir b. Yazid, he from Jabir b. Abdullah al-Ansari. This chain has been confirmed by Ayatollah Syed Muhammad Husayni al-Shirazi in his commentary of Hadith al-Kisaa, *'Min Fiqh al-Zahra',* volume 1, Hadith al-Kisaa.'

'Yes, your grandfather is lying underneath the cloak.' Hasan went near the cloak and said: 'Peace be upon you, O my grandfather, the Prophet of Allah; May I enter the cloak with you?' He ❀ replied: 'And upon you be peace, my son and the master of my fountain (kauthar), you are given the permission to enter.'

So, Hasan entered the cloak with him.

After a while, my son Husayn came in and said: 'Peace be upon you, O mother.' I replied: 'And upon you be peace, O light of my eyes, and the delight of my heart.' He then said: 'Mother! I smell a sweet fragrance like that of my grandfather, the Prophet of Allah.' I replied: 'Yes. Your grandfather and your brother are lying underneath the cloak.' Husayn went towards the cloak and said: 'Peace be upon you, my grandfather, the Chosen of Allah; may I enter the cloak with you?' He replied: 'And upon you be peace, my son and interceder of my followers, you are given permission to enter.'

So, Husayn entered the cloak with them.

After a while, Abul Hasan, Ali b. Abi Talib ❀ came in and said: 'Peace be upon you, O daughter of the Prophet of Allah.' I replied: 'And upon you peace, O father of Hasan, and the Commander of the Faithful.' He then said: 'O Fatima! I smell a sweet fragrance like that of my brother, (my cousin), the Prophet of Allah.' I replied: 'Yes. He is underneath the cloak with your two sons.' So, Ali went near the cloak and said: 'Peace be upon you, O Prophet of Allah; may I enter the cloak with you?' He replied: 'And upon you be peace, my brother, my legatee, my successor, and my standard bearer, you are given the permission to enter.'

So, Ali entered the cloak with them.

Then I went forward and said: 'Peace be upon you, O my father, and Prophet of Allah; May I enter the cloak with you?' He replied: 'And upon you be peace, my daughter, O part of my self; you are given the permission to enter.' So, I entered the cloak with them. Getting together underneath the cloak, my father, the Prophet of Allah], held the two ends of the cloak and raised his right hand towards the heavens and prayed: 'O Allah, these are the people of my Household (Ahl al-Bayt). They are my confidants and my supporters. Their flesh is my flesh and their blood is my blood. Whoever hurts them, hurts me too. Whoever displeases them, displeased me too. I am at war with those who are at war with them, and I am at peace with those who are at peace with them. I am the enemies of their enemies, and I am the friend of their friends. They are from me and I am from them. O Allah! Bestow Your blessings, benevolence, forgiveness and Your pleasure upon me and upon them; and remove impurity from them and keep them thoroughly pure.'

Then the Lord, Almighty Allah said: 'O My angels! O residents of My heavens, verily, I have not created the erected sky, the stretched earth, the illuminated moon, the bright sun, the rotating planets, the flowing seas, and the sailing ships, but for the love of these five lying underneath the cloak.' Jibra'il, the trusted angel, asked: 'Who are under the cloak?' The Almighty answered: 'They are the Household of the Prophet ﷺ and the assets of prophethood. They are: Fatima, her father, her husband and her two sons.' Jibra'il said: 'O Lord, may I fly to earth to be the sixth one of them?' Allah replied: 'Yes. You are given permission.' Jibra'il, the trusted one, landed near them and said: 'Peace be upon you, O Prophet of Allah. The All-Highest One conveys His peace upon you and His greetings and says: 'By My Honour and Glory, O My angels! O residents of My heavens, verily, I have not created the erected sky, the stretched earth, the illuminated moon, the bright sun, the rotating planets, the flowing seas, and the sailing ships, but for your sake and your love.' Jibra'il continued: 'Allah has given me permission to enter the cloak with you. May I join you, O Prophet of Allah?' The Prophet ﷺ replied: 'And peace be upon you, O trusted bearer of Allah's revelations! You are granted permission.'

So, Jibra'il entered the cloak with us and said to my father: 'Allah sends His revelations to you. Verily Allah desires to remove blemish from you, O People of the Household (Ahl al-Bayt) and purify you with a perfect purification.' (33:33)

Then Ali said to my father: 'O Prophet of Allah, tell me: What significance has Allah reserved from His grace for this gathering of ours under this cloak?' The Prophet ﷺ replied: 'I swear by He who rightfully appointed me a Prophet ﷺ and selected me with prophethood as a saviour that this episode of ours will not be recounted in any gathering from the gatherings of the people of the earth where a group of our Shias and lovers are present - except that there will descend upon them mercy! As well angels will encircle them asking Allah the remission of their sins until the assembly disperses!'

Ali said: 'In that case, we have attained success, and our Shias have attained success, by the Lord of the Ka'bah!'

Then the Prophet replied a second time: 'O Ali! I swear by He Who rightfully appointed me a Prophet and selected me with prophethood as a saviour that this episode of ours will not be recounted in any gathering from the gatherings of the people of the earth where a group of our Shias and lovers are present, and there be a person present full of grief, except that Allah will remove his grief; and no person in distress, except that Allah will dispel his distress; and no seeker of any wish, except that Allah grants his wish!'

Ali stated: 'In that case, by Allah! We have attained success and felicity, and our followers also have attained success and felicity, in this world and the hereafter, by the Lord of the Ka'bah!'"[295]

---

[295] *Min Fiqh al-Zahra*, Ayatollah Muhammad al-Husayni al-Shirazi, vol. 2, pp. 8-10.

Chapter 7

Jabir and the Ansar in the Final Year of the Prophet's ﷺ Life

The Prophet ﷺ Announces the Hajj Pilgrimage

Jabir narrates that after living nine years in the city of Medina, the Prophet ﷺ had not performed *hajj* until it was announced that he should perform it that year. A great number of people from across the nation arrived in Medina to join him and participate in it. There were still five days left of the month of Dhul Qa'dah when the Prophet ﷺ left with his companions. When they reached Dhul Hulayfah, the Prophet ﷺ instructed them, "Take a bath and enter into the *ihraam*."

The Prophet ﷺ then proceeded to Baydaa where he called out the talbiyyah and began reciting, "At your service, O Allah, at your service! No partner do You have, we are at your service!"

Jabir continues, "The people in front of the Messenger of Allah ﷺ reached as far as I could see. They were on foot and on animals. Behind the Prophet ﷺ were just as many people and there were just as many on his left and on his right. We would do exactly as the Prophet ﷺ did by imitating his actions."[296]

---

[296] *Al-Bidaaya wa al-Nihayah*, vol. 5, p. 146.

The Prophet's Statement on the Day of 'Arafah

Jabir states, "I saw Allah's Messenger 🌿 performing the *hajj* seated on his she-camel al-Qaswa on the Day of 'Arafah giving a talk and I heard him saying, 'O people, I have left among you something of such a nature that if you adhere to it you will never go astray: Allah's Book and my close relatives, my Ahl al-Bayt 🌿.'"[297]

The Prophet's Actions at Jabal al-Rahmah

Imam Ali b. Musa al-Ridha 🌿 states, "I heard my father 🌿 narrate on the authority of his father 🌿, on the authority of his grandfather 🌿, on the authority of Jabir b. Abdullah who said, 'Allah's Messenger 🌿 was at the Dome of Adam 🌿 (Mountain of Mercy). I saw Bilal al-Habashi come out with the water leftover from the Prophet 🌿 making his ablutions. The people gathered around him and everyone took some of the water with which he had washed his face. Whoever could not get any water would touch the other people who had (gotten it) and get the residue to rub on their own hands and face. They used to do the same thing with the water leftover from Ali's 🌿 ablutions.'"[298]

The Prophet's Predictions and Warning at the Ka'bah During the Farewell Pilgrimage

Jabir b. Abdullah al-Ansari narrates, "I completed my *hajj* with the Prophet 🌿 during his 'farewell pilgrimage.' When the Prophet 🌿 finished what Allah had decreed upon him of the pilgrimage, he 🌿 came to bid farewell to the holy Ka'aba. He stayed at the door ring and called out loudly, 'O people!' Then the people in the Masjid and those of the market place gathered around.

Then he 🌿 said, 'Listen to me - I am saying what is going to happen after me, so those of you who are witnessing this shall tell the ones who are absent.' Then the Messenger of Allah 🌿 cried and so did the people as well. When he stopped crying, he 🌿 said, 'You must know, may Allah have mercy

---

[297] *Sunan al-Tirmidhi*, vol. 3, p. 543, Hadith 3786
[298] *Uyun Akbar al-Ridha*, Al-Sadooq, vol. 2, Chapter 31, Hadith 320, p. 114.

upon you, that today you are like leaves without spikes until a hundred and forty years. Then a time will come after that where there will be spikes and leaves for two hundred years. Then a time will come after that where there will be spikes with no leaves, until nothing will be seen except for an iniquitous ruler (Sultan), or a greedy and wealthy person, or a scholar who is tempted by money, or a liar or poor person, or a licentious Sheikh, or a rude boy or a stupid woman.'

At this the Messenger of Allah ﷺ cried. Salmaan al-Farsi stood and asked, 'O Messenger of Allah, tell us when will this be?' The Prophet ﷺ replied, "O Salmaan, when your scholars decrease, your reciters go away, you stop giving alms (zakat), you (openly) show your abominable (detestable) actions, your voices are raised in your masajid, you put this world (dunya) above your heads and put the knowledge under your feet, you make telling lies as your normal speech, and backbiting as your fruits, and you make the impermissible (haram) as your gain (profit, benefit), your old will not have mercy upon your young, and your young will not respect your old. Then the curse will come down upon you, and your animosity will be made towards each other, spoken through your tongues. When you reach to having these traits, then you should expect a red wind (storm), or a monstrosity, or being thrown by stones- and the endorsement of this is in Almighty Allah's book when He ﷺ said, 'Say: He has the power that He should send on you a chastisement from above you or from beneath your feet, or that He should throw you into confusion, (making you) of different parties; and make some of you taste the fighting of others. See how We repeat the communications that they may understand." (6:65)

Then a group of the companions came to him ﷺ and said: 'O Messenger of Allah tell us when will this be?' The Prophet ﷺ replied, 'When prayers are delayed, desires are followed, coffee is drunk, insults of the fathers and mothers are normal, when the impermissible (haram) is seen as a gain, and alms (zakat) is seen as a constraint, and a husband obeys his wife and ignores his neighbours and cuts his family ties, and the mercy of the old [ones] perishes, and the shame of the young [ones] lessens. As well, high built up buildings will be made, and the slaves and the bondmaids will be severely oppressed, and the desires will be adhered to, and governments will rule with injustice, and men will curse their own fathers and envy their brothers, and the co-partners will be treated with betrayal, and loyalty (trustfulness) will decrease, and prostitution will become popular, and men will dress with women's clothing, and the veil of shyness will be taken off of them. Pride will spread in the hearts as the toxins spread in the bodies, the good will be lessened, and the crimes will become apparent, and the tremendous will be made easy, and people will seek praise by virtue of wealth, and vast money will be spent on singing, and people will be distracted from the hereafter by this world. When piety will decrease, and greed, disorder and corruption will be all abound, and a believer will become humiliated, and the hypocrite will become popular, and the *masaajid* will be engaged with *adhaan*, but the hearts will be devoid of any belief, and when the Qur'an will be taken lightly; and when it is conveyed to the people about their shame, then you see their faces as the faces of humans, but their hearts will be like the hearts of the devils, and their speech will be sweeter than honey, but their hearts will be more bitter than a colocynth (a very bitter plant).

Verily, they will be like wolves clothed. Indeed there is no day except the one when Allah, the Blessed and Exalted says, 'Do you invent things and attribute it to Me or are you being insolent to Me? Do you think that We have created you needlessly, and that you will not have to return to Us?' I swear by My Honour and Majesty, that had it not been because of the ones who worship Me with honesty, I would have not granted a respite [delay] for those who disobey Me with even twinkling of an eye; and had it not been because of the devotion of the devotees of My believers, I would have not brought down a drop of water and would have not grown a green leaf.'

The Prophet ﷺ continued, 'So how strange it is for people to be distracted by their money and have their hopes lengthened - while all along their lives are shortening, yet they covet the neighbourhoods of their peers; and all along they do not reach to any of it except by action, and action will not be accomplished except by a good intellect.'

'From us the Ahl al-Bayt is the Mahdi ﷺ of this nation. If this world becomes full of disorder, corruption, affliction, and sedition becomes apparent, and the paths become broken, and people attack one another, and the elderly do not have mercy upon the young, and the young do not respect the old, then Allah will send our Mahdi ﷺ, the ninth from the progeny of Imam Husayn ﷺ. He will open the castles of aberrance and deviance, and raise the heedless hearts in the name of religion at the end of time, just like

I raised it at the beginning of time; and he will fill the earth with justice as it was filled with injustice.'"[299]

The Announcement of Ali b. Abi Talib ؏ as the Master of all Muslims at the Event of Ghadeer al-Khumm

On the 18th of Dhul Hijjah, as the *hujjaaj* (*hajj* pilgrims) began to disperse to their various regions of living, Prophet Muhammad ﷺ called for all of those ahead of him to return and those behind to catch up as he has been ordered to announce something grand. The verse, "O Apostle! Deliver what has been sent down to you from your Lord; and if you don't do it, you have not delivered His message (at all); and Allah will protect you from the people ..." (5:67) was revealed.

They gathered at a pond known as Ghadeer al-Khumm. The prophet spent approximately five hours there of which three hours he spent delivering a lengthy sermon, surmising his teachings, forewarning the Muslims of their futures and emphasising what needed to be remembered in lieu of his death.

At the end of the sermon Prophet Muhammad ﷺ announced what was the coronation ceremony of the leadership and absolute authority of Ali b. Abi Talib ؏ after him with the words, "For whoever I am his Leader (*mawla*), Ali is his Leader (*mawla*)." This was followed the revelation of the verse, "Today I have perfected your religion and completed my favour upon you, and I was satisfied that Islam be your religion" (5:3).

Jabir narrated this event to such an extent that there are thirty-one different chains of narrations across more than a dozen leading historical books from him testifying this prophetic pronouncement.[300] This makes him one of histories most prolific narrators of this event with companions like Abdullah b. Abbas, Abu Sa'id al-Khudhri, Zayd b. Arqam, Al-Bara' b. 'Azib and Buraydah b. al-Husayb al-Madani.[301]

---

[299] *Noor al-Absar*, Mahdi al-Mazandarani, p. 452; *Qasas al-Sahaaba wa al-Tabi'in*, pp. 81-3.
[300] This can be found at: https://bit.ly/2M027UO
[301] This can be found at: https://bit.ly/2M0g6do

The Prophet's ﷺ Arrival Back into Medina and Meeting the Ansar

After the sermon at Ghadeer al-Khumm and the appointment of Imam Ali ؑ as caliph of the Muslim community, the seed of hypocrisy and envy grew in the hearts of some of the people. They would say that these words of appointment of Imam Ali ؑ were not from Allah, but rather that the Prophet ﷺ only wanted to promote his own cousin.

Imam Ja'far al-Sadiq ؑ states that, "When the Prophet ﷺ arrived in Medina, the Ansar came to see him for a certain issue. They said, 'O Messenger of Allah, Allah has granted us a great deal of favours. He granted us the honour of bringing you to this town among us. In doing so He brought joy to the hearts of our friends and sorrow to our enemies. We know that many delegates come to see you, and there is not enough to give them so the enemies call it degrading. We would like it very much if you accept one third of our properties so when the delegates from Mecca come to see you, you will have enough means to accommodate them."

The Messenger of Allah ﷺ did not reply to them as he ﷺ was waiting for Angel Jibra'il to bring a message from Allah. Jibra'il descended and said, "Muhammad say: I do not ask you for any payment for my preaching except love for my near relatives" (42:23). He ﷺ did not accept their property.

The hypocrites (continued to say), "Allah has not said this to Muhammad. He only wants to lift up the shoulder of his cousin to promote him. He is imposing his family upon us. Yesterday he said, 'Over whoever I have divine authority, this Ali also has the same degree of divine authority over them' and today he says this."

Imam al-Sadiq ؑ continues, "Thereafter came the verse of the Qur'an about khums (8:41). They said, 'He (the Prophet) only wants to take away our properties and interests!' Then Jibra'il came and said (from Allah), 'O Muhammad, you have completed the task of prophethood and the duration of your life is coming to a close. You must now place the greatest name, the legacy of the knowledge, and the symbols of knowledge of prophethood with Ali b. Abi Talib. This is because I (Allah) do not want to leave the earth without having a scholar therein so that people may learn from him how to obey Me and know through him My guardianship and authority.'"[302]

The Prophet ﷺ Addresses the Ansar Before He ﷺ Dies

Amr b. al-Auf al-Ansari narrates that the Prophet ﷺ sent Abu Ubaydah b. Jarrah to collect the tax (*jiziya*) from Bahrain. When he returned and the Ansar heard about his arrival, they all gathered and presented themselves at the time of the *fajr* prayer. After performing the prayer, the Prophet ﷺ began to leave and the Ansar came and stood before him.

When he saw this, the Prophet ﷺ smiled and said, "I assume that you all heard about the return of Abu Ubaydah from Bahrain?" They replied, "We certainly did, O Messenger." The Prophet ﷺ responded, "I have good news for you and you may also hope for some joy (as you will be receiving a portion of the wealth and more in the future). But, I swear by Allah that it is not poverty that I fear for you. Rather I fear that the whole world could be spread before you, as it was spread for the people before you, after which you will vie with one another in acquiring it, just as they competed in acquiring it; and it will eventually destroy you, just like it destroyed them."[303]

On another occasion shortly before the Prophet's ﷺ death, he was informed that the Ansar men and women had gathered in the Masjid and were crying. "What makes them cry?" the Prophet ﷺ inquired, to which he was informed that it was due to their fear and grief at him passing away. The Prophet ﷺ wrapped himself in a shawl, and with a stained bandage on his head, he went to the Masjid and ascended the pulpit. After praising Allah ﷻ he ﷺ said, "People will multiply, just like the Ansar will dwindle in numbers, until they are only as much as salt in food."[304] [305]

---

[302] *Al-Kafi*, vol. 1, The Book about People with Divine Authority, Chapter 60, Tacit and Explicit Testimony as Proof of Ali's Divine Authority over the People after the Messenger of Allah, Hadith 3, pp. 261-2.

[303] *Targheeb wa Tarheeb* vol. 5, p. 141.

[304] The meaning of this statement is that 'Know that you too will also die soon, whereas Islam will grow because of your efforts, to the extent that your proportion will be as small as how much salt is placed in food.'

[305] Haythami, *Majmau' al-Zawa'id wa Manba' al-Fawa'id*, vol. 10, p. 37; *Tabaqat al-Kubra*, vol. 2, p. 252.

Zayd b. Sa'ad reports from his father that just before the Prophet's ﷺ death, he came out of his room wrapped in old clothing and sat on the pulpit. When the people heard about this they left what they were doing and gathered around him ﷺ. After praising Allah ﷻ, the Prophet ﷺ said, "O people, keep me in mind when dealing with the Ansar, for they are like my stomach where I deposit my food (my source of strength), and they are my treasure chest (where I place my trusts)."[306]

Lady Fatima ﷺ Asks her Father ﷺ where She will Meet Him on the Day of Judgement

Jabir narrates from Imam Ali b. Abi Talib ﷺ who said, "Once Fatima said to the Apostle of Allah, 'O my dear father, where shall I meet you on the Day of the Great Station, the Day of Dreads, and the Day of Great Terror?'

The Prophet ﷺ replied, 'O Fatima, at the door of heaven, while I will have the banner of praise and will be interceding for my nation with my Lord.' Lady Fatima ﷺ sought further, 'O my dear father, what if I do not meet you there?' The Prophet ﷺ replied, 'Then meet me at the Spring while I am serving my nation with its drink.' Lady Fatima ﷺ again asked, 'O my dear father, but what if I do not meet you there either?' The Prophet ﷺ replied, 'Then meet me while I am at the Balance saying, 'My Lord, protect my nation.''

Lady Fatima ﷺ again asked, 'And what if I do not meet you there?' The Prophet ﷺ responded, 'then meet me at the edge of the fire while I prevent its flames from reaching my nation.' Upon this, Lady Fatima ﷺ became pleased."[307]

Jabir Narrates a Testimony (Wasiyyah) from the Prophet ﷺ

Among the famous narrations from Jabir is a deeply powerful and spiritual testimony from the Prophet ﷺ advising on how to take care of one's self and time.

---

[306] Ibid., p. 36.
[307] Qummi, Abu Ja'far Muhammad b. Ali b. Babwaih al, *al-Amaali*, p. 276.

Jabir states, "The Messenger of Allah ﷺ addressed us saying, 'O people! Repent to Allah before you die. Hasten to do good deeds before you become preoccupied (because of sickness and old age). Uphold the relationship that exists between you and your Lord by remembering Him a great deal and by giving a lot of charity in private and openly. (Then) you will be granted provision and Divine support, and your condition will improve. Know that Allah has enjoined Friday upon you in this place of mine, on this day, in this month, in this year, until the Day of Resurrection. Whoever abandons it, whether during my lifetime or after I am gone, whether he has a just or an unjust ruler, whether he takes it lightly or denies it (that it is obligatory), may Allah cause him to lose all sense of tranquility and contentment, and may He not bless him in his affairs. Indeed, his prayer will not be valid, his charity will not be accepted, his pilgrimage will not be counted, his fasting will not be effective, and his righteous deeds will not be accepted, until he repents. Whoever repents, Allah will accept his repentance. No woman should be appointed as an Imam over a man, no Bedouin should be appointed as an Imam over a Muhajir, no immoral person should be appointed as an Imam over a (true) believer, unless that is forced upon him and he fears his sword or whip.'"[308]

Death of the Prophet ﷺ

When the Prophet ﷺ passed away, Imam Ali ؏ locked the door for privacy. Members of Banu Abd al-Muttalib stood guard. Addressing the Prophet ﷺ, Imam Ali ؏ painfully said, "May my parents be sacrificed for you! You were

---

[308] *Sunan Ibn Majah*, Book of Establishing Prayer and its Practice, Chapter on the Fardh of Jum'ah, Hadith 1081. The Arabic text of this passage is as follows:

عَنْ جَابِرِ بْنِ عَبْدِ اللَّهِ، قَالَ: خَطَبَنَا رَسُولُ اللَّهِ صَلَّى اللهُ عَلَيْهِ وَسَلَّمَ فَقَالَ: يَا أَيُّهَا النَّاسُ تُوبُوا إِلَى اللَّهِ قَبْلَ أَنْ تَمُوتُوا، وَبَادِرُوا بِالْأَعْمَالِ الصَّالِحَةِ قَبْلَ أَنْ تُشْغَلُوا، وَصِلُوا الَّذِي بَيْنَكُمْ وَبَيْنَ رَبِّكُمْ بِكَثْرَةِ ذِكْرِكُمْ لَهُ، وَكَثْرَةِ الصَّدَقَةِ فِي السِّرِّ وَالْعَلَانِيَةِ، تُرْزَقُوا وَتُنْصَرُوا وَتُجْبَرُوا، وَاعْلَمُوا أَنَّ اللَّهَ قَدِ افْتَرَضَ عَلَيْكُمُ الْجُمُعَةَ فِي مَقَامِي هَذَا، فِي يَوْمِي هَذَا، فِي شَهْرِي هَذَا، مِنْ عَامِي هَذَا إِلَى يَوْمِ الْقِيَامَةِ، فَمَنْ تَرَكَهَا فِي حَيَاتِي أَوْ بَعْدِي، وَلَهُ إِمَامٌ عَادِلٌ أَوْ جَائِرٌ، اسْتِخْفَافًا بِهَا، أَوْ جُحُودًا لَهَا، فَلَا جَمَعَ اللَّهُ لَهُ شَمْلَهُ، وَلَا بَارَكَ لَهُ فِي أَمْرِهِ، أَلَا وَلَا صَلَاةَ لَهُ، وَلَا زَكَاةَ لَهُ، وَلَا حَجَّ لَهُ، وَلَا صَوْمَ لَهُ، وَلَا بِرَّ لَهُ حَتَّى يَتُوبَ، فَمَنْ تَابَ تَابَ اللَّهُ عَلَيْهِ، أَلَا لَا تَؤُمَّنَّ امْرَأَةٌ رَجُلًا، وَلَا يَؤُمَّ أَعْرَابِيٌّ مُهَاجِرًا، وَلَا يَؤُمَّ فَاجِرٌ مُؤْمِنًا، إِلَّا أَنْ يَقْهَرَهُ بِسُلْطَانٍ، يَخَافُ سَيْفَهُ وَسَوْطَهُ

so pure in life and now you are so pure in death." A beautiful fragrance, that had not been experienced before, could be smelt from the Prophet's ﷺ body.

Imam Ali ؑ asked for Fadhl b. Abbas to assist him. Outside of the house were groups of the Ansar calling, "We plead to you in the name of Allah and by the affinity that we have for the Messenger of Allah that you allow one of us to be part of the burial preparations!" The family of the Prophet ﷺ allowed Aws b. Khawlay from the Ansar to help who carried a bucket of water for the bathing.

Before starting a voice was heard saying, "Do not remove the Prophet's clothing. Bathe him as he is in his clothing." Imam Ali ؑ washed the Prophet ﷺ by placing his hand under his clothing as Fadhl held up the clothing for him and Aws brought the water.[309]

After the Prophet ﷺ was shrouded, he was placed on a bed in the corner of the room. People were then allowed to come in and perform their funeral prayers and bid him farewell. As many of the Ansar and Muhajireen that could fit in the room at one time would come in and go, they would say, "Peace be upon you O Prophet ﷺ and the Mercy of Allah and may His blessings be upon you."[310]

Lady Umm Salamah ؑ narrates that when the sound of shovels started to be heard, we the family, started crying loudly and so the people in the Masjid also started crying loudly. This caused all of Medina to shudder. When Bilal recited the call to prayer in the morning and recited the name of the Prophet ﷺ, he was unable to carry on, and burst out crying." [311]

---

[309] *Tabaqat al-Kubra*, vol. 2, p. 63.
[310] Ibid., p. 69.
[311] Ibid., vol. 4, p. 121.

Chapter 8

Jabir in the Period of the Caliphs

The Role of the Ansar during the Event of Saqifah

The Ansar of Medina were one of the important parties of the Muslim community. When Prophet Muhammad ﷺ died, some members of the Ansar upheld their sworn allegiance to Imam Ali ؏, while some others vied for political authority.

A gathering was held at a place called Saqifah to argue about which party would support who and - fearing the rule of the Quraysh, some members of the Ansar decided to join this gathering, even though the Prophet ﷺ had still not even been buried yet. This was because some members of the Ansar felt that they were better than the Quraysh, and thus more deserving of leadership should it be contended. Hubab b. Mundhir, one of the leaders of the Ansar said, "It was their (referring to the Ansar) sword that gained victory for Islam." Historians Tabari and Ibn Athir state that some members of the Ansar present kept their allegiance to Imam Ali ؏.[312]

At the Saqifah, a spokesman said, "We the Ansar, are the unified army of Islam and you, O Quraysh, are a small group of us and a minority among us." When Abu Bakr retorted that the Arabs would only recognize Caliphate from being among the Quraysh, the spokesman relinquished all allegiance to Imam Ali ؏ saying, "Then let there be a leader from us and another one from you." The response came, "Two swords cannot be put into one scabbard," and then Abu Bakr's hand was raised for allegiance. The

---

[312] *Tareekh al-Tabari*, vol. 3, p. 208; *Al-Kamil fi al-Tareekh*, vol. 2, p. 325

representatives of the Muhajireen and Ansar then swore their allegiance to him.[313]

It appears that the Prophet ﷺ predicted that some of the Ansar would turn against Imam Ali ؑ. It is narrated that the Prophet ﷺ said, "O Ali, Allah created you from the tree of which I am the root and you are the trunk. Al-Hasan and al-Husayn are its branches. Those who love us are the leaves. The honourable and Exalted God ﷻ will give Paradise to whoever grabs onto any of the branches. Only those of the Ansar will despise you whose fathers were Jews."[314]

Imam al-Baqir ؑ Replies to the Ansar's Claim that they were Most Proximate to the Prophet ﷺ for Authority after him ؑ

Abd al-Rahim b. Ruh al-Qasir narrates, "I asked Imam al-Baqir ؑ about who the words of Allah were revealed, 'The Prophet has more authority over the believers than they themselves do; and his wives are (in the position of) their mothers. The relatives are closer to each other, according to the Book of Allah, than the believers and the emigrants. However, you may show kindness to your guardians. This is also written in the book' (33:6).

He (the Imam) said, 'It (the verse) was revealed about the governance (leadership). This verse continued to apply to the lineage of al-Husayn ؑ after him. We have the right to exercise governance and we are closer to the Messenger of Allah than the believers of the emigrants and the Ansar.'"[315]

Imam Ali ؑ Acknowledges that a Majority of the Ansar were Excluded from the Talks at Saqifah

Sulaym b. Qays narrated from Salmaan al-Farsi that: "A few people paid allegiance to Abu Bakr." Salmaan came to Imam Ali ؑ to inform him about what happened and said, "You know what the people have done while you

---

[313] *History of the Caliphs*, Rasul Ja'farian, Ansariyan Publications, 2003, pp. 11-2.
[314] *Uyun Akhbar al-Ridha*, vol. 2, Chapter 31, Hadiths 233 & 234, p. 96.
[315] *Al-Kafi*, vol. 1, The Book about People with Divine Authority, Chapter 64, The Book of Proof of Leadership with Divine Authority in the Words of Allah and His Messenger, Hadith 2, pp. 252-3.

were busy washing the Messenger of Allah ﷺ? Abu Bakr is on the pulpit of the Messenger of Allah ﷺ, and the people are not happy with pledging allegiance, some are giving it with one hand (reluctantly), while others are pledging their allegiance with both of their hands (joyful), right and left."

Imam Ali ﷺ said to Salmaan: "O Salmaan, do you know who was the first one to pledge allegiance to Abu Bakr on the Pulpit of the Messenger of Allah ﷺ?" Salmaan said, "No, except that I saw him in the shade of the Clan of Sa'da when the 'Ansar' were excluded, and that the first one who pledged allegiance to him was Mugheira b. Sha'ba, then Basheer b. Sa'eed, then Abu Ubeyda al-Jarrah, then 'Umar b. al-Khattab, then Saalim Mowla Abu Huzayfa, and Ma'adh b. Jabal."

Imam Ali ﷺ said: "I am not asking you about those ones, but do you know who was the first one to pledge allegiance to him when he ascended the Pulpit?" Salmaan replied, "No, but I saw an older person leaning on a staff, with a severe mark of prostration between his eyes, climb upon the Pulpit first, come down and said while weeping, 'Praise is due to Allah who did not cause me to die until I saw you in this place. Extend your hand!' Abu Bakr extended his hand, and he paid allegiance to him, then said, 'This day is like the day of Adam,' then he came down and went out of the Masjid."

Imam Ali ﷺ said: "That was Iblees, may the curse of Allah be upon him gloating at the passing away of the Messenger of Allah."[316]

The Sermon of Lady Fatima ﷺ Complaining about the Ansar

In the famous sermon known as Khutbah al-Fadakiyyah, Lady Fatima ﷺ entered Masjid al-Nabawi to scold Abu Bakr for usurping the land of Fadak from her, pressed for her rights to be given back to her, and gave evidences for her claims. During the sermon she also made claims for the right of caliphate to be given back to Imam Ali b. Abi Talib ﷺ.

At the end of the sermon she addressed the Ansar with an intense criticism of their lack of fortitude in standing up for what they knew to be correct. She also rightly predicted their weaknesses in doing so in the future. Here we will only quote her address to the Ansar.

---

[316] *Kitab Sulaym b. Qays.* Hadith 4. p. 27.

Lady Fatima ؏ turned towards the Anṣar and said, "O group of valorous men! The aides of the nation! The helpers of Islam! What is this slackness (that you display) in regards to me while you are witnessing the oppression being meted upon me, but you still lie in a deep sleep! Did my father not say that the rights of a father for his children must be considered? How soon have you changed your tracks, even though you possess the strength to stand up for my rights and are capable of supporting me regarding my claim!

Do you then say that Muhammad ﷺ has passed away and there remains no responsibility upon us?

His loss is great and the crack that has appeared (in Islam) is severe and the division is immense. Unity has been shattered, the earth is engulfed in darkness due to his concealment, the sun and the moon have eclipsed, and the stars have scattered away! Hopes have broken, mountains have crumbled, the family of the Prophet has been lost, and their sanctity has been dishonoured after his death! This is, by Allah, a great calamity and a grand adversity, while this calamity is incomparable, and there is no other greater calamity than the death of the Prophet!

This (the death of the Prophet) had already been conveyed to you in the Book of Allah, may He be Glorified. You were reading the Quran day and night in a loud voice, lamenting, in a normal tone and in a pleasant voice. As for what happened in the past to Allah's Prophets and Apostles - the command is decisive and destiny is enjoined: 'And Muhammad is not but an Apostle, (other) Apostles have already passed away prior to him, therefore if he dies or is killed, will you turn upon your heels? And he who turns upon his heels will by no means do harm to Allah in the least, and soon shall We reward the grateful ones.' (3:144)

Be aware! I have said what I wanted to say, even though I know that you will not assist me as this slackness of yours to assist us has become a part of your heart (your practice). But all of this complaint is the result of the grief of my heart and the internal rage (that I feel) and (I know that) it is of no use, but I have said this to manifest my internal sorrow and to complete my proof upon you.

Thus usurp it (Fadak) and fasten it firmly, for it is weak and feeble, while its shame and disgrace will always remain over you. The sign of the rage of the Supreme Allah has been cast upon it, and it will be an everlasting disgrace upon you and it will lead you to the fire of Allah which will engulf the heart. Surely Allah sees whatever you do, 'And soon shall those who deal unjustly know what an (evil) turning they will be turned into.' (26:227)

I am the daughter of that Prophet who was sent to warn you against the severe wrath of Allah, 'Act (you) whatever you can, and verily we (too) act, and wait, indeed we too are waiting' (6:158 & 11:121-122)."[317]

In the Period of Abu Bakr

After the death of the Prophet ﷺ, Abu Bakr waged wars on those who denied his Caliphate, those who claimed false prophethood, and decided to fight the Romans and invade Syria. Asides from not accepting the rule of Abu Bakr, many tribes severed their connections with Medina. Mecca and Medina were in states of discord and many were on the verge of apostasy.[318]

He gathered the companions and said, "O my people, may Allah have mercy upon you. Remember that Allah has blessed you with Islam, made you the nation of Muhammad, increased your faith and conviction and granted you complete victory. Allah has said, "This day those who disbelieve have despaired of [defeating] your religion; so fear them not, but fear Me. This day I have perfected for you your religion and completed My favour upon you and have approved for you Islam as religion" (5:3).[319] Know that the Messenger of Allah intended to wage war in Syria and desired that effort should be made in that direction but then Allah recalled him to Himself. So be clear on this point that I intend to send a Muslim army together with their families and dependents to Syria." Abu Bakr thereafter wrote to the kings of Yemen, the Arab chiefs and the people of Mecca about his intentions to send an army to Syria to the expel those present there. He gave these letters to Anas b. Malik to deliver and waited for their replies.

Jabir b. Abdullah narrates, "Anas returned after a short while with the glad tidings that the people of Yemen were coming. He told Abu Bakr 'Whoever I read your order out to immediately obeyed Allah and accepted your orders. These people will present themselves with their equipment and

---

[317] Shareef al-Qurashi, Baqir, *The Life of Fatima al-Zahra*, Qum: Ansariyan Publications. p. 228.

[318] Ibid., p. 33.

[319] Abu Bakr wrongly used this verse to imply Jihad - when it had been revealed at the event of Ghadeer, and the coronation ceremony of Imam Ali ﷺ when he was appointed as the first Imam and Caliph of the Muslim community.

war materials and armour. O representative of the Messenger of Allah, I have presented myself ahead of their coming to give you glad tidings. In obeying you they have accepted to have their hair disheveled and their bodies covered in dust. They are extremely brave and excellent horsemen - the chiefs of Yemen. They will soon be arriving with their families and dependents. You should prepare to meet them.'"[320]

The Battle of Yamamah ended the first bloody civil war between the Muslims, and 58 from the Muhajiroon and 13 from the Ansar who had fought in the Battle of Badr were killed in this war.[321] According to Ibn Qutaybah, the majority of the companions held a disdain for the wars of Abu Bakr to secure his power, but they obeyed on account of his rulership.[322]

After the Prophet's ﷺ passing away, a great deal of wealth was sent from Bahrain. Abu Bakr announced, "Whoever the Prophet owed money to or whoever he had promised some money to should come and collect his dues." Jabir stood up and said, "The Prophet had told me that when wealth comes from Bahrain, he would give me an amount" indicating three handfuls. Abu Bakr told him to take that amount from the money, but when he did so, he only took one handful. Abu Bakr then gave instructions for the other two handfuls to be given to Jabir completing his portion.

According to narrations, there was a stark difference between the practices of Abu Bakr and 'Umar b. al-Khattab when they were caliphs in their treatment of the Ansar and Muhajireen. In the year following the above incident, a greater amount of money was sent from Bahrain. Abu Bakr distributed it among the people. Some people, including 'Umar, asked him, "Why do you not give more money to the Muhajireen and the Ansar since they were the earliest Muslims, and because the Prophet ﷺ held them in the highest esteem?" Abu Bakr replied, "Their rewards are reserved with Allah in the hereafter. In this world, equality is better than giving preference."[323] Another narration mentions something similar, but adds that Abu Bakr also asked, "Should I buy their virtues from them? With regards to peoples' existence in this world, equality is better than preference."[324]

---

[320] *The Islamic Conquest of Syria*, Al-Imam al-Waqidi, pp. 7-9.
[321] *History of the Caliphs*, Rasul Ja'fariyan, Ansariyan Publications, 2003, p. 26.
[322] *Al-Imamah wa al-Siyasah*, vol. 1, p. 35.
[323] *Kanz al-Ummal*, vol. 3, p. 127.
[324] *Sunan al-Bayhaqi*, vol. 6, p. 347.

In the period of 'Umar however, he refuted this practice stating, "While Abu Bakr had his opinion about the distribution of this wealth, I have another opinion. I do not hold those who fought against the Prophet ﷺ in the same esteem as those who fought alongside him"; therefore he gave preference to the Muhajireen and Ansar, stipulating additional amounts for the veterans of the Battle of Badr and those who accepted Islam prior to Badr. Narrations detail the varying amounts that 'Umar arbitrarily set for various categories of companions and family members.[325]

Towards the end of his life, 'Umar changed his views stating, "Abu Bakr was of the opinion that the distribution of wealth should be with total equality, whereas my opinion was that some people should be given more. However, if I live this next year, I will switch to the opinion of Abu Bakr because his opinion was better than mine."[326] [327]

In Period of 'Umar b. al-Khattab

One of the great battles of the Muslim Empire's expansion was that of the Battle of Yarmouk, in the month of Rajab, 15 A.H. It was led against the Byzantine Empire near the Yarmouk River, along what today are the borders of Syria and Jordan, and Syria and the illegal state of Israel. The victory of it ended the Byzantine rule in Syria and marked the first wave of conquests after the death of the Prophet ﷺ.

Upon arrival into Yarmouk, negotiations took place between Jabalah b. al-Ayham and the companion 'Ubadah b. Samit. When these failed Khalid b. al-Waleed, commander of the Muslim army sent a delegation to Jabalah. Jabir b. Abdullah al-Ansari was in this and he told them: "O Ansar of Allah and His Messenger. These Christian Arabs wish to fight us. They are from the Banu Ghassaan, Lakhm and Jutham and are your cousins in lineage. Go

---

[325] *Majma'uz Zawa'id*, vol. 4, p. 6; *Sunan Bayhaqi*, vol. 6, p. 350; *Kanz al-Ummal*, vol. 2, p. 315.

[326] Haythami, vol. 6, p. 6.

[327] The opinion and practice of Abu Bakr was closer to that of Imam Ali ؑ. It is narrated that Imam Ali ؑ said in this matter, "I have studied the Book of Allah and have not found in it anything denoting that the progeny of Isma'il (Arabs) be given preference to the progeny of Ishaq (non-Arabs)" and so Imam Ali ؑ would distribute equally to everyone whether they were a Muhajir, Ansar or those that came later. (*Hayaat al-Sahaaba*, vol. 2, p. 241)

out and speak to them. Persuade them not to fight. If they refuse, then our swords will deal with them. We are enough to meet them in battle." The delegation approached and called out, "We are your cousins desiring to speak with you." Jabalah granted them permission and opened the dialogue in his tent. "O my cousins, we have common blood and ancestry. I have come out from this army which has come upon you. A man then came from your army and transgressed the limits of speech when addressing me, so now what brings you to me?"

Jabir b. Abdullah led the response saying, "Do not take us to task for what our friend has said. Our religion is based on the truth and we wish well upon others. To wish you well is obligatory since you are a relative. We therefore invite you to Islam and to become part of our community. You will be entitled to whatever we are entitled to, and will be obligated with whatever we are obligated with. Our religion is most noble and our Prophet was most grateful." Jabalah replied, "I do not like that religion or any other. I am attached to my religion. You, O Aws and Khazraj, are pleased with a thing for yourself while we are pleased with something else. You keep to your religion, while we will keep to ours."

Jabir continued, "If you will not leave your religion then at least refrain from fighting us. Wait and see who is victorious. If we are victorious and you want to accept Islam then we will still welcome you, and you will be a brother unto us. If however you wish to remain a Christian, then we will be satisfied with the specified tax from you and will leave you in control of your lands and the lands of your ancestors as well."

Jabalah responded to this "I fear that should I refrain from fighting and the Romans are victorious, then I will not be safe and will lose my territory. They will only be satisfied with me if I fight against you and have proclaimed me as a leader over all of the Arabs. If I was to become a Muslim then I will be reduced to a low status and it is not in my nature to be a mere follower."

Jabir responded with a show of strength, "Bear in mind that if you refuse our offer and we win we will certainly execute you. Therefore stay away from us and our swords which crack open skulls and break bones. However, we would much rather if the battle was to take place without you and your men participating in it." Jabalah responded with his own preparedness for battle saying, "(I swear) by Christ and the Cross, I will definitely fight on

Rome's behalf even if it has to be against all my relations." The Ansar mounted their horses and returned to report that Jabalah was set on fighting them.[328]

Khalid began preparations for war and made an audacious plan. "O Muslims, know that the Devil's army is 60,000 Christian Arabs. We, the army of the Most Merciful, amount to 30,000 horsemen. We will have to fight this big force but if we fight them with our entire force, that will be quite cowardly. All we need to do is send our select and elite warriors against the Christian Arabs. I propose selecting thirty horsemen, each of whom will have to face 2,000 Christian Arabs. I am selecting those Muslims whom I know for their patience, steadfastness and the way that they forge ahead in battle. I will offer them this mission and if they love to meet Allah and desire His reward, then they will accept it."

Khalid then summoned sixty companions of the Prophet ﷺ calling them out by name one by one, including Jabir b. Abdullah. Then he said: "Where are those who were patient at the Battle of Uhud, for Allah has mentioned them in his Book?" (8:66).

When the Ansar heard the frequency with which their names were being called out they remarked, "Today Khalid is mostly calling out the Ansar and rarely the Muhajireen. Is it because he prefers for us to be destroyed?" When Khalid heard this he rode his horse until he was right in the middle of the Ansar and said, "By Allah, O descendants of 'Aamir, I only call you because of your pleasing qualities. I also have firm trust in you and have selected you for your faith. You are among those whose faith is firmly anchored in the heart. O Ansar, what do you say about joining me in an assault against this army which has come to fight us?" to which the Ansar agreed shouting, "We place our trust in Allah, the Most High and in His power. We will give up our lives in desire for the Hereafter." Thereafter, the sixty of them set out.[329]

The battle went on from the morning through to sunset.[330] The result brought a resounding victory for the Muslim warriors. After the battle, Khalid began searching for his sixty men, but only found twenty of them

---

[328] *The Islamic Conquest of Syria*, pp. 271-2.
[329] Ibid., pp. 273-6.
[330] Ibid., p. 279.

(alive).[331] Jabir narrates "I participated in the Battle of Yarmouk and did not see a boy braver than Jundub b. 'Aamir b. al-Tufayl when he was fighting Jabalah. He struck Jabalah with a blow which weakened him, but Jabalah struck back and killed him and Allah sped his soul to Paradise."[332]

The war however, had not ended. Five men from the Muslim army had been captured and so reinforcements were sought for another battle. The Roman army was led under the supreme command of Bannes, King of Armenia. Jabalah had returned to convey news of the battle and deliver the captives. Together they devised a scheme to capture the Muslim commanders to add them to the captives and have them all killed together. Bannes dispatched a sage telling the Muslims to send an envoy, which must include Khalid b. Walid. Abu Ubaydah addressed Khalid saying, "Go, may Allah keep you safe. Perhaps Allah will guide them, or they will surrender and pay the tax, and then Allah will spare bloodshed through you." Khalid selected one hundred Muhajireen and Ansar to accompany him, including Jabir b. Abdullah. They put on their good clothes and war gear, attached daggers to their waists, and took their swords, ready for any event.

Arriving at the camp of Bannes, they walked to where the King was sitting on his throne. Cushions, rugs and brocade decorated the tent. When the companions saw all of the pomp, they declared Allah's greatness and refused to sit on the chairs that were brought for them. They went to the extent of removing the rugs and preferred to sit on the bare ground. Bannes responded to this, "O Arabs, you refuse our hospitality? You show no etiquette towards us and trample on our rugs?" The response came, "To show etiquette to Allah is much better than to show etiquette to you. The mat of Allah, the earth, is much purer than your filthy mat, and our Prophet had told us, "The earth has been made a masjid and a means of purification for us.""[333]

A lengthy negotiation and heated argument ensued between Bannes and Khalid both posturing for war and victory over the other. Khalid demanded their acceptance of Islam, or for them to pay the specified tax. Bannes refused both saying, "Once upon a time this land belonged to neither us nor you, but to another nation. We fought them until we took it from them. So

---

[331] Ibid., p. 280.
[332] Ibid., p. 340.
[333] Ibid., p. 282-98.

now there will be war between us." Khalid responded, "You cannot be more eager for war than us. It is as if I already see you defeated with victory ahead of us. You will be dragged with a rope around your neck in disgrace and humiliation. You will be brought before 'Umar b. al-Khattab who will behead you." Bannes became furious shouting, "(I swear) by Christ, I will now bring your five captured men and behead them in front of you." Khalid responded to keep the captives alive, "You are indeed disgusting enough to do such a deed. Know that they are of us and we are of them. I swear that if you kill them, then I will kill you with this sword of mine and each one of my men will kill one or more of your men." Khalid then sprang up unsheathing his sword. His men, including Jabir, imitated him shouting, "There is no god but Allah, and Muhammad is His Messenger!" convinced that they would be killed.

Once Bannes understood the reality, and not wanting to risk such bloodshed, he sought to calm the situation and called out, "Respite, Khalid! Do not be hasty in destruction. I only uttered those words to test you and to see what you would do. Out of honour for you I am freeing the captives. They may help you, but you will still be helpless tomorrow." The confrontation ended with another battle expected the following day.[334]

After the battle, the spoils were divided. Abu 'Ubaydah announced, "I divided the booty in the same manner that the Prophet ﷺ had divided it amongst his companions," however many from the army did not accept the divisions of the gold, silver and horses. Abu 'Ubaydah wrote to Caliph 'Umar seeking his approval who wrote back, "You have implemented the practice of the Prophet ﷺ, so do not change your decision." However Abu 'Ubaydah had actually failed to correctly implement the Prophetic practice, as did 'Umar by endorsing Abu 'Ubaydah's distribution.

Ibn Zubayr narrates, "I saw my father Zubayr b. al-Awwam in the Battle of Yarmouk with two horses which he took turns in riding to battle. Abu 'Ubaydah gave him three shares (of the spoils), a share for himself and two for the horses. So Zubayr asked him, "Will you not treat me as the Prophet ﷺ treated me at the Battle of Khaybar? He gave me five shares, one for me and four for my two horses." Jabir b. Abdullah then came forward and testified that the Prophet ﷺ had given Zubayr five shares at Khaybar. Abu

---

[334] Ibid., p. 303-6.

'Ubaydah then wrote to 'Umar again who replied, "Zubayr speaks the truth."[335]

The Battle of Qadisiyyah

Jabir states, "I swear by the name of Allah, besides whom there is none worthy of worship, that we found no one among the army fighting at Qadisiyyah who desired the world together with the hereafter. We did however, have doubts about three of them (from among the thousands in the army), but they too turned out to be trustworthy and abstinent."[336]

The Distribution of Wealth by 'Umar and His Tafseer of the Holy Qur'an

It is narrated that 'Umar wanted to know how to distribute the wealth that was now coming into the Muslim community. In order to do so, he called upon people to advise him. He stated, "Gather around to consult and ponder about who should be the recipients of this wealth." When the people gathered to consult, he continued, "I instructed you to congregate here to ponder about who should receive this wealth. I have studied a few verses of the Qur'an in which it says the following:[337]

The booty that Allah granted His Messenger (without a battle being fought) from the people of the villages is for Allah, for the needs of the Messenger, for the close relatives of the Prophet, for the orphans, for the poor and for the travelers so that this wealth may not remain as amassed riches with the wealthy among you. Whatever the Prophet gives you, take hold of its command properly, and whatever he prohibits you from, refrain from that. Be God-conscious, surely the punishment of Allah is severe. For the poor emigrants who were removed from their houses and their possessions, they seek Allah's Grace and Pleasure and assist Allah and His Messenger. These are the ones who are truthful." (59:7-8)

'Umar announced, "This refers to the Muhajireen."

---

[335] Ibid., pp. 369-70.
[336] *Hayaat al-Sahaaba*, vol. 3, pp. 671-2.
[337] According to different narrations 'Umar also recited Surah al-Tawbah, verse 60 and Surah al-Anfaal, verse 41.

He then continued, "Those who adopted the places as their homes before them and adopted faith. They love those who migrated to them and find no want in their hearts for what they are given. They prefer others above themselves, even though they themselves are in need. And the one saved from miserliness of his low self, they truly are the successful ones." (59:9)

'Umar then announced, "This refers to the Ansar."

He further continued: "Those who come after them, who say 'Our Lord, forgive us and our brothers, those who preceded us in faith. And do not place in our hearts any ill-feeling against those who believed. Our Lord, indeed You are the Most Forgiving, the Most Merciful." (59:10)

'Umar then announced, "This verse encompasses all other people. Therefore there is no Muslim apart from your slaves who do not have a right to this wealth. If I live there shall not be a single Muslim who will not receive his right even though he may be a shepherd in the furthest parts of Yemen."[338] [339]

Jabir Narrates 'Umar's Altering of the Prophetic Sunnah

Ati' reports that Jabir b. Abdullah came to perform *'umrah*. We came to his abode and the people asked him about different things, and then they made a mention about temporary marriage, whereupon Jabir said, "Yes, we had been benefiting ourselves by this temporary marriage during the lifetime of the Prophet ﷺ and during the time of Abu Bakr and 'Umar."[340]

Jabir also stated, "We contracted temporary marriage giving a handful of dates or flour as a dowry during the lifetime of Allah's Messenger ﷺ and

---

[338] *Sunan al-Bayhaqi*, vol. 6, pp. 351-2.

[339] In the Chapter on the period of Abu Bakr, it was mentioned that 'Umar distributed wealth unevenly in accordance to his preferences. This narration appears to explain his methodology of preference, as his interpretation of the distribution was that the earlier Muslims should receive a greater share. It appears that he relied on the sequence of these verses from Surah al-Hashr which mention the Muhajireen first, then the Ansar, and then all of the other Muslims, to formulate his understanding about who should receive preference.

[340] *Sahih Muslim*, Book 16, 'Mut'ah Marriage: It was permitted then abrogated', Hadith 18. The Arabic text of this passage reads as follows:

قَالَ عَطَاءٌ قَدِمَ جَابِرُ بْنُ عَبْدِ اللَّهِ مُعْتَمِرًا فَجِئْنَاهُ فِي مَنْزِلِهِ فَسَأَلَهُ الْقَوْمُ عَنْ أَشْيَاءَ ثُمَّ ذَكَرُوا الْمُتْعَةَ فَقَالَ نَعَم اسْتَمْتَعْنَا عَلَى عَهْدِ رَسُولِ اللَّهِ صلى الله عليه وسلم وَأَبِي بَكْرٍ وَعُمَرَ

during the time of Abu Bakr, until 'Umar forbade it in the case of 'Amr b. Huraith."[341]

'Umar's Rebuke of Jabir b. Abdullah

Abdullah b. 'Umar narrates that one day 'Umar saw a dirham in the hand of Jabir. He asked him, "What is the dirham for?" Jabir replied, "I intend to use it to purchase some meat for my family as they are craving some." 'Umar replied, "Will you always buy something merely because you crave it? Where has the verse of the Qur'an left you in which Allah says, 'You have used up your good things in your worldly life." (46:20).[342]

In a similar narration, 'Umar is narrated to have responded by repeating over and over, 'My family has a strong craving' so much that Jabir is narrated to have said that he wished the dirham had dropped from his hand and that he had never met 'Umar.[343]

The Last Hours of 'Umar

Jabir b. Abdullah has been narrated to have said: "I witnessed that 'Umar said the following when he faced death: 'I repent to Allah for the following three things: freeing the atheist slaves from Yemen captured by the Muslims; not obeying Usamah whom Allah's Messenger ﷺ appointed him as the Chief of the Army; and we pledged to each other not to let any of the Prophet's ﷺ family succeed the Prophet ﷺ when Allah took away his life.'"[344]

Period of 'Uthman b. 'Affan

According to historical records, the Ansar were leading opponents of 'Uthman in the events preceding his killing, and Jabir in particular is named as among those companions who opposed the practices of this caliph. Jabir however, is not mentioned as being among those exiled for his stances.

---

[341] Ibid., Hadith 19. The Arabic text of this passage reads as follows:

قَالَ سَمِعْتُ جَابِرَ بْنَ عَبْدِ اللَّهِ، يَقُولُ كُنَّا نَسْتَمْتِعُ بِالْقُبْضَةِ مِنَ التَّمْرِ وَالدَّقِيقِ الأَيَّامَ عَلَى عَهْدِ رَسُولِ اللَّهِ صلى الله عليه وسلم وَأَبِي بَكْرٍ حَتَّى نَهَى عَنْهُ عُمَرُ فِي شَأْنِ عَمْرِو بْنِ حُرَيْثٍ

[342] *Muntakhab Kanz al-Ummal*, vol. 4, p. 406.
[343] Ibid., p. 407; *Targheeb wa al-Tarheeb*, vol. 3, p. 424.
[344] *Al-Khisal*, As-Sadooq, On 'three' numbered characteristics, Hadith 226.

'Allama Amini has listed the names of more than eighty leading companions as instigators of his death, or open opponents to 'Uthman such as: Talha, Zubayr, Ammar b. Yasir, Abu Dharr, Miqdaad b. Aswad al-Kindi, Sahl b. Hunayf, Abu Ayyub al-Ansari, and Jabir b. Abdullah al-Ansari.[345] In fact, when Jabir was eventually tortured by Hajjaaj b. Yusuf al-Thaqafi, the premise of it was that Jabir was among those directly blamed for 'Uthman's assassination by Hajjaaj. Amini narrates that when Hajjaaj reached the city of Medina he began accusing people of having killed 'Uthman. He arrested and handcuffed Jabir b. Abdullah al-Ansari as one of those responsible[346] even though not all of the companions agreed with the murder, or even considered it advisable.

It is generally agreed upon that some from the Ansar and Muhajireen were present at the killing of 'Uthman. Mu'awiyah is narrated to have once asked Abu Tufayl, "Were you one of the killers of 'Uthman?" He replied, "No, I was present, but I did not advocate for him." Mu'waiyah asked why not, to which Abu Tufayl admitted, "Since the Muhajiroon and Ansar didn't come to help him."[347] Despite this, it is not known if Jabir was present at the killing of 'Uthman or to what extent he supported it, if at all.

Period of Abd al-Malik b. Marwan

The Muslims were travelling through the Roman territories under the command of Malik b. Abdullah Khath'ami. Malik passed by Jabir b. Abdullah who was walking and leading his mule along - as opposed to riding it. Malik commented, "O Aba Abdullah (Jabir), ride! For Allah has provided you with convenience (his mule)." Jabir replied, "I have kept my animal in good condition and require nothing from my people. However, I am walking because I heard the Messenger of Allah ﷺ say that "Whenever the feet of a servant of Allah gets dusty in the path of Allah, Allah will forbid the hellfire for them." When the group with Malik heard this they all jumped off of their animals and began to walk in order to gain the merit of what the Prophet ﷺ had said.[348]

---

[345] *Al-Ghadir*, vol. 9, pp. 104-213.

[346] Ibid., p. 188.

[347] *History of the Caliphs*, Rasul Ja'fariyan, Ansariyan Publications, 2003, p. 140.

[348] *Targheeb wa Targheeb*, vol. 2, p. 396; *Majmau' al-Zawa'id*, vol. 5, p. 286; Bayhaqi, vol. 9, p. 162.

Chapter 9

Jabir during the Period of Imam Ali 🕮

Introduction

Jabir's proximity and loyalty to Imam Ali 🕮 stemmed from his direct knowledge about the position of the first Imam as regularly lauded to him by the Prophet 🕮. Since that time, what he saw and experienced with Imam Ali 🕮 ensured Jabir's service to him at all times, including being present in the Battle of Siffeen. Through this service, Jabir became known as one of the choicest companions. Al-Barqi in his biographical works divided the companions of Imam Ali 🕮 into three groups: his disciples; his special guards, and his servants. Amongst those whom al-Barqi named as his disciples were: Salmaan al-Muhammadi, Miqdaad b. Aswad al-Kindi, Abu Dharr, Ammar b. Yasir, Abu Layla, Sa'eed b. al-Khudhri, and Jabir b. Abdullah al-Ansari. They were considered the cream of the followers of Imam Ali b. Abi Talib 🕮.[349]

Ayatollah Syed al-Khoei quotes al-Kishi narrating from the companion al-Fadhl b. Shadhan who said about Jabir, "He was from among the foremost in good deeds (al-sabiqoon), those who followed the Commander of the Faithful Ali b. Abi Talib 🕮."[350]

Sheikh Fawzi Aal Sayf states, "After the death of Allah's Messenger 🕮, Jabir became one the Commander of the Faithful Ali's 🕮 choicest and dearest companions who would call towards the Imam, and spread his virtues. But Jabir never used to do that out of his abstract feeling, instead he

---

[349] *Rijaal al-Burqi.*
[350] *Mo'jam Rijal al-Hadith*, vol. 4, p. 330.

realized that he had a responsibility of making the wise and rightly guided line of the Divine message clear for the nation. Furthermore, he wanted to make it clear to the people who was the one that was able to rescue them from the mistakes that they had made - as he had heard from the Messenger ﷺ that it was Allah ﷻ Himself who had designated Imam Ali ؑ as the guardian of the community after him ﷺ. Thus Jabir found it his responsibility to inform others about this tradition. As well, in the issue of holding firm to the Friends of Allah (awliyaa') he was very strong in applying this, just like he was in the issue of repudiating the enemies of Allah ﷻ."[351]

Imam Ja'far al-Sadiq ؑ describes the choice companions of Imam Ali ؑ as the following: "Those who worship the meaning of Allah's Divine names, with the understanding that the names only point to the attributes that He Himself has said belong to Him. These people firmly tie this to their hearts and make their tongues laud it in private and public. These are certainly the friends of the Commander of the Faithful Ali b. Abi Talib,"[352] and without a doubt, Jabir was among those who possessed these noble qualities.

A Group of Ansar Meet with Imam Ali ؑ

Rabaah b. Harith reports that a group of the Ansar came to Imam Ali ؑ in Rahbah, Kufa and greeted him with the words, "Peace be upon you O our master (mawlana)!" Imam Ali ؑ inquired, "How can I be your master when you are Arabs and not slaves?" They replied, "On the day when the Messenger of Allah ﷺ delivered a lecture at the Pond of Khumm, we heard him say, 'Whomsoever I am their master, so too is Ali their master.'"

Rabaah says that he followed the group for a while after they left and inquired who they were. "I was informed that they were a group of the Ansar and amongst them was Abu Ayyub al-Ansari."[353]

---

[351] *Rijal Hawl al-Rasul wa Ahl Baytihi*, p. 223.
[352] *Al-Kafi*, vol. 1, Part 3, The Book on the Oneness of Allah, Chapter 5, The One Who is Worshipped, Hadith 1, p. 66.
[353] Haythami, vol. 9, p. 104.

Imam Ali 📖 Teaches Jabir the Ta'weel of the Qur'an

Jabir narrates, "I entered the Masjid of Kufa and saw that the Commander of the Faithful Ali 📖 was writing something with his finger and that he had a smile on his face.

I asked him: 'O Commander of the Faithful 📖, what makes you smile?' He 📖 replied, 'I find it strange that some people read this verse but do not reflect upon it.' 'O Commander of the Faithful 📖, to which verse are you referring?' He 📖 replied, 'Allah is the Light of the heavens and the earth. The similitude of His Light is as a lantern - and Muhammad 📖 is the lantern. Wherein is a lamp – and that lamp refers to me. The lamp is in a glass – and Hasan and Husayn are the glass. The glass was as if it was a shining star – and Ali b. Husayn is that shining star. Lit from a blessed tree – and Muhammad b. Ali is that blessed tree. The olive - and Ja'far b. Muhammad is that olive. Neither of the east - refers to Musa b. Ja'far; nor of the west - refers to Ali b. Musa. Whose oil grows of itself - refers to Muhammad b. Ali. Though fire did not touch it - refers to Ali b. Muhammad. Light upon light - refers to Hasan b. Ali. Allah guides unto His light whomsoever He wills – and the Qa'im is His light. And Allah sets forth parables for people. Allah is Aware of all things.'" (24:35)[354]

Jabir Travels with Imam Ali 📖 and Witnesses a Miracle

Imam Ali al-Hadi 📖 narrates from his father Imam Muhammad al-Jawad 📖, who narrates from his father Imam Ali al-Ridha 📖, who narrates from his father Imam Musa al-Kadhim 📖, who narrates from his father Imam Ja'far al-Sadiq 📖, who narrates from his father Imam Muhammad al-Baqir 📖, who narrates from Jabir b. Abdullah al-Ansari, "I was walking with Amir al-Mo'mineen Ali 📖 on the bank of the River Euphrates when a great wave came out and covered Imam Ali 📖 to the extent that he became veiled from me. When it receded, there was no wetness upon him. I was dumbfounded by that and wondered about it, so I asked him how that happened. He 📖 said, 'You saw that?' I replied, 'Yes.' He 📖 said: 'The Angel allocated to the water came to greet me with an embrace.'"[355]

---

[354] *Tafseer al-Burhan*, vol. 5, p. 392.
[355] *Bashaaratu al-Mustafa li Shi'ati Murtadha*, Section 5, p. 21, Hadith 29.

Jabir Teaches in Medina

Ziyad b. Meena narrates that amongst the companions, there were a few of them who would narrate extensively and issue edicts of guidance to others. He says these included people like Abdullah b. Abbas and Jabir b. Abdullah. He states that from the time 'Uthman b. Affan died, Jabir b. Abdullah, Abdullah b. Abbas, Abdullah b. 'Umar, Abu Hurarya, and Abu Sa'eed al-Khudhri narrated the most narrations.[356]

Ayatollah Syed Taqi al-Modarresi specifies the role of Jabir and his influence over other Muslims, especially in responding to fallacies and misconceptions circulating from various schools of thought. Amongst them was the theology of the al-Qadariyyah, those who went to such extremes regarding the Divine Decree (*qadar*) that it led them to say that the human is compelled in all actions by God; he acts without choice. Rather, he has no power over his own actions.

Ayatollah al-Modarresi says, "Jabir b. Abdullah absolved himself and his peers from the belief of the Qadariyyah and advised their followers not to give salutation (salaam), nor to participate in the funeral prayer or visit their sick (of the upholder of absolute *qadr*).[357]

Jabir Corrects a Famous Tabi'i[358]

A famous Tabi'i from Barsa, Talq b. Habeeb narrates, "I was a person who most vehemently denied the concept of intercession, until I met Jabir b. Abdullah al-Ansari. After I recited to him all of the verses of the Qur'an that I could recite which spoke about the people of hell remaining there forever, he said, 'O Talq, do you think that you have more knowledge about the Qur'an and the Prophetic practices than I do? The verses you have recited refer to those who belong in hell. They are the polytheists. However, those

---

[356] *Tabaqaat al-Kubra*, vol. 4, p. 187.

[357] *Al-'Irfan al-Islami*, p. 28, see also *Al-Farq Bayn al-Firq* by Al-Baghdadi for further reading. The Arabic of this passage reads:

قد تبرأ جابر و أقرانه من أفكار القدرية و أوصوا أخلافهم بإلا يسلموا على القدرية و لا يصلّوا على جنائزهم و لا يعودوا مرضاهم

[358] The '*tabi'un*' or 'followers' are the generation of Muslims who were born after the passing away of Prophet Muhammad ﷺ but who were contemporaries of the companions.

for whom intercession will take place are the believing people who have sinned and who will be punished for their sins, but then will be removed from hell.' Talq continued that Jabir then held both of his ears and said, 'May these become deaf if I did not hear the Messenger of Allah 🌸 say that they will leave hell after having entered it (because of the Prophet's intercession). We also recite the Qur'an like you recite it!'"[359]

Yazeed al-Faqeer reports, "I was once sitting with Jabir b. Abdullah al-Ansari as he was busy narrating Prophetic traditions. When he narrated that some people will leave hell, I became very angry because during those days, I was one who rejected such a belief. I therefore responded, 'I am not as astonished when common people making such statements, as I am when you companions of the Prophet 🌸 do so! You believe that people will leave the hellfire when Allah clearly says, 'They will try to escape from the fire but they will not be able to escape. They will have a permanent punishment.'' (5:37)

'His companions started rebuking me, but he was the most tolerant of them all.' 'Leave the man alone!' he told them. 'He then explained to me, 'That verse refers to the rejectors of the Truth.' He then recited the (whole) verse, 'Without doubt even if the disbelievers possessed all of the wealth of the world and as much more in addition to ransom themselves from the punishment of the Day of Judgement, it will not be accepted from them. They shall have to suffer a painful punishment. They will try to escape from the fire, but they will not be able to escape. They will have a permanent punishment.'' (5:37)

'He then asked me, 'Do you recite the Qur'an?'[360] 'I certainly do. In fact I have memorised it,' I replied. Jabir then responded, 'Does Allah not say, 'In a portion of the night perform the night prayer, that is an extra prayer for you. Soon your Lord will accord you a special and praised position?' (17:79) That special and praised position is the position of intercession. Allah will detain some believing people in hell for a period without addressing them

---

[359] *Hayaat al-Sahaaba*, vol. 3, pp. 86-7.

[360] This is a question often asked by members of the Ahl al-Bayt 🕮 to their enquirers to demonstrate that firstly the answer lies in the Qur'an, but also to demonstrate their comprehensive knowledge of the Qur'an. Jabir's asking this question and then answering through the Qur'an reflects his adoption of the practice of the Imam's 🕮 and also his command of and confidence in his knowledge of the Qur'an. This is truly a special rank.

because of their sins. Then when Allah ﷻ wills, He will remove them from hell."

Yazeed says, 'After this I never repeated my mistake of denying this belief.'"[361] [362]

---

[361] *Kanz al-Ummal*, vol. 2, p. 54.

[362] Jabir's correcting these incorrect views were important because as second generation and new Muslims who had just entered into Islam, new theological debates were being raised and confusion reigned on account of people claiming scholarship. Many debates existed as to the Oneness of Allah, Freedom and Predestination, Role of the Intellect, Revelation in Guidance, and the Labelling of Sinners and Major Sins. Another confusion among them was the topic of Intercession.

Chapter 10

Jabir in the Period of the Imams of the Ahl al-Bayt ﷺ

In the Period of Imam Hasan ﷺ

Jabir Travels to Damascus to Hear a Narration

Jabir narrates, "News once reached me that there was a person who heard a particular narration from the Prophet ﷺ so I purchased a camel, tied a carriage to it and rode for a month until I reached Damascus. When I made inquiries, I found out that it was narrated by Abdullah b. Ubays, so I went to his house and told his servant to inform him that I am visiting. When Abdullah heard that it was me, he rushed so quickly that he tripped over his own clothes in a hurry to welcome me. He hugged me and I hugged him, after which I asked, 'A narration from you has reached me concerning retribution. I have come to you because I feared that either you or me would die before I had the opportunity of hearing it from you directly. 'Abdullah b. Ubays responded, 'I heard the Messenger of Allah ﷺ say, 'On the Day of Judgement, Allah will raise a people naked, uncircumcised and empty-handed.' When someone asked one of the narrators what was meant by empty-handed, he replied that people will have nothing of their worldly possessions with them. Then in a voice that those far away can hear just as well as those close by, Allah will announce, 'I am the One who pays back in full! It is not proper for any person destined for hell to enter hell while a person in Paradise owes him some right that I have not claimed for him, even if it is retribution for the smallest of offences.'' Ibn Ubays continued, 'So we asked, 'How will this retribution be done when people will be in this bare state?' to which the Prophet ﷺ replied, 'It will be done with good and bad deeds. People will pay for their injustices by giving away their good deeds to the wronged party, and when their good deeds are exhausted, they will be burdened with the sins of the wronged party.'"[363]

Jabir and Mu'awiyah b. Abi Sufyan

After the martyrdom of Imam Ali ؏, Jabir went to Mu'awiyah in Damascus. Initially he did not give Jabir permission to visit him for a few days. When he gave him permission, Jabir said, "O Mu'awiyah, have you not heard the Messenger of Allah ﷺ saying, 'Whoever makes a barrier to someone who is poor and in need from his needs, Allah will make a barrier for him on the Day (of Judgement) when he is poor and in need'"?[364] To this, Mu'awiyah got angry and replied, "I heard him saying to you 'You will face hardship after me so bear patience until you come to me at the pond,' so could you not just be patient!'" Jabir said, "You reminded me about what I had forgotten" and then he left. Mu'awiyah b. Abi Sufyan sent Jabir six hundred dinars. This was Mu'awiyah's way to buy the weak-minded people and the ones who get defeated in the presence of money and gold; those whose opinions change with respect to the size of the bag of money sent to them. When the messenger brought it, Jabir refused it and wrote for him a poem:

'Surely I choose contentment over wealth. And among people there are the ones who it [the wealth] will destroy and will not fulfil anything [for them]. But I wear the dresses of modesty, and I see the position of wealth [in a way] so as not to affront my honour.'[365]

---

[363] Haythami, vol. 1, p. 133; *Jaami' al-Bayaan al-Ilm*, vol. 1, p. 93.
[364] The Arabic text of this passage reads:

من حجب ذا فاقة و حاجة حجبه الله يوم فاقته و حاجته

[365] The Arabic text of this passage reads:

و إني لأختار القنوع على الغنى و في الناس من يقضي عليه و لا يقضي
و ألبس أثواب الحياء و قد رأى مكان الغنى أن لا أهين له عرضي

He then said to Mu'awiyah's messenger, "Tell him, I swear by Allah, O son of the one who eats the livers, that you will never find in your book a single good deed that is due to me."[366] [367] [368]

Jabir Reburies his Father at the Place of the Battle of Uhud after its Destruction by Mu'awiyah

Jabir states, "It was during the caliphate of Mu'awiyah b. Abi Sufyan that a person came to me and said, 'O Jabir, I swear by Allah that some of Mu'awiyah's workers dug into your father's grave causing some of his body to be exposed.' When I went there, I discovered that his body was exactly as it was when I buried him. The only parts that were not unscathed were of course those that were wounded in the battle. I then buried him again."[369]

Jabir is also narrated to have said, "When Mu'awiyah intended on digging a canal, we were told to move the bodies of our martyrs from the Battle of Uhud. Although this was forty years afterwards, their bodies were still supple and their limbs could even be bent."[370]

Some of the Ansar narrate, "When Mu'awiyah was digging a canal that passed by the martyrs of Uhud, it burst its banks. We hurried there and exhumed the bodies of Amr b. Jumooh and Abdullah (the father of Jabir). They both wore two sheets of cloth that covered their faces, while their feet were covered with some plants. As we removed the bodies from the grave, they were so supple and pliable that it appeared as if they had just been buried yesterday."[371]

---

[366] The Arabic text of this passage reads:

قل و الله يا ابن آكلة الأكباد لا تجد في صفيحتك حسنة أنا سببها أبدا

[367] *Rijal Hawl al-Rasool wa Ahl Baytihi*, p. 224; *A'yan al-Shi'a*, vol. 4, pp. 45-9.

[368] Mu'awiyah intended by his reply to say that the poverty upon the Muslim community was not because of his theft or greed, but because the Prophet ﷺ predicted so and thus nothing could be done about it. This was an abuse and purposeful misinterpretation of the hadith of the Prophet ﷺ because Mu'waiyah was being confronted about his hoarding of wealth away from those in need. Jabir's response was intelligent as he had done his duty and decided not to incur the oppression of Mu'awiyah, and took the matter no further. Indeed one is forced to ask 'Where are the Jabir's of today in the Muslim world?!'

[369] Al-Samhudi, *Wafaa'ul Wafaa*, vol. 2, p. 116.

[370] *Tabaqaat al-Kubra*, vol. 3, p. 563; *Kanz al-Ummal*, vol. 5, p. 274.

[371] *Fath al-Bari*, vol. 3, p. 142.

Jabir narrates, "When Mu'awiyah started to dig the canal near the martyrs of Uhud forty years after the battle, we were summoned to move them from their graves. We went there and while we were busy exhuming the bodies, a spade accidentally hit the foot of Hamza 🕮 and blood actually started to pour out of the wound."[372]

The Threats upon the Life of Jabir

In the year 40 A.H. Mu'awiyah b. Abi Sufyan made a specific threat to Jabir b. Abdullah due to his support for the Ahl al-Bayt 🕮 and his fame as a noble companion of the Prophet 🕮. Mu'awiyah wished to remove this threat to his power, which affected the strength of the resistance against him.

Ibn al-Atheer narrates, "In that year Mu'awiyah sent Serr b. Abi Arta'ah with 3,000 soldiers. He marched until he reached the city of Medina. He then sought Bani Salama, Jabir's tribe and said: 'By God, you do not have any safety with me until you bring me Jabir b. Abdullah.' Jabir went to Lady Umm Salama 🕮, the wife of the Prophet 🕮 and said to her, 'What do you say, this is a deluded misguided allegiance and they seek me, but I am worried to be killed.' She replied, 'I say that you should pay allegiance (to save your life)' and so Jabir went to him and paid allegiance."

In *Tareekh al-Ya'qoubi* it is narrated that he said to Lady Umm Salama, "I am afraid that I will be killed and this is a deluded misguided allegiance." She said, "Then pay allegiance to him. The *taqiyah* (dissimulation of faith) made the Companions of the Cave to wear the cross and attend the festivals with their community."[373]

During the Period of Imam Husayn 🕮

Ayatollah Syed al-Khoei mentions in his *Rijal* that Jabir was specifically noted as amongst those who did not abandon Imam Husayn 🕮 after his martyrdom, like so many did out of fear or neglect.[374]

---

[372] *Al-Bidaayah wa al-Nihaayah*, vol. 4, p. 43.
[373] *Qasas al-Sahaaba wa al-Tabi'in*, pp. 78-9.
[374] *Mo'jam Rijal al-Hadith*, vol. 4, p. 331.

Chapter 11

Jabir and his Farewell to Imam Husayn ☙ upon His Leaving Medina

Jabir b. Abdullah al-Ansari is narrated to have said, "When Husayn b. Ali decided to leave for Iraq, I went to him and said, 'You are the son of the Messenger of Allah ☙ and one of his grandsons. I do not see a way other than that you make peace, as your brother Hasan ☙ made peace as it was a rational stand.' He ☙ said to me, 'O Jabir, whatever my brother did was ordained by Allah and the Prophet, and whatever I shall do will be according to the command of Allah and His Messenger as well. Do you wish that at this very moment I invite the Messenger of God, Imam Ali and my brother Hasan to testify regarding my action?'

Then the Imam ☙ looked towards the skies. Suddenly I saw the doors of the heavens open up and the Messenger of Allah ☙, Ali ☙, Hamza ☙ and Ja'far al-Tayyar ☙ descended from the heavens to the earth. Seeing this I became frightful. Then the Messenger of Allah ☙ addressed me saying, 'O Jabir! Did I not inform you with regard to the matter of Hasan even before that of Husayn, in that you would not become a believer unless you surrender to the Imams, and not object to their actions? Do you desire to see the place where Mu'awiyah will dwell and the place of my son Husayn and his murderer Yazeed?'

I replied, 'Yes O Messenger of Allah.' Then the Prophet struck his foot onto the ground and it split apart and a sea appeared and it ripped apart, and another ground appeared beneath and it split apart. Seven layers of the ground split apart and seven seas ripped apart (one below the other) until I saw beneath it all a great fire. I saw Waleed b. Mughirah, Abu Jahl,

Mu'awiyah and Yazeed (may Allah curse them all) were bound together in a chain along with the other rebellious Satans; and their torment was more severe than that of the other people of hell.

Then the Holy Prophet ﷺ commanded me to lift up my head. I saw that the heavens had opened their doors and paradise was apparent. Then the Messenger ﷺ and whoever was with him ascended to the heavens and all of them ascended. When he ﷺ was in the air he ﷺ called out to Husayn, 'O my son, the Truth is with me, and the Truth is with Husayn' and they continued to elevate until I saw them entering the paradise from its highest levels.

Then the Holy Prophet ﷺ looked at whoever was there and took hold of the hand of Husayn and said: 'O Jabir! This son of mine is here along with me, therefore submit to him and do not fall in doubt so as to become a disbeliever.' Then Jabir said: 'May both of my eyes become blind if whatever I have seen and related from the Messenger of Allah ﷺ is false.'"[375] [376]

---

[375] *Ma'ali al-Sibtayn*, Muhammad Mahdi Mazandarani, vol. 1, p. 216; *Qasas al-Sahaaba wa al-Tabi'in*, pp. 90-1; As-Sayyed al-Bahrani also narrated in *Medinat al-Ma'ajez*.

[376] Sheikh al-Hakimi comments, "And when Jabir knew that Imam Husayn ﷺ would not raise a foot or put a foot down, and would not do anything or say anything except by the command of Allah ﷺ and His Messenger ﷺ, he submitted to him and acknowledged his actions, and bid farewell to him. Thereafter, Imam Husayn ﷺ left and Jabir stayed in Medina waiting for news about the Imam, and tracking his movements; until a person who announces deaths, announced the killing of Imam Husayn ﷺ and his name was Abed al-Malik b. Abi al-Harith al-Selmy and with him was a letter from Obaydullah to Amrou b. Sai'd b. al-A'ass - the commander of Medina announcing to him [happily] the killing of the grandson of the Prophet ﷺ.

When Jabir found out about the killing, he yearned, whined, cried and sighed and he went out of Medina to visit the grave of Imam Husayn ﷺ, and he was the first who visited the Imam ﷺ and with him there was a group of Bani (the sons of) Hashim. When he reached Karbala, he approached the River of Euphrates..." until the end of what will follow if God wills.

(I, the author say that) I found in some books that when Imam Husayn ﷺ wanted to go out of Medina, his children, his wives, his brothers and sisters, his cousins, his brother's (Imam Hasan ﷺ) children, his daughters, his bondmen, bondwomen, the maids, and a lot of his relatives from Bani Hashim - males, females, men and women gathered with him [at his place]. In total, they were 220 people, including the baby Ali al-Asghar."

Chapter 12

During the Period of Imam Zayn al-Abideen ﷺ

Introduction

During the time of the Imamat of Imam Husayn ﷺ and Imam Ali b. Husayn Zayn al-Abideen ﷺ, Jabir had been afflicted with the trial of blindness, losing his power of sight. This condition kept him from participating in the revolution of Imam Husayn ﷺ in Karbala - otherwise with certainty, just like he had participated in eighteen battles with the Prophet ﷺ and three with Imam Ali ﷺ, he would have been alongside Imam Husayn ﷺ despite his elder age.

Sheikh Aal Fawzi states, "Although Jabir became blind at the end of his life, he was insightful, and because of that he persevered in his stand of being a friend and supporter of the Ahl al-Bayt ﷺ openly. Though he could not take part in the battle of Karbala for this reason, he used to see himself – due to what he believed about his support for Imam Husayn ﷺ and due to how he advocated calling others to the path of Ahl al-Bayt ﷺ – as one of those who participated in that battle."[377]

Jabir had a special affinity to Imam Zayn al-Abideen ﷺ and their interactions demonstrated a unique type of caring towards this Imam ﷺ. It is likely because of his knowledge about the extent of grief and torture that the fourth Imam ﷺ underwent from the events of Karbala, their captivity, parading through the cities of Kufa and Shaam, and the house arrest of the Ahl al-Bayt ﷺ in Medina. The historian 'Allama Baqir Qarashi states,

---

[377] *Rijal Hawl al-Rasool wa Ahl Baytihi*, p. 224.

"Among those who adored the Imam 🕮 was the great companion Jabir b. Abdullah, who said, 'I have never seen a son of the Prophet 🕮 similar to Ali b. Husayn 🕮.'"[378]

The Story of the Mother of Imam Zayn al-Abideen 🕮

Jabir b. Abdullah al-Ansari narrates from Imam Muhammad al-Baqir 🕮 who said, "The girls of Medina used to love to see the daughter of Yazdjurd when she was brought before 'Umar b. al-Khataab.

When she entered the Masjid it became all delightful and bright. When 'Umar looked at her she covered her face and said in her own language, '*Uff, bay ruj ba' da Hurmuz* (may the life of Hurmuz turn black)' (Hurmuz was the Persian king). 'Umar asked, 'Is she abusing me?' He turned to her (with a certain attitude). Amir al-Mu'mineen Ali 🕮 said, 'You do not have such a right (over her). Give her the chance to choose whoever of the Muslims she likes and then count that as his share of the booty (of the properties seized from the Persian army).'

He ('Umar) allowed her to choose and she came all the way to place her hand on the head of Imam Husayn 🕮. Amir al-Mu'mineen Ali 🕮 asked her, 'What is your name?' She said, 'It is Jahan Shah.' Amir al-Mu'mineen Ali 🕮 said, 'In fact, it is Shahra Banu.' He then said to Imam Husayn 🕮, 'O Aba 'Abdullah, she will give birth to a son for you who will be the best of the inhabitants of earth.' She gave birth to Imam Zayn al-Abideen 🕮."

Imam Zayn al-Abideen 🕮 was called the son of the two best - from the Arabs it was the tribe of Hashim, and from the non-Arab it was the Persians.[379]

The Story of Jabir's being the First Visitor to Karbala after the Martyrdom of Imam al-Husayn 🕮

Among the famous traditions of Imam Hasan al-Askari 🕮 is the narration, "The signs of belief (*al-imaan*) are five: Wearing a ring on the right hand; reciting fifty-one units of prayer daily, reciting '*Bismillahi ar-Rahmani ar-*

---

[378] *The Life of Imam Muhammad al-Baqir*, Ansariyan Publications, 2003, p. 32.
[379] *Al-Kafi.* vol. 1, Hadith 1259, Chapter. 117, The Birth of Ali ibn al-Husayn, Hadith 1, p. 441-42.

Rahim' out loud; rubbing the forehead with soil/dirt in prayer, and performing the *Ziyarat al-Arba'een* of Imam Husayn."

Sheikh al-Hakimi states, "The first person who visited Imam Husayn on the day of Arba'een (The fortieth day after his martyrdom) was Jabir b. Abdullah al-Ansari.[380] All of those who visit the Imam knowing his rights - perform the visitation with the necessary etiquettes. Jabir knew the rights of Imam Husayn and what realities there are in his *ziyarat*, as well as the rewards and bounties of it because he had heard them from the Messenger of Allah who had said that 'Whoever visits Imam Husayn in Karbala, it is as if he visits Allah on His throne' and he used to know that for every step taken towards this Imam is the reward equivalent to one *hajj* and one *umrah*."[381]

Ateyah al-Auwfy, Jabir's companion, helper and guide, narrates the event as following:

"I went out with Jabir b. Abdullah al-Ansari, may Allah be pleased with him, to visit the grave of Imam Husayn. When we arrived to Karbala, Jabir approached the shore of the River Euphrates, and performed his ghusl (ceremonial bath for purification and preparation). He wore a wrapper (cloth worn round the hips, as a sole garment) and dressed with another one. Then he opened a bag which contained a *sa'ad* (type of fragrance) and he sprinkled it on his body.

He did not proceed to take any steps towards Imam Husayn unless he remembered Allah, the Exalted (and performed dhikr). When he approached the grave he said to me, 'Help me to touch it' and so I helped him reach it.[382]

---

[380] Some authors claim that Jabir visited Karbala with a group from Medina. Muhammad Hasan Mustafa al-Kaleedaar Aal Tu'mah states, "He visited the grave of Imam Husayn on the 20th of Safar 62 A.H. with a group of Muslims from the people (city) of Medina." (*Medinatu al-Husayn, Mukhtasaru Tareekh Karbala*, vol. 1, p. 35, Markaz Karbala Li ad-Dirasat wa al-Bahooth).

عندما زار قبر الامام الحسين عليه السلام في عشرين من صفر عام (٦٢ ه) مع جماعة من المسلمين من اهل المدينة

[381] *Qasas al-Sahaaba wa al-Tabi'in*, p. 96.

[382] Sheikh al-Hakimi comments that Jabir, "walked bare foot and he did not step forward even one step without reciting the *dhikr* of Allah (remembrance of God). This from the etiquettes of the *ziyarat* of Imam Husayn." Indeed the actions of Jabir, who visited seven infallibles in his lifetime knew best how to approach this Imam in Karbala and therefore it becomes evidence for all of those who wish to visit Imam al-Husayn about its etiquettes and mannerisms. Ibid., p. 96.

Suddenly he fell unconscious on the grave. I sprinkled some water on him and when he woke up he lamented 'O Husayn, O Husayn, O Husayn! Does a beloved not answer his beloved?[383] But how can you answer[384] when your neck veins were cut causing your blood to flow on your back [on the area between the upper back and the lower back] and your head and body have been separated?!'

Jabir continued his lamentations, 'I bear witness that you are the son of the best of the Prophets, and the son of the master of the believers, and the son of the ally of piety, and the descendant of the guidance towards the right path. You are the fifth of the *Ashab al-Kisaa* (people of the Cloak) and the son of the master of the chiefs! The son of Fatima, the Leader of all women. How can you be anything but that since the hand of the master of all of the Messengers fed you and you were brought up in the laps of the pious, fed from the chest of faith itself, and weaned by Islam in its reality?![385] So you were blessed when you were alive and you are blessed in your death, however the hearts of the believers are suffering because of your departure, and they were not doubtful in your life while you were alive. So upon you is Allah's peace and contentment, and I bear witness that you have

---

[383] Sheikh al-Hakimi comments Jabir was one of the people of knowledge and he was knowledgeable in regards to the Imam's existential reality such that he hears the speech and replies with the answer because he is alive with Allah and receiving sustenance, as per the verse: "*And do not ever assume that those who are killed in Allah's path are dead; in fact they are alive with their Lord, receiving sustenance. (3:169)*" Ibid., p. 96. This question however was an expression at the grief of the loss of the physical response of Imam Husayn ⚔. Sheikh al-Hakimi continues, "So Imam Husayn ⚔ will answer Jabir when he called him, and speak to him like he ⚔ talked (may my soul be of ransom to him) with his daughter Sakina while he was a headless body and said: 'O my people, whenever you drink fresh water, remember me, etc...'" Ibid., p. 96.

[384] Sheikh al-Hakimi comments, "Jabir's apology for his saying, 'And where would you get the answer' is his wanting to show the state of his master and his martyrdom for whoever was present there (and in the future) to cry upon Imam Husayn ⚔." That is why he next said: "And your neck veins were ensanguined (flowing) [the blood was flowing from the neck veins] on your back [on the area between the upper back and the lower back] and your head and body were separated." Ibid., pp. 96-7.

[385] Sheikh al-Hakimi comments, "And his saying: 'And you were fed from the bosom of faith (Imaan)' is an analogy of the Prophet's tongue; 'And you were weaned by Islam' which is an analogy of the antecedence of Islam, because Ali was the first of the people to embrace Islam and the foremost to believe. Ibid., p. 97.

proceeded upon the same path that your brother Yahya b. Zakarriyah proceeded upon.'"[386]

Ateyah continues: "Then he (temporarily) got his eyesight back while he was at the grave and he said:

'Peace be upon you, O the souls who accompanied Husayn 🖎 to his death and came to his camp to put themselves at his disposal. I bear witness that you established the prayer, gave alms to the needy, commanded others to do that which is right and lawful, forbade that which is wrong and unlawful, you strived hard against the unbeliever, and you served Allah until the inevitable (death) came unto you. I swear by He Who sent Muhammad with the truth that we have taken part in what you underwent.' Ateyah recounts that at this point he asked Jabir, 'How is it that we partook with them, yet we did not go down into a valley, nor go up a mountain, and we did not even strike with a sword - while the heads and bodies of the people were separated and their children were made orphans and their women were made widows?!'

Jabir replied, 'O Ateyah, I heard my beloved Messenger of Allah 🖎 say that: 'Whoever loved a nation (community or group of people) he will be resurrected with them, and whoever loved the actions of a nation (community or group of people) will be considered involved in their actions.' I swear by He Who sent Muhammad 🖎 with the truth, that my intention and the intention of my companions is on what Imam Husayn 🖎 and his companions proceeded in.'"

Ateyah continues, "And while we were like that, a blackness came from the direction of Shaam and so I said: 'O Jabir, a blackness is coming from the direction of Shaam.' Jabir said to me, 'Go to that blackness and inform me about it - if they are from the companions of 'Umar b. Sa'ad then come back to us so we can try to get into a shelter for protection; and if it is Zayn al-Abideen, then you will be free in the way of Allah.'"

---

[386] Sheikh al-Hakimi comments, "And his saying: 'And I bear witness that you have proceeded upon the same path that your brother Yahya b. Zakariyyah proceeded upon' this means that, 'O my master Aba 'Abdullah you were killed in the path of God as Yahya b. Zakariyyah was killed in the path of God; and you were killed tyrannized (oppressed), and they roamed (paraded) carrying your head in the towns as they roamed with the head of Yahya, and they put your head in a bowl like the head of Yahya b. Zakariyyah was put in a bowl, however how could this (the slaughter of Imam Husayn 🖎 even be) be compared with that?!'" Ibid., p. 98.

Ateyah went and could not be any faster in coming back saying, "O Jabir, stand up and receive the womenfolk of the Messenger of Allah ﷺ! This is Zayn al-Abideen ؏; he has come with his aunts and sisters."

Jabir stood up and walked bare-footed and bare-headed (representing a state of urgency and grief) until he reached Imam Zayn al-Abideen ؏. Imam ؏ asked him, "Are you Jabir?"

"Yes, O the son of the Messenger of Allah." "O Jabir, here by Allah, our men were killed and our children were slaughtered and our women were taken as captives and our tents were burnt."[387]

This inaugural visitation of Imam al-Husayn ؏ by Jabir after the events of Karbala is a momentous moment in history, especially from the theological and spiritual perspectives. There is great debate as to the permissibility of visitation of saintly figures in Islam, the practices that take place and their boundaries. Jabir, being a great companion of the Prophet ﷺ, and having been considered as a leading jurist, commentator of the Qur'an and authority on the Prophetic practice considered it highly recommended to visit Imam Husayn ؏ and address him in such a way.

It appears that this was not just a practice of the great companions at that time, rather even the generations that followed felt it necessary to visit Imam Husayn ؏ as a demonstration of understanding his movement, loyalty to it and gain inspiration from it. In the year 65 A.H., upon the death of the tyrant Yazid b. Mu'awiyah, the group known as the *Tawwabeen*, or those penitent for not aiding Imam Husayn ؏ rose to fight the Banu Umayyah (though their activities started in 61 A.H.). They were led by Sulayman b. Surad Khuza'ee, and coined the phase, 'O seekers for the revenge of the blood of Husayn ؏.'

Beginning their uprising in 65 A.H., they first visited the grave of Imam Husayn ؏, wept bitterly and sent blessings upon him. History has also recorded their statement of allegiance and intent, saying, "O Lord! Bestow Your blessings upon Husayn ؏, the Martyr and son of the Martyr! The guided one and the son of the guided one! The truthful one and son of the truthful one! O Lord! Bear witness that we are steadfast upon their religion and their customs, and we bear enmity to their murderers and are friendly towards their friends. O Lord! We abandoned the grandson of our

---

[387] *A'yan al-Shi'a*, vol. 4, p. 48.

Prophet ☙, but please forgive our past sins, and accept our repentance; and bestow Your blessings upon Husayn ☙ and his companions, who were the martyrs and the truthful ones. We hold You as a witness that we are steadfast upon their religion and upon that belief for which they were martyred. If You do not overlook our sins and do not bestow your blessings upon us, then we will be of those who are in loss."[388] [389]

Given that Jabir and the subsequent generations visited Imam Husayn ☙ in such ways, is a strong precedent as to how the companions and the *tabi'een*, those who followed, viewed such practices. Jabir therefore became an aid in understanding these visitations, primarily for the wider Muslim community who consider the actions of the companions and their followers as religious precedent, and in keeping with one of the goals of this book. If a great companion like Jabir visited Imam Husayn ☙, then surely the wider Muslim community should be following his precedent as well.

Jabir's Interactions with Imam Zayn al-Abideen ☙ after the Arba'een

Sheikh Aal Fawzi says, "Jabir went back to Medina al-Munawwara as did Imam Zayn al-Abideen ☙. He used to see in the Imam ☙ a resemblance to that of his great grandfather - the Messenger of Allah ☙ and Amir al-Mu'mineen Ali b. Abi Talib ☙ and used to visit him every day to attain something from his fountain of knowledge, and follow the grace of his exemplary actions.

Just like Imam Zayn al-Abideen ☙ had seen the extent of the Umayyad oppression and its brutality in its worst forms in Karbala, he ☙ also saw another version of this Umayyad transgression against the sanctity of the family of the Prophet ☙. In response to that, the Imam ☙ saw that bringing back the balance to the nation which had been obliterated by the Umayyad transgressions should start by promoting the real meaning of worship and

---

[388] The Arabic text of this passage reads:

اللهم ارحم حسينا الشهيد ابن الشهيد، المهدي ابن المهدي، الصديق ابن الصديق، اللهم انا نشهدك أنا على دينهم و سبيلهم و أعداء قاتليهم، و أولياء محبهم، اللهم انا خذلنا ابن بنت نبينا صلى الله عليه و آله و سلم، فاغفرلنا ما مضى منا و تب علينا، و ارحم حسينا و أصحابه الشهداء الصديقين، و انا نشهدك انا على دينهم و على ما قتلوا عليه وَإِن لَّمْ تَغْفِرْ لَنَا وَتَرْحَمْنَا لَنَكُونَنَّ مِنَ الْخَاسِرِينَ

[389] *Tareekh al-Islami*, Ayatollah Syed Muhammad Taqi al-Modarresi, p. 121.

focusing on the relationship between the servants and their Creator. The Imam ﷺ was an exemplary role model in this endeavour and such was his devotion for worship and supplication that he attained the title of Zayn al-Abideen, 'The adornment of the worshippers.'"

Fatima ﷺ, the daughter of Imam Husayn ﷺ, looked at the intensity of her brother's diligence in worship and she became so worried about him harming himself due to his devotions that she approached Jabir b. Abdullah out of concern and said to him, "O companion of the Messenger of Allah. We, the family of the Prophet have rights upon you! One of these rights is that if you saw one of us tiring ourselves excessively in diligent worship, then you should remind us and ask that person to look after oneself. Here is Ali b. Husayn ﷺ, the remanence of his father Husayn ﷺ! His nose has become pressed, his forehead is rough along with his knees and palms as a result of his diligence in worship."

Therefore at the request of Fatima bt. Husayn, Jabir came to Imam Zayn al-Abideen ﷺ. The Imam ﷺ was in his *mehrab* (prayer niche) exhausted by his surrendering to Allah ﷻ. As Jabir approached, the Imam ﷺ stood up for him and inquired about his well-being in a very caring manner. Then Jabir said to him ﷺ, "O the son of the Messenger of Allah, did you not know that Allah, the Exalted created paradise for you the Ahl al-Bayt and for whoever loves you; and He created the hellfire for whoever hates and opposes you?! So what is this diligence that you burden yourself with?"

The Imam ﷺ responded, "O companion of the Messenger of Allah, do you not know that Allah has forgiven all of that which preceded from my grandfather's dues, and all of that which will come later, but yet he ﷺ did not leave the diligence of his worship - I swear by my father and my mother – even though his legs were throbbing and his feet were swollen. He was also told 'You do all of this yet Allah has forgiven all what preceded from your dues and all of that which will come later' to which he ﷺ replied, 'Should I not be a thankful servant?'"[390]

---

[390] It appears that Imam Zayn al-Abideen ﷺ was following the tradition of his grandfather the Prophet ﷺ in this response, as is narrated by Anas b. Malik that the Prophet ﷺ would stand all night in prayers until his feet would swell up. When he asked, 'Has Allah not forgiven you all of your past and future sins, so why do you exert yourself as such?' He ﷺ replied, 'Should I not then be a grateful servant?' (*Kanz al-Ummal*, vol. 4, p. 36)

When Jabir heard this he tried a different approach imploring him, "O the son of the Messenger of Allah, you should look after yourself for you are from the family due to which the hardships of this world can be repelled, the calamities can be relieved, and because of whom the sky can be made to rain!" The Imam 🖼️ replied, "O Jabir, I am still on the path of my parents, following them as my example, peace be upon them, until I meet them."

Jabir took his leave and whoever he met, he felt compelled to express his feelings and said, "By God, I do not see in the children of the Prophets any person like Imam Ali b. Husayn 🖼️ - except Prophet Yusuf b. Ya'qoub 🖼️, but I swear by Allah 🖼️, that the progeny of Ali b. Husayn 🖼️ is better than the progeny of Yusuf b. Ya'qoub 🖼️, because it is them who fill the earth with justice as it is filled with inequity and injustice."[391]

8th Imam 🖼️ Narrates from Imam Zayn al-Abideen 🖼️ who Narrates from Jabir

Imam Ali b. Musa al-Ridha 🖼️ said, "I heard my father (Imam al-Kadhim) narrate on the authority of his father (Imam al-Sadiq), on the authority of his grandfather (Imam Zayn al-Abideen), on the authority of Jabir b. Abdullah who said, "Allah's Messenger 🖼️ was at the dome of Adam (the dome upon the Mountain of Mercy/Jabal al-Rahmah) and I saw Bilal al-Habashi come out with the water leftover from the Prophet making his ablutions. The people gathered around him and each person took some of that water with which he had washed his face. Whoever could not get any water would touch the other people and get their wetness and then rub their hands on their face. They used to do the same thing with the water leftover from Imam Ali's 🖼️ ablutions."[392]

Jabir Narrates the Merits of Imam Ali 🖼️

Shu'bah narrates, "I heard the Chief of the Hashimites, the Adornment of the Worshippers, Ali b. Husayn 🖼️ say in Medina that, 'It was narrated to me by my uncle Muhammad (al-Hanafiyyah), son of Imam Ali 🖼️ that, 'I heard Jabir b. Abdullah saying, 'The Messenger of Allah 🖼️ said, 'Shut the

---

[391] *Bihar al-Anwar*, vol. 46, p. 61.
[392] *Uyoon Akhbar al-Ridha*, vol. 2, Chapter 31, Hadith 320, p. 114.

doors (of the Prophet's *masjid*), all of them, except for the door of Ali' – and he pointed with his ﷺ hand towards his ؑ door.'""[393]

Jabir Advises the Tyrant Caliph Abdul Malik

Jabir entered upon Caliph Abdul Malik b. Marwaan who welcomed him and brought him closer. Jabir said to him: "O Amir al-Mo'mineen, this is Tayba (the township). Have you looked at establishing its inhabitants' rights by maintaining family ties (*silat al-rahim*) for its people?" Abdul Malik disliked this suggestion and turned away from him. Jabir began to insist until Abdul Malik signaled him to desist and so Jabir stopped. Jabir decided to leave and on his way out a worker for Abdul Malik named Qubaysah told him that: "These people have become kings." Jabir replied, "May God test you with a good test (that you may succeed in), as there is no excuse for you (to not also insist on these rights) while your friend (Abdul Malik) can hear (listens to you)." Qubaysah replied, "He only can hear what he agrees with. Amir al-Mo'mineen has commanded us to give you 5000 dirhams, so use it to seek assistance for your time." Jabir took the money and left.[394]

Jabir's Sadness at the Demise of Abdullah b. Abbas

When the news of Abdullah b. Abbas's death in 67 A.H. reached Jabir, he hit one hand against the other and said, "A very knowledgeable and forbearing person has passed away. By his demise the nation has been afflicted with a calamity that cannot be rectified."[395]

---

[393] *Bashaaratu al-Mustafa li Shi'ati Murtadha*, Section 9, p. 24, Hadith 30.
[394] *Qasas al-Sahaaba wa al-Tabi'in*, p. 80.
[395] *Tabaqaat al-Kubra*, vol. 4, p. 187.

Chapter 13

Jabir During the Time of Imam Muhammad al-Baqir ﷺ

Introduction

Sheikh Aal Fawzi says, "Since Jabir knew the Imams of the Ahl al-Bayt ﷺ one after the other by virtue of the expressed indications by the Messenger of Allah ﷺ about their Imamate, Jabir ensured that his footsteps followed them in all matters."[396]

The last of those whom he served was Imam Muhammad al-Baqir b. Ali b. Husayn ﷺ. Jabir's first duty towards him ﷺ was to convey the salutations of Prophet Muhammad ﷺ, something which Jabir regularly repeated in as many audiences as possible so that the audience might become aware of the position of the Imam ﷺ.

'Allama Baqir Qarashi states that, "The great companion of the Prophet ﷺ Jabir was famous for following members of the Ahl al-Bayt ﷺ. He loved them very much. It was he who sent the greetings of the Prophet ﷺ to Imam al-Baqir ﷺ. He was amongst those who understood the high rank of the Imam ﷺ, and he glorified and respected the Imam from his childhood. When Jabir addressed him ﷺ, he would say, "You are the son of the best of all of the creatures. Your father is the leader of the Youth of Paradise."[397]

Jabir had a key role in reuniting the Shi'a who had been scattered and had lost solidarity after the defeat of the Tawwabeen (the Penitents), the killing of Mukhtar al-Thaqafi and the Kaysaniyyah movement in support of Muhammad al-Hanafiyyah between 65 A.H. and 67 A.H. respectively.

---

[396] *Rijal Hawl al-Rasool wa Ahl al-Baytihi*, p. 224.
[397] *Bihar al-Anwar*, vol. 11, p. 64; *The Life of Imam Muhammad al-Baqir* ﷺ, p. 94.

Moreover, Hajjaaj b. Yusuf al-Thaqafi used to rejoice in the killings of the Shi'a of Imam al-Baqir ﷦ which made many Shi'as turn to Jabir for his experience and knowledge of the 5th Imam's ﷦ commands as well as Muslims generally, who were facing the rise of multiple theological sects at that time.

As such, he would visit and learn from Imam al-Baqir ﷦ daily. Initially people thought that he was teaching the Imam, but instead this daily meeting between them was designed as such so as to subtly demonstrate who really was the teacher and who was the student, without attracting attention from the authorities. This led to other intriguing historical peculiarities whereby Imam al-Baqir ﷦ would often quote from Jabir narrations about Prophet Muhammad ﷺ, despite the Imam ﷦ knowing the Prophet ﷺ better. This resulted in a unique historical phenomenon in Shi'a texts where a distinct number of Imam al-Baqir's ﷦ traditions were linked to the Messenger of Allah ﷺ but through Jabir. Both of these matters we will expand on in detail Insha Allah.

Indeed Jabir was not just a profoundly influential and tactical Medinan figure in drawing support for Imam al-Baqir ﷦; but rather the Imam ﷦ enjoyed Jabir's company, high spirituality, and appreciated his first-hand experience of the previous Imams ﷦. For example, in a beautiful narration, Imam al-Baqir ﷦ said, "Meeting a person whom I trust gives more strength to my soul than working for an entire year!"[398]

Having visited Imam al-Baqir ﷦ daily, the Imam ﷦ would then visit Jabir when he was afflicted at the end of his life by weakness, old age and torture. He ﷦ once asked him about his condition to which Jabir replied, "I am in the state whereby oldness is what I prefer most over youth, illness is what I like most over good health, and death is what I love most over life." Imam al-Baqir ﷦ responded, "For me, it is whichever state that Allah chooses is what I like between youth and old age, illness and good health, and life and death." When Jabir heard this, he took Imam al-Baqir's ﷦ hand and kissed it and said: "The Messenger of Allah ﷺ was truthful (about your imamate)."[399] Even in that state Jabir continued to take benefit from the 5th Imam ﷦.

---

[398] *Al-Kafi*, Part 2, The Book on the Excellence of Knowledge, Chapter 8, Hadith 81.
[399] *Rijal Hawl al-Rasool wa Ahl al-Baytihi*, p. 227.

Strategy of Conveying Wilayat between Imam al-Baqir 🕮 and Jabir

This next part will detail arguably the most important contribution from the life of Jabir b. Abdullah al-Ansari after helping in the establishment of Islam alongside the Messenger of Allah 🕮. It was the culmination of a lifetime of his service to the Prophet 🕮 and his immaculate family 🕮 - in that all of Jabir's efforts in the refinement of his soul, courage on the battlefield, persistence in learning the realities of Islam, and humility to the Divine message, provided him with the opportunity to help establish the Imamate of Muhammad al-Baqir 🕮. This was first done by feigning tutorship of Imam al-Baqir 🕮 to later openly declaring his studentship of the 5ᵗʰ Imam 🕮. Being a trusted and pious companion, warrior and a prolific narrator gave Jabir immense respect in the Muslim nation, and seeing his submission to Imam al-Baqir 🕮 had a profound impact on Medina's understanding of the Ahl al-Bayt 🕮 at a time when new Muslims lands were increasing, civil war was rife, and formal centres of learning and schools of thought were being established.

In order to analyze this, we will review four important collections of narrations: The salutations of the Prophet 🕮 to Imam al-Baqir 🕮; the rejection of Imam al-Baqir 🕮 by the people of Medina; narrations from Imam al-Baqir 🕮 when he quotes Jabir; and narrations of Jabir from Imam al-Baqir 🕮. We will also refer to Eton Kholberg's work 'An unusual Shi'i Isnad' to appreciate his understanding of this issue, but also demonstrate where we depart from his analysis.

A necessary question to this examination is: 'Why would Imam al-Baqir 🕮, a Divinely appointed Imam and authority over all of mankind, need to quote narrations from Jabir b. Abdullah, a companion of the Prophet 🕮? Did Imam al-Baqir 🕮 need to cite Jabir in order to verify his statements, or was the Imam 🕮 unaware of what the Prophet 🕮 had said and done?'

The answer lies in the narration that we will quote, about how the people of Medina rejected the sayings of Imam al-Baqir 🕮. When we view all of these narrations together and not in isolation, and build a holistic picture, then we will see that between Imam al-Baqir 🕮 and Jabir, they both understood their social circumstances and how to impact them delicately. These were times when revolutions against the Bani Umayyah were plenty, people were not trusted, students of all sciences and lands were flocking to Medina, oppression and misguidance was at its peak and multiple sects were being created at the behest of other faiths and government influence.

As a result, Imam al-Baqir ◎ and Jabir together created a strategy for disseminating the *wilayah* of Ahl al-Bayt ◎ - which first took the form of building the trust of Medina towards Imam al-Baqir ◎ through the fame and authority that Jabir had, and then it saw Jabir openly declaring Imam al-Baqir ◎ as his teacher, master and guide. In the narrations, we can see five distinct stages of this strategy between them.

First Jabir conveyed the salutations of the Prophet ◎ to Imam al-Baqir ◎.

Second, when Imam al-Baqir ◎ would narrate from his forefathers ◎, the people would reject his words because he had not met them, and they did not understand the divinity of his Imamate nor that he did not have to meet the Prophet ◎ to narrate from him. This was supported by the Umayyad government who sought to tarnish his reputation.

Thirdly, Imam ◎ was perceived to have been visiting Jabir to learn from him. When this occurred, Imam al-Baqir ◎ would either narrate from Jabir or directly from the Prophet ◎, whereby people would think that this was from Jabir's teachings. This stopped the rejection of Imam al-Baqir ◎ by the people of Medina, and initiated their trust and admiration of him.

Fourth, Jabir would then visit Imam al-Baqir ◎ and learn from him. People began to see the extent of Imam al-Baqir's ◎ knowledge and purity, unrivalled by any other person. It became normal that Jabir, this great companion, trusted and lauded by the people of Medina, was now learning from Imam al-Baqir ◎. Instead of Imam al-Baqir ◎ quoting narrations from Jabir, Jabir was now quoting from Imam al-Baqir ◎.

Fifth, Jabir would eventually declare the narrations that he heard from the Prophet, the earlier Imams ◎ and Imam al-Baqir ◎ about the authority (*wilayat*) of the Ahl al-Bayt ◎. With trust Medina had for Jabir, his testimony about their authority was evidence of what the Prophet ◎ had declared as proper Islam.

What will follow now are the details and development of this strategy.

Jabir Conveys the Salutations of the Prophet 🖼 to Imam al-Baqir 🖼

As mentioned in the chapter on Jabir's being informed about the Imams of the Ahl al-Bayt 🖼, Prophet Muhammad 🖼 also asked Jabir to convey his salutations to Imam al-Baqir 🖼.[400] Jabir undertaking this action is one of his most famous interactions with Imam al-Baqir 🖼, and by the number of times and number of ways that it has been reported, it appears not to be a unique or single event, but rather, Jabir repeatedly conveyed the Prophet's 🖼 salutations to Imam al-Baqir 🖼 - at different times, different locations, and in different gatherings.

A legitimate question to raise would be, 'Why would Jabir not convey these salutations just once? Had he not discharged his duty?' To answer this question we must first ask why did the Prophet 🖼 seek to convey his salutations in the first place, and why not to any of the other Imams 🖼, such as Imam Zayn al-Abideen 🖼 or any other person generally that Jabir would meet? The answer lies in the Prophet 🖼 wanting to establish his link, proximity and love for Imam al-Baqir 🖼 - to the exclusion of all other people in that period. No other person could claim that the Prophet 🖼 had sent him salutations, therefore this elevated Imam al-Baqir 🖼 above all others. This

---

[400] Narrations mention that Imam Ali 🖼 also specifically asked for his salutation to be sent to Imam al-Baqir 🖼. Sulaym b. Qays mentions, "I witnessed the will of (Imam) Ali which was made before me in which he appointed his son Hasan as the executor of it. He called Husayn, Muhammad (al-Hanafiyyah), his other sons, and the leaders amongst his followers and family to bear testimony to his will. He then delivered the Book and the Armament to his son Hasan and said, 'My son, the Messenger of Allah 🖼 commanded me to appoint you as the executor of my will. He commanded me to deliver to you my books and armament, just like the Messenger of Allah 🖼 did. He made his will in which he appointed me as the executor, delivered to me his books and armament, and ordered me to command you to deliver them to Husayn when you are about to depart this world.' Then he (Ali) addressed Husayn and said, 'The Messenger of Allah 🖼 has commanded you to deliver them to your son, this one.' Then he held with his hand Ali b. Husayn (Zayn al-Abideen) and said to him, 'The Messenger of Allah 🖼 has commanded you to deliver them to your son Muhammad (al-Baqir) and convey to him the greetings of the Messenger of Allah 🖼 and my greetings.'"

Al-Kafi, vol. 1, Chapter of the Tacit and Explicit Testimony as Proof of Hasan b. Ali's Authority over the People, Chapter 66, Hadith 1, p. 263.

also raises the query that why salutations upon Imam al-Baqir ﷺ only? Did the Prophet ﷺ not want this salutation to be conveyed to the rest of his community that he only gave precedence to Imam al-Baqir ﷺ over all others?

Jabir constantly repeated this salutation in as many gatherings as possible, so that numerous people would come to know about it, ponder upon its meaning and significance, and seek more details such as when, where and why the Messenger of Allah's ﷺ salutations were passed; then they would hear from Jabir which individuals had been appointed as the leaders of the Muslim community by Allah ﷺ in explaining the revelation of the verse, "O you who have believed, obey Allah and obey the Messenger and those in authority among you. And if you disagree over anything, refer it to Allah and the Messenger, if you should believe in Allah and the Last Day. That is the best [way] and best in result" (4:59).

In this section we will mention some of the different times that Jabir fulfilled the command of the Prophet ﷺ in conveying his salutations, and discuss some further points which will elaborate on the true and lofty position of Jabir in the eyes of the Ahl al-Bayt ﷺ.

Hadith 1: Jabir Conveys the Salutation while Imam al-Baqir ﷺ was a Youth

When Fatima, the daughter of Imam Husayn ﷺ saw the extent of her nephew's (Imam Zayn al-Abideen ﷺ) diligence in worship, she came to Jabir b. Abdullah b. Amrou b. Haraam al-Ansari and said to him, "O companion of the Messenger of Allah, we have rights upon you and one of our rights is that if you see one of us over-engrossed in worship, then you should remind us and ask us to look after ourselves. Here is Ali b. Husayn - the remainder of his father Imam Husayn, his nose is pressed in, his forehead is wounded, and his knees and palms as well, and he has confined himself away in worship."[401]

Then Jabir b. Abdullah came to the door of Imam Ali b. Husayn ﷺ. At the door was a young Abu Ja'far Imam Muhammad b. Ali al-Baqir ﷺ with

---

[401] This part of the narration has already been mentioned in the chapter on Jabir's interactions with Imam Zayn al-Abideen ﷺ.

a group of youth who had gathered there. Jabir looked at him while he was approaching and said, "This is the walk of the Messenger of Allah ﷺ and his character! Who are you, O young man?" He ﷺ replied, "I am Muhammad b. Ali b. Husayn."

Jabir ﷺ began to cry and then said, "Truly, by God, you are the splitter of knowledge. Come closer please, may my father and my mother be ransom for you." When Imam al-Baqir ﷺ came closer, Jabir undid the button of his ﷺ shirt and put his hand on his chest and kissed it. He then put his cheek and face on it and said to the Imam ﷺ, "I convey to you the greetings of your grandfather the Messenger of Allah and it was he ﷺ who instructed me to do what I just did to you. He ﷺ said to me, 'You will live until you meet my children, one of whom is called Muhammad, he who splits open the knowledge thoroughly.' Then he ﷺ told me, 'You will stay until you become blind, and then you will get your eyesight back.'[402]

Jabir asked him, "Please allow me to see your father." Abu Ja'far al-Baqir ﷺ entered upon his father and told him the story saying, "There is a Sheikh at the door and he did so and so." Imam Zayn al-Abideen ﷺ said, "O my son, that is Jabir b. Abdullah al-Ansari." Then Imam al-Baqir ﷺ allowed Jabir in. He entered and found Imam Zayn al-Abideen ﷺ in his *mihrab*, in which he was exhausted by worship. Imam Ali Zayn al-Abideen ﷺ stood for Jabir and asked about him in a very caring manner, and made him sit next to him..."[403] [404]

Hadith 2: Jabir would Call Out for Imam al-Baqir ﷺ when He ﷺ was a Young Man

Jabir used to sit in the Masjid of the Messenger in Medina and call out: "O Baqir! O you who will split open knowledge!" The people of Medina used to say, "Jabir is hallucinating!"

---

[402] According to the narration mentioned about Jabir's visit to the grave of Imam Husayn ﷺ, it was there that he miraculously regained his vision; however according to this narration Jabir's sight returned by the blessing of Imam al-Baqir ﷺ.

[403] The rest of this narration has been mentioned in the Chapter on Jabir's interactions with Imam Zayn al-Abideen ﷺ.

[404] *Bihar al-Anwar*, vol. p. 60; *Qasas als-Sahaaba wa al-Tabi'in*, pp. 84-6.

Jabir would reply, "I swear by Allah that I have never hallucinated, but I have heard the Messenger of Allah 🕮 say, 'Indeed, you will live until you meet a man who belongs to me from the children of Husayn. His name is Muhammad and he will split open the knowledge of the Prophets thoroughly. When you meet him convey to him my greetings.'"

Jabir was waiting for his arrival until one day he met the 5th Imam 🕮 and said to him: "O young man, come here." He 🕮 approached. Then Jabir said to him, "Turn around." He 🕮 turned around. Then Jabir exclaimed, "I swear by He in whose hand is my soul, these are the qualities of the Messenger of Allah 🕮. O young man, what is your name?" He 🕮 replied, "My name is Muhammad."

Jabir inquired further, "The son of who?" The Imam 🕮 said, "The son of Ali b. Husayn."

Then Jabir said, "O my master, may my soul be ransomed for you, so you are al-Baqir?"

The Imam 🕮 said, "Yes, tell me what the Messenger of Allah asked you to deliver!"

Jabir came closer to him, kissed his head and said, "May my father and mother be ransom for you, your grandfather, the Messenger of Allah, has sent you his greetings."

Imam al-Baqir 🕮 replied, "O Jabir, as long as the earth and the heavens exist, upon the Messenger of Allah and upon you - for what you have conveyed, O Jabir, are greetings and salutations."[405]

In the narration of Imam Ja'far al-Sadiq 🕮 he continued the description of this event saying, "So Muhammad b. Ali returned back to his father in a state of trepidation and conveyed the event. Imam Zayn al-Abideen 🕮 responded, 'O my dear son, did Jabir do this?' to which Imam al-Baqir 🕮 confirmed, 'Yes.' The Imam 🕮 told him, 'O my dear son, remain at home.'[406]

---

[405] *Ma'ali al-Sibtayn*, p. 44; *Qasas al-Sahaaba wa al-Tabi'in*, pp. 91-2.
[406] The 5th Imam's trepidation upon receiving the greetings of Jabir is mentioned in many traditions. Some state that Imam Zayn al-Abideen 🕮 told Imam al-Baqir 🕮 not to grieve because Jabir intended no harm. What is meant by this is that Jabir's eagerness to convey the salutations and love for Imam al-Baqir 🕮 in public could certainly have placed the young Imam 🕮 in great danger by virtue of the enmity held by the Banu Umayyah for him. For this reason he became fearful, and his father 🕮 reassured him that Jabir meant no harm, and told him to remain inside the house until the danger subsides.

So Jabir visited the next the day. To this event the people of Medina said, 'What an astonishing level of admiration Jabir approached this young boy with while he is the last remaining companion of the Prophet, and soon Imam Zayn al-Abideen will pass away.'"[407]

Hadith 3: Jabir Calls out for Imam al-Baqir 🖑 while Entering into Medina

It is narrated that Jabir walked into Medina and said, "O Baqir! When shall we meet?!" Another time as Jabir was passing through the streets, a boy ran out and sat on his lap. Jabir said to a lady present (either Jabir's retainer or the young boy's), "Who is this?" to which she replied, "Muhammad b. Ali b. Husayn."

So Jabir brought him close to his chest and kissed his head and hand and said, "O my son, your grandfather, the Messenger of Allah, sends his salutations!"[408]

Hadith 4: Jabir Attempts to Kiss the Feet of Imam al-Baqir 🖑 before Conveying the Greetings of the Prophet 🖑

Imam Muhammad al-Baqir 🖑 said,[409] "I came to Jabir b. Abdullah al-Ansari and greeted him. He replied my salutations and then asked, "Who are you?" since by then he had become blind. I said to him: "Muhammad b. Ali b. Husayn."

Jabir responded, "O my son come closer to me." When I came close to him he kissed my hand, and then bent down to my foot to kiss it, however I pulled it away from him. Then he said, "The Messenger of Allah sent his greetings to you."

I replied, "Peace and God's mercy and blessings be upon the Messenger of Allah. But how is that the case, O Jabir?" He replied, "One day I was with him when he said to me, 'You will live until you meet one of my descendants

---

[407] *Mo'jam Rijal al-Hadith*, vol. 4, p. 332.
[408] *Al-Wafi*, Faydh Kashani, vol. 4, p. 103.
[409] Chain of narrators: Maymoun al-Kaddah, from Imam Ja'far b. Muhammad 🖑 from his father Imam al-Baqir 🖑.

called Muhammad b. Ali b. Husayn upon whom Allah will bestow light and wisdom. Then convey to him my greetings.'"410

Hadith 5: Imam al-Baqir ﷺ Kisses Jabir on his Forehead and Conveys his Salutations

Abi Zubayr b. Muhammad b. Aslam al-Makki narrates, "We were with Jabir b. Abdullah when Imam Ali b. Husayn approached with his son Imam al-Baqir who was a young child. Imam Zayn al-Abideen said to Imam al-Baqir, 'Kiss you uncle's head' so Imam al-Baqir kissed Jabir on the forehead. Jabir asked, 'Who is this?' (as he had become blind.) Imam Zayn al-Abideen replied, 'This is my son Muhammad al-Baqir.'

Jabir embraced Imam al-Baqir and said, 'O Muhammad (al-Baqir). The Messenger of Allah, your grandfather, sends his greetings to you.' Imam al-Baqir ﷺ responded, 'How is that so, O Aba Abdillah (Jabir's title)?' He replied, 'I was with the Messenger of Allah and Imam Husayn was in his room playing. He said to me 'O Jabir, from my son Husayn will be a son named Ali (Zayn al-Abideen). On the Day of Judgement a caller will call out 'Come forth Master of the Worshippers' and so Ali b. Husayn will arise, and from Ali b. Husayn will be his son Muhammad al-Baqir. O Jabir, when you see him, convey my salutations.'"411

Jabir Attempts to Make the People of Medina see the Divine Hand in Imam al-Baqir ﷺ from His ﷺ Youth

In order to help the people of Medina realize the immaculate nature and Divine link between Prophet Muhammad ﷺ and Imamate, Jabir would speak about Imam al-Baqir ﷺ through verses of the Holy Qur'an. In particular, Jabir would refer to the God-given knowledge that was bestowed upon Prophet Yahya ﷺ as a boy (19:12). Referring to Imam al-Baqir ﷺ in this way was not only a subtle form of provoking the minds of the Medinan community toward the realities of Imamate, but it also demonstrated Jabir's

---

410 The link to this is: https://bit.ly/2GL1tqj
411 The link to this is: https://bit.ly/2GL1tqj

understanding of theology, long before these verses were linked to Imam Muhammad al-Jawad ﷺ and his appointment to Imamate at a young age.

The narration states, "When Imam al-Baqir ﷺ was in his youth, a sign from among the signs of his intelligence was that even Jabir, who was in his old age, would come and sit with the Imam ﷺ who in turn taught him. Jabir was dazzled by this capacity of knowledge and insight and said "O Baqir, surely you have been given Divine judgement as a boy."[412]

The People of Medina Call Imam al-Baqir ﷺ a Liar and Jabir Verifies His Testimony

The following narration is one of the most insightful regarding the role of Jabir b. Abdullah towards Imam Muhammad al-Baqir ﷺ and this agency of revealing Wilayah without compromising the Imam ﷺ. Before we narrate the tradition, due to its central role in our theory of understanding how Jabir revealed the Imamate of Imam al-Baqir ﷺ, we will introduce some context and analysis around the hadith.

The narration demonstrates that due to many factors, the people of Medina did not trust or care for the views of Imam al-Baqir ﷺ at a certain period of time during his youth and early adulthood. This may have been because he was young or less known due to house arrest and oppression by the Bani Umayyah. It may also have been due to the pressure on the people of Medina to show hatred to the children of Imam Ali ﷺ and Lady Fatima ﷺ by the rulers; or as a result of the jealousy that certain family members around him had such that they spread mischief and doubts about him amongst the people of Medina. This is indicated towards in the narrations of Falih b. Abu Bakr al-Shaybani where he narrated, "I swear by Allah, I was sitting in the presence of Ali b. al-Husayn (Zayn al-Abideen) whose sons were also there when Jabir b. Abdullah al-Ansari came. He offered his greetings and then held the hand of Abu Ja'far (Imam al-Baqir). He took him

---

[412] The Arabic text of this passage reads:

وكان (عليه السلام) في طفولته آية من آيات الذكاء حتى أن جابر ابن عبد الله الانصاري على شيخوخته كان يأتيه فيجلس بين يديه فيعلمه... وقد بهر جابر من سعة علوم الإمام ومعارفه وطفق يقول: «يا باقر لقد أوتيت الحكم صبياً

'Ilal al-Shara'i', p. 234.

aside for privacy and said, 'The Messenger of Allah informed me that I will find myself with a man from Ahl al-Bayt who will be called Muhammad b. Ali, also called Abu Ja'far. When I meet him I must convey to him my greetings from him (the Messenger of Allah)'. When Abu Ja'far returned to the meeting, he sat near his father and his brothers. When the Imam 🕮 performed the evening prayer, Ali b. al-Husayn asked Abu Ja'far, 'What did Jabir b. Abdullah al-Ansari say to you?' He (Abu Ja'far) replied, 'Jabir said that the Messenger of Allah told me to convey his greetings of peace to him.' Imam Zayn al-Abideen then said, 'Success for you my son, for what Allah has granted to you exclusively through His Messenger from among the members of your family! Do not tell this to your brothers, otherwise they may plan against you like the brothers of Prophet Yusuf did.'"[413]

Kohlberg however suggests a more correct historical reasoning for the people of Medina to have rejected him and that is due to Imam al-Baqir's 🕮 narrating directly from the Prophet 🕮 - though having never met him. This would have been of particular issue considering the number of competing sects, each vying to prove their authority and proximity to the Prophet 🕮. He states, "The Medinese were infuriated by what they considered al-Baqir's impudence. In their view, since neither he, nor his father had ever met Muhammad, he had no right to transmit (narrate hadith) from the Prophet in this manner." Furthermore, Imam al-Baqir 🕮 would have maybe been twelve or fifteen or maximum eighteen years old when narrating directly from the Prophet 🕮.

Kohlberg's study questions the existence of unique narrations, primarily found in the Shi'a hadith corpus (less so in the Sunni literature)[414] of a Ma'sum immaculate Imam narrating from a non-Ma'sum, the only time of which is Imam al-Baqir 🕮 quoting from Jabir b. Abdullah or other Imam's narrating from their forefathers who narrate from Jabir, as mentioned above such as from Imam ar-Redha 🕮. Kohlberg questions, "How can an omniscient Imam gain knowledge from a person, however worthy he may be, who is not a member of the Ahl al-Bayt?" He further claims that: "This question must have proved rather awkward, as may be inferred from the

---

[413] *Al-Kafi*, vol. 1, Chapter 68 on Tacit and Explicit Testimony as Proof of Ali b. Husayn's Divine Authority over the People, Hadith 4, p. 270.

[414] See al-Dhahabi, *Seer A'lam al-Nubala'*, vol. 3, p. 126; Al-Qunduzi, Sulayman, *Yanabi al-Mawadda*, p. 564.

variety of solutions to be found in Shi'a literature." Though never demonstrating its being theologically problematic for any Shi'a scholar, Kohlberg cites Zurahah b. A'yun's questioning al-Baqir, and Ibn Taymiyyah's quoting of al-Baqir's 🕮 transmitting from Jabir as part of his refutation of Shi'a doctrine[415] suggesting Ibn Taymiyyah being the first to formally raise such an issue.

Returning to the introduction of the particular narration that we are about to explore, (when Imam al-Baqir 🕮 narrated from his father Imam Zayn al-Abideen 🕮, about how the people of Medina were skeptical and rejected his words) when Imam al-Baqir 🕮 narrated directly from the Prophet 🕮, and the people of Medina called him an outright liar - we seek refuge in Allah from that! This was because Imam al-Baqir 🕮 had not met the Prophet 🕮 and so they perceived no authority from him for narrating directly from the Messenger 🕮. This called into question, in their eyes at least, Imam al-Baqir's 🕮 quoting from his father - as their distrust extended even to this. They did not understand the fact that a Divinely appointed Imam's 🕮 words are the same as the Prophet's 🕮, and he is not in need of hearing a tradition directly from him 🕮 in order to narrate it, nor is he in need of explicating the chain of narrators from his father 🕮 through Imam al-Husayn 🕮 through Imam Ali b. Abi Talib 🕮 to the Prophet 🕮.

Kohlberg lays out the challenge about the existence of Imam al-Baqir's 🕮 narrations from Jabir given that "virtually all Shi'a asanid (chains of narrators) have three basic forms: They go back to an Imam; they go back to an Imam who transmits it from his forefathers; or else they go back to an Imam who transmits from Muhammad, either directly or via the Imam's forefathers." It is the latter that caused the Medinan's to distrust and revile Imam al-Baqir 🕮.

When the people of Medina rejected Imam al-Baqir's 🕮 narrations from his father 🕮 and grandfather 🕮, the Imam 🕮 adjusted his methodology and instead narrated from Jabir b. Abdullah those traditions about the Prophet 🕮 so that they would then believe the Imam 🕮. This was the weight of Jabir's testimonies in the eyes of the people of Medina, and thought to be

---

[415] See *Minhaj al-Sunnah al-Nabawiyyah*, ed. Muhammad Rashad Salim, vol. 2, p. 362.

a reason for Imam al-Baqir ☙ visiting Jabir so often, that he ☙ was learning these traditions (from Jabir).

As a result they belied Imam al-Baqir's ☙ claim of salutations from the Prophet ☙ and Jabir would come and intervene by repeating them at every opportunity the salutations of the Prophet ☙. This explains why there are so many versions and occasions of Jabir narrating the Prophetic salutations to Imam al-Baqir ☙, in front of various audiences for how could the citizens of Medina reject and revile the very person who the Prophet ☙ sent his salutations to - and evidently the only person that he fore-sent them to?! It appears that the salutations of the Prophet ☙ were in themselves strategic and with knowledge of the challenges that Imam al-Baqir ☙ would face. These salutations in essence had a resounding impact on the people of Medina who then came to realize the status of Imam al-Baqir ☙. As a result, their respect and love for Imam al-Baqir ☙ increased and they changed their attitude towards his speeches and lessons.

This event must be noted as one of the greatest contributions that Jabir made for the Ahl al-Bayt ☙ and should be understood for the immediate and historical impact that it has made up until today. Moreover, the fact that Jabir's speech was so readily accepted, later laid the groundwork as having been prepared through these sorts of events, and as such when Jabir then testified to the Imamate of Imam al-Baqir ☙ it awoke the people of Medina finally, to who Imam al-Baqir ☙ really was. This was because if the people of Medina accepted the salutations of the Prophet ☙ to Imam al-Baqir ☙ through Jabir, then they had to accept his testimony of Imam al-Baqir ☙ for Imamate and Caliphate from the Prophet ☙ as well. As for the one who rejects this, the Holy Qur'an questions such logical inconsistencies asking, "Do you then believe in a part of the Book and deny another part of it? Then what is the reward for those who do that except disgrace in this worldly life and on the Day of Resurrection?" (2:85).

Let us now see this particular and very important narration:

Ayatollah Syed al-Khoei mentions in his *Rijal* in the narration continuing from Jabir where he conveys the Prophet's ☙ greeting and Imam al-Baqir ☙ felt trepidation by this (Hadith 2 above), from Imam Ja'far al-Sadiq ☙, "Imam al-Baqir ☙ would regularly visit Jabir showing him great honour. Afterwards the Imam ☙ would sit with the people of Medina and narrate to them from his father Imam Zayn al-Abideen ☙, but the people of Medina would say, 'For sure we have not seen anyone as bold as this person!' So when Imam al-Baqir 🕮 saw what they were saying about him, he would narrate traditions to them from the Messenger of Allah 🕮. But the people of Medina would say, 'Certainly we have not seen anyone lie more than this person, to narrate from someone that he has not even seen!' Then when Imam al-Baqir 🕮 narrated from Jabir b. Abdullah, the people of Medina believed in him and testified to him. But I swear by Allah 🕮 that Jabir would regularly come and learn from him (Imam al-Baqir 🕮)."[416]

Let us mention here some examples of such narrations from Imam al-Baqir 🕮 who narrated directly from Prophet Muhammad 🕮, the ones which may have been rejected by the people of Medina on the basis that al-Baqir 🕮 never met the Messenger of Allah 🕮. Jabir narrates from Imam al-Baqir 🕮, "When the verse, 'On the Day when We will call every nation with their leaders' (17:71) was revealed, people asked the Messenger of Allah 🕮, 'Are you not the Imam (leader) of all of the people together?' The Messenger of Allah 🕮 replied, 'I am the Messenger of Allah to all of the people, but after me there will be Imams from my family for the people. They will be among the people, but they will be rejected. The leaders of the unbelievers and misguidance, and their followers will do injustice to them. Those who support, love, follow and acknowledge their authority are from me, they are with me, and they will meet me. People must know that whoever will do any injustice to the Imams or reject them is not from me and is not with me. I will denounce them and have no association with them.'"[417]

Another example is when Abdul Rahman b. Kathir narrated from Imam al-Baqir 🕮 who said, "The Messenger of Allah 🕮 said, 'The first successor and executor of the will on earth was Hibbat Ullah (gift from Allah), the son of Prophet Adam 🕮. No Prophet ever left this world without first leaving behind one who would execute his will. The Prophets numbered 124,000. Five of them were commissioned as *Ulul Azam* (prophets who had divine books and independent teachings. See Qur'an (42:13)) Messengers and they were: Nuh, Ibrahim, Musa, Isa and Muhammad 🕮. Imam Ali b. Abi Talib 🕮 was the Hibbat Ullah (gift from Allah) for Prophet Muhammad 🕮. He 🕮

---

[416] *Mo'jam al-Rijal*, vol. 4, p. 332.
[417] *Al-Kafi*, The Book about People with Divine Authority, Chapter 25 'Two Kinds of Imams', Hadith 1, p. 183.

inherited the knowledge of the executors of the wills of the Prophets, and the knowledge of those who were before him."[418]

Other such narrations exist, and Imam al-Baqir 🕮 narrates some directly from Imam Ali b. Abi Talib 🕮, also whom he did not meet. Here we will mention some examples of these in order to demonstrate what the Imam 🕮 would have said and what may have been rejected by the people of Medina. Jabir narrates from Imam al-Baqir 🕮 who said, "Amir al-Mo'mineen (Ali) 🕮 said about the words of Allah, 'In this there are signs for the distinguished ones' (15:75) that, 'The Messenger of Allah 🕮 was the 'Distinguished One,' and I am as such after him and the Imams from my children are (also) the distinguished ones.'"[419]

Also, Isma'il b. Abi Ziyad narrates from Imam Ja'far al-Sadiq 🕮, who narrated from Imam Muhammad al-Baqir 🕮, who said, "Amir al-Mo'mineen Ali 🕮 said, 'We, the Ahl al-Bayt 🕮 are the tree of Prophecy, the station of the Messengership, the location for the coming and going of the angels, the house of mercy, and the mine of knowledge.'"[420]

Although there are many other narrations where Imam al-Baqir 🕮 narrates directly from the Prophet 🕮 and Imam Ali 🕮, the theme of this collection expresses the position and authority of the Ahl al-Bayt 🕮 and in particular Amir al-Mo'mineen 🕮. Given the culture of abuse against Imam Ali 🕮 during that period, the norm of narrating through a chain, the many theological groups, government influence and new Muslims' unawareness of the Imam's position, it is understandable why people ignorant of Imam al-Baqir's 🕮 authority would question the legitimacy of such direct narrations.

Narrations of Imam al-Baqir 🕮 from Jabir b. Abdullah

Given that Jabir b. Abdullah was considered an authoritative and trustworthy narrator by the people of Medina, and the political climate of oppression was so prevalent upon the Ahl al-Bayt 🕮, we have mentioned

---

[418] Ibid., Chapter 33, 'The Imam Inherited the Knowledge of the Holy Prophet and All of the Prophets and Their Successors before Them', Hadith 2, p. 191.

[419] Ibid., Chapter 28, 'The People with Whom Allah has Called Mutawassimeen Who are also, The Straight Path', Hadith 5, p. 186.

[420] Ibid., Chapter 31, 'Imams are the Mines of Knowledge, the Tree of Prophecy and a Centre of Movement of the Angels', Hadith 2, p. 188.

that Imam al-Baqir 🕮 would seek Jabir's testimony in order to validate his own. Later on when the ground had been prepared and the opportunity arose, Jabir began testifying to the Imamate of Imam al-Baqir 🕮.

While this is understandable from the pragmatic perspective of history, it also demonstrates two other important points that any lover and servant of the Ahl al-Bayt 🕮 must learn from Jabir. The first is that the view of the people of Medina was not necessarily important in the eyes of Imam al-Baqir 🕮, but rather he, the immaculate Imam 🕮 himself trusted the tongue of Jabir to be truthful and accurate from what he had heard from the Prophet 🕮! This means that an Imam of the Ahl al-Bayt 🕮, Divinely appointed by Allah 🕮, referred to a non-divine companion for testimony and verification! This demonstrates the level that a companion can reach such that a Divine Imam 🕮 narrates from a non-divine companion!

Secondly, it demonstrated the role of great companions in the establishment of Imamate, just as the great companions had such a role in the establishment of the message of the Prophet 🕮. This is a lesson for those hoping to be a companion of the Awaited Saviour of humanity, Imam al-Mahdi 🕮 in that the Imam 🕮 will be in need of companions like Jabir to establish his movement. This is mentioned in the Holy Qur'an that there will be those who will pave the way for the coming of Imam al-Mahdi 🕮 by stating: "(And they are) Those who, if We give them authority in the land, they establish the prayer, give the charity, enjoin what is right and forbid what is evil." (22:41)

In keeping with our theory of Jabir's role in revealing the Imamate of Imam al-Baqir 🕮 tentatively and intelligently, the next stage of the cooperation was for Imam al-Baqir 🕮 to reduce and remove the distrust and repulsion of the people of Medina. Having been lavished with salutations and lauded by his title al-Baqir from the Prophet 🕮, their daily meetings allowed Jabir to attain vast degrees of knowledge from Imam al-Baqir 🕮. Kohlberg also notes that these meetings allowed the Imam 🕮 to gain reverence from the people of Medina: "Al-Baqir used to come and visit Jabir out of respect for his status as a companion." He also states, "When al-Baqir heard about these objections (to his narrating directly from the Prophet 🕮), he began to transmit traditions on the authority of Jabir so as to guarantee their acceptance."

In this chapter we will view some of the narrations of Imam al-Baqir 🕮 from Jabir b. Abdullah. As we do so, in addition to the content of the narrations, let us appreciate the value of Jabir in the eyes of the Imam 🕮 for him 🕮 to have used the testimony of Jabir. It is also noteworthy that the Imams after the 5th Imam also narrated from Jabir through the chains of their fathers, going as far as Imam al-Hadi 🕮 who narrated from his forefathers, to Imam al-Baqir 🕮 who narrated from Jabir, (see Hadith 10) - demonstrating their upkeep of this tradition and their individual trust in the statements of this great companion Jabir.

Hadith 1: Regarding the Month of Ramadaan

Abu Ja'far Muhammad b. Ali al-Baqir 🕮 said, "The Messenger of Allah 🕮 said to Jabir, 'This is the month of Ramadaan. Whoever fasts during its day, spends a portion of its night saying prayers, abstains from eating anything unlawful, safeguards his modesty against anything illicit, and withholds his tongue against saying anything prohibited, will depart from his sins just like the month also departs.'"

Jabir said, "O Messenger of God 🕮! What a beautiful tradition (hadith) this is!" The Messenger of God 🕮 replied, "O Jabir, yes but what difficult conditions they are to fulfil."[421]

Hadith 2: The Prophet 🕮, Imam Ali 🕮 and the Shi'a are from One Essence

Imam Muhammad al-Baqir 🕮 narrates from Jabir b. Abdullah al-Ansari who said, "The Messenger of Allah 🕮 said to Ali b. Abi Talib 🕮 'Shall I give you glad tidings? Shall I converse with you?'

The Imam 🕮 responded, 'Yes, O Messenger of Allah!' The Prophet 🕮 stated, 'Certainly me and you were created from one clay (essence). Then there remained some remnants from it, and our Shi'a were created from what remained (sharing in our essence). On the Day of Judgement, people will be called by the names of their mothers except for our Shi'a, for they

---

[421] *Fawai'd al-Ibadah*, Sheikh al-Hakimi, p. 213; *Qasas al-Sahaaba wa al-Tabi'in*, p. 89.

will be called by the names of their fathers, due to the goodness of their births.'"[422]

Hadith 3: The Position of Lady Fatima ﷺ on the Day of Judgement

Imam Abu Ja'far Muhammad al-Baqir ﷺ narrates that he heard Jabir b. Abdullah al-Ansari say, "The Messenger of Allah ﷺ said, 'When it will be the Day of Judgement, my daughter Fatima will come upon a she-camel from the she-camels of paradise with decorated reins, their seals being made of white pearls, its legs having green emeralds, its tail perfumed with al-Azfar musk, and its two eyes being red rubies. Upon it will be a dome of light, such that its outside will be seen from its inside, and its inside will be seen from its outside. Its interior will be the Forgiveness of Allah, and its exterior will be the Mercy of Allah. Upon Fatima's head will be a crown of light, which will have seventy corners, each corner embedded with gemstones and rubies. It will illuminate brightly just like the brilliant star in the horizon of the sky.

On her right side will be 70,000 angels, and on her left side will be 70,000 angels. The Arch-Angel Jibra'il will be holding the reins of the she-camel and will call out in a high voice 'Close your eyes until Fatima passes by!' So she will travel until she is parallel to the Throne of her Lord. She will go by herself from her she-camel and will say: 'My God and my Master! Judge between me and the ones who oppressed me! O Allah! Judge between me and the ones who murdered my children!'

So there will be a Call from Allah, Majestic is His Majesty: 'O My Beloved and daughter of My Beloved! Ask Me for I will Grant it! As for My intercession, you can intercede. I swear by My Might and My Majesty, I will not allow the oppression of the oppressor.' So Fatima ﷺ will say, 'My God and my Master! My offspring and my Shi'as, and the Shi'as of my offspring, and the ones who loved my offspring.'

So there will be a Call from Allah ﷺ, 'Where are the children of Fatima and her Shi'as, and those who adore her and the ones who love her children?' So they will be gathered, and the angels of divine mercy will

---

[422] *Bashaaratu al-Mustafa li Shi'ati Murtadhza*, Section 1, p. 22.

encircle them. Thus, Fatima 🌹 will precede them until she leads them into paradise."[423]

Hadith 4: The Remembrance of Ali b. Abi Talib 🌹

Imam al-Baqir 🌹 narrates from his father Imam Zayn al-Abideen 🌹 who narrates from Jabir that the Messenger of Allah 🌹 said, "Adorn your gatherings with the remembrance of Ali b. Abi Talib 🌹."[424]

Hadith 5: The Command of Allah 🌹 to the Prophet 🌹

Imam al-Baqir 🌹 narrates from Jabir b. Abdullah al-Ansari who said, "The Messenger of Allah 🌹 stated, 'Arch-Angel Jibra'il descended unto me and said, 'Allah commands that you stand and address your companions regarding the merits of Ali b. Abi Talib 🌹 in order for those merits to reach those who come after you; and He has commanded the entirety of the angels that they should listen to what you are mentioning. Allah reveals unto you O Muhammad that the ones who oppose you in regards to this matter, for them will be the Hellfire, and the ones who obeys you, for them will be the paradise.'

'The Prophet then ordered a call for congregational prayers and the people gathered. The Prophet 🌹 came out until he ascended to the top tier of the pulpit. The first thing that he said was, 'I seek refuge with Allah from the accursed Satan. I begin in the Name of Allah, the Beneficent, the Merciful.'

Then he continued, 'O people! I am the giver of good news and the warner and I am the Ummi (unlettered or from Ummu al-Qur'a (Meccan)) Prophet. I am delivering something to you all on behalf of Allah, the Mighty and Majestic, regarding the matter of a man whose flesh is my flesh, and his blood is my blood. He is the receptacle of knowledge, and the one who Allah has nominated from this community, chosen, guided and made a guardian.'

'And He created me and him. He graced me with the Message, and graced him with the delivery on my behalf; and He made me the city of knowledge, and made him the treasurer of the knowledge; the source of the Judgements

---

[423] *Bashaaratu al-Mustafa li Shi'ati Murtadha*, Section 1, pp. 29-31.
[424] Ibid., Section 2, p. 45.

are from Him, and He specialized this man with successorship. He clarified His matter and scared people from being inimical to him and drew closer the ones who befriended him and forgave for him his Shi'a, and commanded the people in their entirety with obeying him (Imam Ali 🕮).

'And He the Mighty and Majestic says, 'The one who is inimical to him is inimical to Me, and the one who befriends him is befriending Me; the one who is hostile to him is hostile to Me, and the one who opposes him is opposing Me; and the one who disobeys him is disobeying Me and the one who harms him is harming Me; and the one who hates him hates Me and the one who loves him loves Me; and the one who intends (to hurt) him is intending (to hurt) Me; and the one who plots against him is plotting against Me, and the one who helps him is helping Me.'

'O people! Listen to what I am ordering you with! Obey him for I am fearing for you all the punishment of Allah 'On the Day when every soul will find present what it has done of good and what it has done of evil, it shall wish that between it and that (evil) there was a long duration of time' (3:30) and Allah is cautioning you about His 'Nafs.'"

Jabir continued, "Then the Prophet 🕮 grabbed the hand of Amir al-Mo'mineen Ali and said, 'O Group of people! This is the master of the believers and a Divine authority of Allah upon the creatures altogether, and a holy warrior against the disbelievers. O Allah! I have delivered your message and these are Your servants, and You are able upon correcting them, therefore correct them, O most Merciful of the merciful! I seek the forgiveness of Allah for myself and for all of you.'

Then he 🕮 descended from the Pulpit, and Jibra'il came to him 🕮 and said, 'O Muhammad! Allah, Mighty and Majestic, conveys greetings to you! Allah recompenses good for your preaching, and you have delivered the message of your Lord and advised your community, and you have pleased the believers and compelled the disbelievers. O Muhammad! The son of your uncle will be afflicted and tested. O Muhammad! Say during every time, 'The Praise is for Allah, Lord of the worlds 'and they who act unjustly shall come to know the turning they shall be overturned with' (26:227).'"[425]

---

[425] *Bashaaratu al-Mustafa li Shi'ati Murtadha*, Section 2, pp. 51-3.

Hadith 6: Imam al-Sadiq ☬ Narrates from Jabir

The companion Muhammad b. al-Samit al-Ju'fi narrates: "We were a group of people from the city of Basra in the presence of Abu Abdullah Ja'far al-Sadiq ☬. He narrated to us a tradition from his father Imam al-Baqir ☬ who narrated it from Jabir b. Abdullah, during the hajj, dictating upon them how to act. When they finished discussing and party stood up, Abu Abdullah al-Sadiq ☬ said, 'The people are taking to the right and left (going in any direction and taking from other paths), and you all are forcing your companion (the Imam ☬ to speak). So to where do you see he would be returning (meeting) with you all?! To the paradise! By Allah, to the paradise! By Allah to the paradise! By Allah.'"[426] [427]

Hadith 7: Attach Yourself with Love to the Wilayah of Ali ☬

Abu Aasim al-Zahhak b. Makhlad al-Nabeel narrates from Imam Ja'far al-Sadiq ☬, who narrates from his father Imam al-Baqir ☬, who narrated from Jabir that, "I was in the presence of the Prophet ﷺ. I was on one side and Ali ☬ was on the other side when 'Umar b. al-Khattab came over and there was a man with him who was muttering. So the Prophet ﷺ said, 'What is the matter with him?' 'Umar replied, 'He is repeating from you O Messenger of Allah ﷺ what you said, 'The one who says 'There is no god except Allah, and Muhammad is the Messenger of Allah will enter into paradise' and when the people hear it, they will be abandoning the other deeds. Did you say that, O Messenger of Allah?' The Prophet ﷺ replied, 'Yes, when you attach yourself with the love of this (Ali) and his Wilayah.'"[428]

---

[426] Ibid., Section 2b, p. 31, Hadith 100.

[427] It appears that the Imam ☬ is suggesting that the public discourse will ultimately place the Imam ☬ in difficulty from the tyrannical government. He therefore is announcing his, their, or all of their impending deaths and that they will soon meet again in paradise.

[428] *Bashaaratu al-Mustafa li Shi'ati Murtadha,* Section 3, p. 36, Hadith 38.

Hadith 8: The Story of Lady Fatima's 𐓒 Pendant

Imam Muhammad al-Baqir 𐓒 narrates from Imam Zayn al-Abideen 𐓒 who narrates from Jabir, "The Messenger of Allah 𐓒 prayed Salaat al-'Asr with us. When he 𐓒 finished, he 𐓒 sat in his position and the people were around him. While they were like that an old man from the emigrants came over. He was wearing worn out clothes which were hanging and ripped, and he was almost unstable out of weakness and old age. The Prophet 𐓒 turned to the old man and inquired from him about his situation.

The old man said, 'O Prophet of Allah. I am so hungry please feed me, and I am bare on the body so please clothe me, and I am poor so please sprinkle me with wealth.' The Prophet 𐓒 said to him, 'I do not have anything for you, but the one who points towards the good is like its doer. Go to the house of the one who loves Allah and His Messenger, and Allah and His Messenger love them. They prefer Allah over themselves. Go to the house of (Lady) Fatima.'

Her house was adjacent to the house of the Prophet 𐓒. He 𐓒 addressed his companion and said, 'Rise up O Bilal and wait with him at the house of Fatima.' So the Bedouin went with Bilal. He paused at the door of Fatima 𐓒, and called out at the top of his voice, 'Greetings be upon you, O People of the Household of prophethood, and the place of the coming and going of the angels, and the place of descent of the Arch-Angel Jibra'il 𐓒 - the Trustworthy Spirit with the Revelation from the Presence of the Lord of the worlds!' So (Lady) Fatima 𐓒 replied, 'Who are you, O person?' He said, 'An elderly from the Arabs. I went to your father, the chief of the mortals, emigrating from a great distance, and I, O daughter of Muhammad, am bare on the body and hungry. Therefore, be sympathetic to me, may Allah have mercy on you.'

'It was so that Fatima and Ali were also in that situation, as was the Messenger of Allah 𐓒 for three days, in that they had not eaten a meal during it either, but the Prophet 𐓒 had not known that about their state. So Fatima 𐓒 turned to a sheep skin which had been tanned with al-karz (some material). It was what Hasan 𐓒 and Husayn 𐓒 used to sleep on. So she said, 'Take this, O visitor! Perhaps Allah will help you to feel comfort with what is better than it.' So the Bedouin said, 'O daughter of Muhammad! I complained to you about hunger, and you are giving me a sheep skin? What am I to do with it for my hunger?'

(Jabir continues) 'So Fatima ⁕ deliberated upon what she heard and took off the pendant which was on her neck which had been gifted to her by Fatima, the daughter of her uncle Hamza b. Abdul Muttalib ⁕ and gave it to the Bedouin and said, 'Take it and sell it. Perhaps Allah will give you instead of it what is better than it.'

So the Bedouin took the pendant and went to the Masjid of the Prophet where the Prophet ⁕ was seated among his companions. The man said, 'O Messenger of Allah! Fatima gave me this pendant and she said, 'Sell it, perhaps He will do something for you.'' The Prophet ⁕ wept and said, 'How can Allah not do something for you when it was given to you by Fatima daughter of Muhammad, the Leader of the daughters of Prophet Adam?'

Ammar b. Yasir stood up and said, 'O Messenger of Allah! Will you allow me to buy this pendant?' He ⁕ said, 'Buy it, O Ammar, for (it will be such a good deed that) if the jinns and mankind were to participate with you, Allah would not punish them with the fire.' Then Ammar said, 'How much is this pendant, O Bedouin?' He replied, 'For satiation from bread and meat, and a Yemeni cloak to cover my bareness with which and I can make my prayers to my Lord in, and a dinar to make me reach back to my family.'

It happened that Ammar gave his share which the Prophet ⁕ had apportioned him from Khayber and nothing remained from it. Then he said, 'For you are twenty dinars and two hundred dirhams and a Yemeni cloak, and my rider to help you reach your family, and satiation with wheat, bread and meat.' So the Bedouin responded, 'How generous you are with wealth!' Ammar went with him and fulfilled what he had guaranteed to him, and the Bedouin returned to the Prophet ⁕.'

The Prophet ⁕ asked him, 'Have you been fed and clothed?' The Bedouin said, 'Yes, O Messenger of Allah and I have been enriched. May my father and my mother be sacrificed for you.' He ⁕ said, 'So recompense Fatima for what she did'. The Bedouin said, 'O Allah! You are the One Who created us, and there is no god for us that we worship besides You; and You are our Sustainer in every aspect. O Allah! Give Fatima what neither the eye has seen, nor has the ear heard before.'

Thereafter the Prophet ⁕ said 'Ameen' upon his supplication and turned to his companions and said, 'Allah has already given that to Fatima in this world. I am her father and there is no one from the universe like me; and Ali is her husband, and had it not been for Ali, there would have never been a match for Fatima! Plus He gave her Hasan and Husayn and there is nothing in the universe the likes of them. They are the chiefs of the tribes of the Prophets and the chiefs of the people of the paradise.'

At this point the Prophet ﷺ was with Miqdaad, Ibn 'Umar, Ammar and Salmaan and he ﷺ said, 'Shall I increase for you all (expand further)?' They said, 'Yes, O Messenger of Allah!' He ﷺ said, 'The Trustworthy Spirit (Arch-Angel Jibr'aeel) came to me and said, 'Certainly when she (Fatima) passes away and is buried, the two angels in her grave will ask her, 'Who is your Lord?' So she will reply, 'Allah is my Lord.' Then they will ask, 'Who is your Prophet?' She will reply, 'My father.' Then they will ask her, 'Who is your Guardian?' So she will reply, 'This one standing on the edge of my grave, Ali b. Abi Talib.'

'Indeed! Shall I further elaborate for you all of her merits? Allah has allocated a group of angels with her, protecting her from the front and from the behind, from her right and from her left, and they will be with her during her lifetime, and by her grave after she passes away. They will frequently send blessings upon her, her father, her husband and her two sons.'

The Prophet ﷺ continued: 'So the one who visits me after my death, it is as if he visited me during my lifetime, and the one who visits Fatima, it is as if he has visited me. The one who visits Ali b. Abi Talib, it is as if he has visited Fatima; and the one who visits Hasan and Husayn, it is as if he has visited Ali, and the one who visits their children, it is as if he has visited the two of them.'

Ammar then deliberated upon the pendant which he had purchased and decided to perfume it with musk and enveloped it in a Yemeni cloth. He had a servant whose name was Sahm who he had bought from that share which he had attained at Khayber. So he handed over the pendant to Sahm and said to him, 'Take this pendant and give it to the Prophet ﷺ and you are also for him.' So he went to the Prophet ﷺ with it and informed him ﷺ about Ammar's words, may Allah have mercy on him.'

The Prophet responded, 'Go to Fatima and give the pendant to her and you also are for her.' So Sahm went with the pendant and informed her about the words of the Prophet ﷺ. Fatima ﷺ took the pendant and freed the servant, so Sahm laughed. Fatima ﷺ inquired, 'What makes you laugh O servant?' He said, 'It is the greatness of this pendant which makes me laugh! It satiated a hungry one, clothed a bare one, enriched a poor one, freed a slave, and returned back to its original owner!'"[429]

Hadith 9: The Prophet's ﷺ Hopes

Imam Musa al-Kadhim ؏ narrates from Imam Ja'far al-Sadiq ؏ who narrates from Imam Muhammad al-Baqir ؏ who narrated from Jabir that the Prophet ﷺ said, "I am hoping for my community regarding the love for Ali ؏ just as I have hope regarding the words 'There is no god but Allah.'"[430]

Hadith 10: How to be a Neighbour of Prophet Ibrahim ؏ in Paradise

It is narrated by Imam Ali al-Hadi ؏ who narrated from his father Imam Muhammad al-Taqi ؏ who narrated from his father Imam Ali al-Ridha ؏, who narrated from his father Imam Musa b. Ja'far ؏, who narrated from his father Imam Ja'far b. Muhammad ؏ who said, "It was narrated to me by my father (Imam) Muhammad b. Ali al-Baqir ؏ who narrated from Jabir b. Abdullah al-Ansari who said, 'The Prophet ﷺ said, 'The one who ardently desires that he wants to be a neighbour of the Friend of Allah (Prophet Ibrahim) in his house, and be safe from the heat of His Fire, let him befriend Ali b. Abi Talib.''"[431]

Hadith 11: Ali ؏ is the Key to the Treasure of Knowledge

It is narrated by Imam Ali b. Musa al-Ridha ؏, who quoted on the authority of his father, Musa b. Ja'far ؏, who quoted on the authority of his father Ja'far b. Muhammad ؏, who quoted on the authority of Imam Muhammad al-Baqir ؏, who quoted from Jabir b. Abdullah that Prophet Muhammad ﷺ said, "I am the treasure of knowledge and Ali is its key. Whoever wants the treasure should go through its key."[432]

---

[429] Ibid., pp. 42-6, Hadith 44.
[430] Ibid., Section 4, p. 5, Hadith 2.
[431] Ibid., Section 5, p. 11, Hadith 11.
[432] *Uyun al-Akhbar al-Ridha*, vol. 2, Chapter 31, Hadith 343, p. 124.

Hadith 12: The Preference of Ali ﷺ over All of the Other Companions

Imam al-Baqir ﷺ narrates from Jabir that the Prophet ﷺ said, "Jibra'il came to me and said, 'Allah has ordered you to give preference to Ali b. Abi Talib when speaking to your companions. This is so that the companions may inform those who come after them (that Ali is the best companion by the Prophet's ﷺ own words). Also Allah has ordered all of the angels to what you say (about Ali). Allah reveals to you, Muhammad, that whoever disobeys you regarding Ali will enter Hell and whoever obeys you will enter Paradise.'"[433]

Hadith 13: End Result for Hating the Ahl al-Bayt ﷺ

Imam al-Baqir ﷺ narrates from Jabir that, "The Messenger of Allah spoke to us and said, 'O people, whoever hates us, the Ahl al-Bayt, will be resurrected on the Day of Judgement as a Jew.' I said, 'O Messenger of Allah, will this happen even to someone who fasts and prays and claims to be a Muslim?' He answered, '(Yes), even to someone who fasts and prays and claims to be a Muslim.'"[434]

Jabir openly calls people towards the leadership of Imam Ali ﷺ during the period of Imam al-Baqir ﷺ and warns them against the tyrant rulers of the time

During the time of Imam al-Baqir ﷺ, Jabir would not let people forget about the initial causes of the seizures of power and splits in the Muslim community. The nation had grown as far as the borders of modern day China, Spain and Northern Africa by this time, inviting potentially millions of new Muslims, ignorant of the Islamic political history, and at the mercy of whichever preachers the government would empower. Moreover, during the period of Imam al-Baqir ﷺ, the city of Medina was evolving into more than a capital city, for it was at the head of Islamic learning. Despite the

---

[433] *Amali*, pp. 73-4.
[434] *Bihar al-Anwar*, vol. 7, p. 405.

potential of reprisal and oppression, Jabir called people towards Imam Ali and continuously spread his virtues. This was the foundation of eventually calling the people towards Imam al-Baqir for once the authority of the Ahl al-Bayt could be established, the illegitimacy of any other rulership would be realized. This means the strategy, after the people of Medina had rejected Imam al-Baqir, was in its penultimate stage: Jabir had spread the Prophet's salutations far and wide; he was continually visiting the Imam who in turn was narrating from Jabir. Now Jabir was spreading the Wilayah of Imam Ali and the Ahl al-Bayt.

Abi al-Zubair narrates:[435] "I saw Jabir leaning on his stick. He used to pass by the streets of the city and their gatherings and say, 'Ali is the best of the people and whoever denies this has surely disbelieved. O the people of Ansar, discipline your children on the love of Ali b. Abi Talib and whoever denies this (is an offender against his love), should look into the affair (chastity) of his mother.'"

Then when someone would ask him:[436] "Tell me what type of man Ali b. Abi Talib was?" The narrator says, "Jabir would raise his eye-brows over his eyes because they had fallen over his eyes." He would then reply: "He is the best of the people! I swear by Allah that if we wanted to know (recognize) the hypocrites at the time of the Messenger of Allah, we would recognize them by their hatred towards him (meaning Imam Ali)."[437]

Ibn Asakir narrates that Jabir said, "I entered towards Hajjaaj b. Yusuf al-Thaqafi but I did not salute him." Zaid b. Aslam said, "Jabir had lost his eyesight, and once it was mentioned in his presence what the king wears of silk and ornaments and how he behaves to which Jabir replied that he wished he has lost his hearing how he lost his sight so that he would not have to hear any of the king's news nor see him."[438]

When Hajjaaj b. Yusuf al-Thaqafi, the Umayyad tyrant king would visit Medina, the inhabitants of the city would go to Jabir and ask him about how the Prophet would pray. This may have been because the Caliphs

---

[435] Chain of narrators: Muhammad b. Masoud said: Ali b. Muhammad told me: Muhammad b. Ahmad b. Yahya told me from Muhammad b. al-Mounkary (Ibn al-Taghlouby) from Ali b. al-Hakam from Fadeel b. 'Uthman from Abi al-Zubair.

[436] Chain of narrators: Asem b. Hameed from Mo'awiyyah b. Amaar from Abi al-Zubair al-Makki said: I asked Jabir b. Abdullah.

[437] *Rijal Hawl al-Rasool wa Ahl Baytihi*, p. 223; *Qasas al-Sahaaba wa al-Tabi'in*, p. 77.

[438] *Qasas al-Sahaaba wa al-Tabi'in*, p. 80.

themselves did not or did not know how to pray, or maybe because they wished to use Jabir as a means of reminding the Caliphs to pray, or perhaps they did not trust the Caliph to give the correct answer. It is most likely that the Caliphs attempted to change the prayer and so Jabir was seen as the authority of Prophetic practise (*sunnah*) for them. Muhammad b. 'Amr b. al-Hasan b. 'Ali reports: "When Hajjaaj came to Medina, we asked Jabir b. Abdullah about the timings of the prayers as observed by the Prophet."[439]

Ibn Askir also narrates about this in his book, *Taareekh Demashq* with his reference from Jabir that he replied, "The midday prayer (*dhuhr*) with the Messenger of Allah 🕮 used to be at the time when the shadows of things are no longer than a shoe lace; and he offered the afternoon ('*asr*) prayer at the time when the shadows of things stretched in length to match the height of the thing. He offered the evening (*maghrib*) prayer at the time when the sun vanished below the horizon; and he offered the night (*isha*) prayer at the end of dusk. He 🕮 used to lead us in the morning (*fajr*) prayer when the dawn breaks.[440]

It was then asked of Jabir, "So how can we pray with Hajjaaj while he delays the prayer for so long?" Jabir advised, "When he prays it on time then pray it with him, but if he delays it then pray it on its time, and make the prayer with him as a supererogatory prayer (*nafelah*)."[441]

Abu al-Ja'ad narrates, "Jabir b. Abdullah al-Ansari was asked about Ali b. Abi Talib. So he replied, 'He is the best of creation, from the former ones and the latter ones, apart from the Prophets and Messengers.[442] Allah, the Mighty and Majestic did not create a creature after the Prophets and the Messengers more honourable to Him than Ali b. Abi Talib and the Imams from his son after him.'

---

[439] *Sahih Muslim*, The Book of Prayers, Book 4, Hadith 1348.

[440] The narration is lengthy explaining the different times that the Prophet 🕮 would pray.

[441] *Qasas al-Sahaaba wa al-Tabi'in*, pp. 80-1; *Sahih Muslim*, The Book of Prayers, Book 4, Hadith 1349.

[442] The unanimous belief of the Shi'a Imamiyyah is that Imam Ali b. Abi Talib 🕮 is the best of creation but only after Prophet Muhammad 🕮, to whom the Imam 🕮 was a servant to. Certainly Jabir was aware of this. Either there is a mistake in this part of the narration, or else Jabir was forced to conceal part of his faith (taqiyyah) in order to convey the rest of his message. Allah knows best.

I asked, 'So what are you saying regarding the one who hates him and attempts to diminish his status?' Jabir responded, 'No one would hate him except for a disbeliever, nor would anyone try to diminish him except for a hypocrite.' I said, 'What do you say regarding the one who befriends him and befriends the Imams from his son after him?' Jabir replied, 'The Shi'a of Ali and of the Imams from his sons after him, they will be the successful ones and the secured ones on the Day of Judgement.'

Then Jabir continued, 'What do you say regarding a man if he was to come out calling the people to a straying path? Certainly the one who was the closest of the people to him would say that he is his follower (Shi'a) and his helper. Similarly, if one was to come out calling the people to the path of guidance, the one who was the closest of the people to him would say that he is his follower (Shi'a) and his helper. Such is the case with Imam Ali b. Abi Talib. On the Day of Judgement, in his hand will be the 'Flag of Praise' and the closest of the people from him will be his Shi'as and his helpers.'"[443]

Jabir's Narrations from Imam Muhammad al-Baqir

In the previous sections we saw the historical evolution of the circumstances of Jabir's relationship with Imam al-Baqir. Engulfed by ravenous oppressions upon the Ahl al-Bayt, his testifying to the position of Imam al-Baqir provoked legitimate fear for the life of Imam al-Baqir. Jabir initiated his publicising of *wilayah* by conveying the Prophetic salutations. The Imam would regularly visit and narrate from Jabir, further establishing Jabir's own reputation and shifting the attitude of the people of Medina towards Imam al-Baqir.

It then appears that Jabir ceased to convey the Prophet's salutations, and also Imam al-Baqir refrained from narrating from Jabir. As the reputation of Imam al-Baqir and the understanding of the people towards him grew, Jabir then began narrating from Imam al-Baqir.

Imam al-Baqir would have been maybe fifteen or eighteen years old at this point. This certainly would have raised questions initially that since Jabir was a companion of the Prophet, Imam Ali, Imams Hasan, Husayn and Zayn al-Abideen, and a scholar in his own right, why does he now narrate from Imam al-Baqir - who used to visit and narrate

---

[443] *Bashaaratu al-Mustafa li Shi'ati Murtadha*, Section 4, p. 61, Hadith 92.

from him in the beginning! This of course was because all along, Jabir knew the rights and position of Imam al-Baqir 🕮 in the eyes of Allah 🕮 and this had been a strategy for disseminating his leadership; and now that the opportunity had risen to testify to Imam al-Baqir's 🕮 Imamate, he did so.

One may rightly speculate that this political and emotional intelligence was a guidance from Imam al-Baqir 🕮 himself, and their private discussions were used to discuss the climate in Medina and how best to execute their responsibilities at that time. This is also because they were both aware of the narration from Imam Ali b. Abi Talib 🕮 which states that: "The one most aware of the circumstances of his time will not be surprised or overcome by the events therein."[444] This indeed is another great lesson to be learned from Jabir and his interactions with the Imam 🕮 of his time for those hoping to be companions of Imam al-Mahdi 🕮.

In this section we will mention some of the narrations of Imam al-Baqir 🕮 that Jabir then conveyed to others.

Hadith 1: Having Love for the Ahl al-Bayt

Jabir narrates from Imam al-Baqir 🕮 who narrates from his father Imam al-Sajjad 🕮, who narrates from his father Imam Husayn 🕮, who narrates from the Messenger of Allah, Prophet Muhammad 🕮 who said, "Having love for me and the members of my family will benefit a person in seven places when their state will be grievous: During death; in the grave; during the raising of the dead on the Day of Judgement; during the presenting of one's deeds; during the time of divine accountability and reckoning; at the scales; and at the bridge."[445]

Hadith 2: Death of the Scholars

Jabir narrates from Imam al-Baqir 🕮 who would say about his father, Imam Ali b. Husayn 🕮: "My soul shows generosity in accepting the quickening of death or being martyred. This is due to the Words of Allah when He says,

---

[444] The Arabic text of this passage reads:

أعرف الناس بالزمان، من لم يتعجّب من أحداثه

Ghurar al-Hikam, Hadith 3252.

[445] *Bashaaratu al-Mustafa li Shi'ati Murtadha*, Section 1, p. 29.

'Have they not considered that We have taken over the land and reduced its borders?' (13:41). The reference here is to the death of the scholars."[446]

Hadith 3: The Tax on Knowledge

Jabir narrates that Imam al-Baqir 🕮 said: "The tax on knowledge is teaching it to the servants of Allah."[447]

Hadith 4: Calmness Should Lead One To...

Jabir narrates from Imam al-Baqir 🕮 who said, "There is no one without the characteristics of excitement and calmness. But whoever's calmness leads one towards the ways (*sunnah*) of the Prophet 🕮 is rightly guided, but if it leads one towards innovations and heresy, then that person has gone astray."[448]

Hadith 5: Those who Believed and then Disbelieved

Jabir narrates, "I asked Muhammad b. Ali al-Baqir 🕮 about the following words of the Qur'an, 'Surely as for those who believe and then disbelieve' (4:137); to which he 🕮 replied, 'It is them (the *shaykhaan* – Abu Bakr and 'Umar), the third ('Uthman), the fourth (Mu'awiyah), Abd al-Rahman, and Talha. There were seventeen men mentioned in total.'"[449]

Hadith 6: The One Killed Unjustly

Jabir narrates from Imam al-Baqir 🕮, "The verse, 'And whosoever is killed unjustly, then we have indeed given his heir an authority, but let him not exceed the limits in killing. Indeed he is the helped' (17:33) was revealed

---

[446] *Al-Kafi*, vol. 1, Part 2, The Book on the Excellence of Knowledge, Chapter 7, The Loss of a Scholar, Hadith 6, p. 25.

[447] Ibid., Chapter 10, Giving Knowledge as Charity, Hadith 3, p. 27.

[448] Ibid., Chapter 22, Following the Sunnah and the Evidence of the Book, Hadith 10, p. 54.

[449] *Tafseer al-Burhan*, vol. 1, p. 267; *Tafseer al-Safi*, vol. 1, p. 237.

about the killing of Imam Husayn 🕮.[450] The 'helped' one in this verse refers to Husayn 🕮."[451]

Hadith 7: The Approaching Torment

Jabir narrates, "I asked Imam al-Baqir 🕮 about the words of Allah in the verse, 'So when they felt our approaching torment, lo! They began to flee from it.' (21:12) The Imam 🕮 replied, 'The approaching torment refers to the rising of the Qa'im (Imam al-Mahdi) 🕮.'"[452]

Hadith 8: Chastisement that will Befall

Jabir narrates, "Imam al-Baqir 🕮 asked me, 'How do the people read Surah al-Ma'arij?' I replied, they read it as: 'A demander demanded the chastisement that is to befall the disbelievers - which none shall be able to repel - from Allah, the Lord of the Ways of Ascent.' (70:1-3)

The Imam 🕮 replied, 'It should not be read as: 'A demander demanded the chastisement that is to befall.'[453] Rather it should be read, 'A flood will flow with a chastisement that is to befall.' This refers to the fire that will begin in Thawiyyah[454] and will reach the church of Banu Asad. Then it will continue until it reaches Banu Thaqeef. It will not leave anyone who participated in the spilling of the blood of the members of the family of the Prophet 🕮 without burning him.'"[455]

Hadith 9: To Establish the Truth

Jabir narrates, "I asked Imam al-Baqir 🕮 about the meaning of the verse, 'Allah intends to establish the Truth by His Words and to cut off the roots of the disbelieving rejectors.' (8:7) He 🕮 replied, 'The explanation of this verse is in its deeper meaning (ta'weel). It means that Allah intends something, but He has not done it as of yet. 'To establish the Truth by His

---

[450] *Tafseer al-Burhan*, vol. 4, p. 560.
[451] *Tafseer al-Ayyashi*, vol. 2, p. 290.
[452] *The Qa'im in the Qur'an*, p. 143. (add author if 1st time mentioned)
[453] This does not refer to the changing of the words of the verse, but rather the deeper meaning (ta'weel) of the verse.
[454] An area in Kufa where the companion Kumayl b. Ziyad is buried.
[455] No'mani, *al-Ghaybah*, p. 272.

Words' means that Allah will establish the right of the family of the Prophet ﷺ, and the meaning of 'His words' specifically refers to Ali b. Abi Talib ؑ; and 'To cut off the roots of the disbelieving rejectors' refers to the Banu Umayyah whose roots Allah will 'cut off.' 'In order that He may establish the Truth' (8:8) means that Allah will establish the right of the family of the Prophet ﷺ at the time of the rising of the Qa'im ؑ. 'And bring to naught what was false' (8:8). This means that when the Qa'im rises, he will destroy the falsehood of the Banu Umayyah. This is the meaning of the verse 'In order that He may establish the Truth and bring to naught what was false.' (8:8)'"[456]

Hadith 10: Ulul Azam Prophets

Jabir narrates from Imam al-Baqir ؑ, about the verse: "'Indeed we had made a covenant with Adam before, but he forgot; and We did not find in him any firm resolve.' (20:115) 'This verse means that Allah took a covenant with Adam about Prophet Muhammad ﷺ and the Divine Imams after him but Adam neglected the covenant. Adam did not have the 'firm resolve' to recognize the true status of Prophet Muhammad ﷺ and the Imams ؑ. The reason for giving the title of *Ulul Azam* - those with firm resolve - to the five *Ulul Azam* Messengers is that Allah took a covenant from them about Muhammad ﷺ, his successors ؑ, the Mahdi ؑ and his traditions. The *Ulul Azam* Prophets testified to this covenant and with a 'firm resolve;' they accepted the covenant as the Truth.'"[457]

Hadith 11: What is Al-Islam?

Jabir narrates from Imam al-Baqir ؑ, who narrates from his father Imam Zayn al-Abideen ؑ who narrates from Imam al-Husayn ؑ who said, "When the Messenger of Allah ﷺ fulfilled his rituals at the farewell hajj, he ﷺ mounted upon his ride and said: 'No one will enter paradise except for the one who is a Muslim!'

So Abu Dharr stood up and asked, 'O Messenger of Allah! What is al-Islam?' The Prophet ؑ replied: 'Al-Islam is bare - its clothing is piety; its

---

[456] *Tafseer al-Ayyashi*, vol 2. p. 45.

[457] *Tafseer al-Qummi*, p. 65; A similiar tradition is found in *Basa'ir al-Darajat fi Ulum al-Muhammad wa ma Khassahum Allah bihi*, of al-Saffar al-Qummi, p. 90.

adornment is bashfulness; its framework is devoutness; its beauty is dignity; and its fruit is righteous deeds. For everything there is a foundation and the foundation of al-Islam is having our - the People of the Household's - love.'"[458]

Hadith 12: Advice from Imam al-Baqir 🕮

Jabir narrates, "We visited Abu Ja'far Muhammad al-Baqir 🕮 and we were a group having fulfilled our hajj rituals. So we bid him farewell and said, 'Advise us, O son of the Messenger of Allah!' So he 🕮 said, 'Let your strong ones assist your weak ones, and let your rich ones be kind to your poor ones; and let man advise his brother like the advice to himself; conceal our secrets and do not load the people upon our necks. Look into our matter and whatever comes to you all from us- if you find it to be in accordance with the Qur'an, then take it; but if you do not find it in accordance with the Qur'an, then reject it.'

'If the matter is confusing to you, then pause during it and refer it to us so that we can explain it for you from that which has been explained to us. If you are like I am advising you to be, not having transgressed to something else, and one among you dies before the rising of our Qa'im, then know that he will be counted as a martyr; and the one from you who comes across our Qa'im and is killed with him, there will be for him the recompense of two martyrs. The one who kills an enemy of ours in front of him, will have for him the recompense of twenty martyrs.'"[459]

Hadith 13: Companions of the Right Hand

Jabir narrates from Imam al-Baqir 🕮, who narrates from Imam al-Sajjad 🕮, from Imam Husayn 🕮 that the Prophet 🕮 said to Ali b. Abi Talib 🕮, "Certainly you are the one for who Allah argues by in the beginning of creation when He gathered their resemblances. So He said to them, 'Am I not your Lord? They said: Yes!' (7:172) Then He said, 'And Muhammad is My Messenger?' They replied, 'Yes.' He said, 'And Ali is Master of the Believers?' However, the creatures in abundance refused and were arrogant,

---

[458] *Bashaaratu al-Mustafa li Shi'ati Murtadha*, Section 2b, p. 32, Hadith 102.
[459] Ibid., Section 3, pp. 4-5, Hadith 1.

and they transgressed about your authority except for a small number - and they were fewer than the few, and they are the companions of the right hand.'"[460]

Hadith 14: Who is a True Believer?

Jabir narrates from Imam al-Baqir ☖ that, "A man came over to the Prophet ☖ and said, 'O Messenger of Allah! Is everyone who says, 'There is no god except Allah' a true believer?' He ☖ replied, 'Enmity to us (Ahl al-Bayt) will join you with the Jews and the Christians. You will not enter Paradise until you love me. He has lied, the one who claims that he loves me but hates this one, meaning Ali b. Abu Talib.'"[461]

Hadith 15: Who are the Ahl al-Bayt ☖?

Jabir narrates from Imam Muhammad al-Baqir ☖ that "A man came over to him ☖ and said, 'Inform me about a tradition regarding you (Imams of Ahl al-Bayt ☖) in particular'. He ☖ said, 'We are the treasurers of the Knowledge of Allah, and the inheritors of the Revelation of Allah, and the bearers of the Book of Allah. Obedience to us is an obligation and love for us is faith, while hatred for us is hypocrisy. Those who love us will be in the paradise, and those who hate us will be in the Fire.'

'We were created by the Lord of the Ka'bah from the best clay (essence). None have been created from it besides us and those who love us have been created from a clay lower than that. When it will be the Day of Judgement, the lower will be joined with the higher. Therefore, how do you see Allah dealing with His Prophet and how do you see His Prophet dealing with his children? How do you see his children dealing with those who loved them and their Shi'a? All of them will be in the Gardens of the Lord of the worlds.'"[462]

---

[460] Ibid., p. 13, Hadith 5.
[461] Ibid., p. 16, Hadith 11.
[462] Ibid., Section 4, pp. 26-27, Hadith 42.

Hadith 16: People of the Right Hand

Jabir narrates that when he was sitting with Imam Muhammad al-Baqir 🕮 "A man recited the verses 'Every soul is held in pledge for what it earns. Except the people of the right hand.' (74:38-39). So another man asked, 'Who are the people of the right hand?' Imam al-Baqir 🕮 replied, 'The Shi'a of Ali b. Abi Talib.'"[463]

Hadith 17: Intercession in the Fire of Hell

Jabir narrates from Imam al-Baqir 🕮, "A servant will remain in the fire of hell for seventy *'khareyfas'* and each *'khareyf'* is seventy years. Then he will ask Allah, Mighty and Majestic, by the right of Muhammad 🕮 and the People of his Household 🕮, 'Have Mercy on me!' So Allah, Mighty and Majestic, will reveal unto the Arch-Angel Jibra'il, 'Descend to My servant and extract him from hell!' So Jibra'il will ask, 'O Lord! How can I descend into the Fire?' He 🕮 will respond, "I have commanded it to become a coolness and a safety for you.' So Jibra'il will reply, 'I have no knowledge of his location.' Allah 🕮 will say: 'He is in a pit in the blazing fire of Sijjeen.'

The Imam 🕮 continues, 'So Jibra'il will descend into the Fire and extract him.' Then Allah, Mighty and Majestic, will address him, 'O My servant! How much did you remain seeking Me whilst in the Fire?' He will reply, 'To the extent that I cannot count it, O Lord.' Allah will reply, 'I swear by My Might! Had you not asked Me by it (the intercession of the Prophet 🕮 and the Ahl al-Bayt 🕮), I would have prolonged your shame in it. But I have determined that a servant will not ask Me by the right of Muhammad and the People of his Household, except that I will forgive him whatever sins are between Me and him, thus I have forgiven you today!'"[464]

Hadith 18: Imam Ali 🕮 Reminds the People

Jabir narrates from Imam al-Baqir 🕮 who narrates from Abdullah b. 'Abbas who said, "I was at the door on the day of the consultation (to choose the third Caliph) and I heard Ali b. Abi Talib 🕮 saying, 'I advise you all to Allah,

---

[463] Ibid., p. 34, Hadith 57.
[464] Ibid., Section 7, p. 9, Hadith 11.

O you number who have gathered! Is there anyone among you to who the Messenger of Allah ﷺ had said, 'O Allah! Befriend the one who befriends him and be inimical to the one who is inimical to him' apart from me?' They all said, 'O Allah, no!'"[465]

Hadith 19: People who Take Heed

Jabir narrates about the words of Allah ﷻ in the Qur'an, "'Say, are those who know equal to those who do not know? Only the people of reason take heed,' (39:9) that Imam al-Baqir ﷺ said, 'It is a reference to us (the Ahl al-Bayt ﷺ). We are the people of knowledge and the people who do not know are our enemies, and our followers are the people who take heed and are the people of reason.'"[466]

Hadith 20: Prophet Ibrahim's ﷺ Stages

Jabir narrates, "I heard from Imam Abu Ja'far (al-Baqir) ﷺ who said, 'Allah chose Ibrahim as a servant before He chose him as a Prophet. He chose him as a Prophet before He chose him as a Messenger. He chose him as a Messenger before He chose him as a friend. He chose him as a friend before He chose him as an Imam.'

'When all of these conditions accumulated in him,' the Imam (al-Baqir) holding his hands said, 'Allah said, 'O Ibrahim, I have appointed you as the Imam of the people.'' The position was so great that Ibrahim asked, 'O Lord, can it (Imamate) be in my descendants also?' The Lord replied, 'My covenant will not be made available to the unjust ones.'"[467]

Hadith 21: Those in Error

Jabir narrates, "I heard Imam Abu Ja'far (al-Baqir) ﷺ say, 'Only those people recognise Allah, the Most Holy, the Most High, and worship Him, who are cognizant of Him and are cognizant of their Imam from the family of the Prophet ﷺ. Those who do not recognize Allah, the Most Holy, the Most High

---

[465] Ibid., p. 60, Hadith 52.
[466] *Al-Kafi*, vol. 1, Chapter 21, Hadith 1.
[467] *Al-Kafi*, vol. 1, Chapter 4, The Book about People with Divine Authority, Hadith 433, p. 139.

and do not recognize the Imams from us, such people only recognize and worship something other than Allah, and I swear by Allah, that they are in error.'"[468]

Hadith 22: Fortification Against Satan

Jabir narrates, "Imam Muhammad al-Baqir 🕮 once wanted to visit one of his followers because he was ill. He (the Imam) told me to accompany him and so I followed him. When he arrived at the sick person's door, his small son came out and so Imam al-Baqir 🕮 asked him, 'What is your name?' He replied, 'It is Muhammad.' The Imam asked, 'What is your title (kunya)?' to which he replied, 'It is Ali.'

The Imam 🕮 said, 'Indeed you have fortified yourself against Satan very well. When Satan hears someone calling 'O Muhammad, O Ali' Satan melts like lead until he hears someone calling with the names of our enemies, for then he becomes excited and boastful.'"[469]

Hadith 23: First Thing that Allah 🕮 Created

Jabir narrates from Imam al-Baqir 🕮, "Allah was present when nothing else existed. So the first thing that He began in creation was that He 🕮 created Prophet Muhammad, and then He created us the Ahl al-Bayt with him 🕮 from the greatness of his a divine light. So we were stationed as a green shadow before Him when there existed no sky, no land, no place, no night, no day, no sun and no moon."[470]

Hadith 24: The People of Reason

Jabir says about the verse, "Say, are those who know equal to those do not know? Do the people of reason take heed (39:9)" that Imam al-Baqir 🕮 said, 'It is a reference to us. We are the people of knowledge. The people who do

---

[468] Ibid., Hadith 463, p. 146.
[469] Ibid., vol. 6, Hadith 10308, Chapter 10, Hadith 12, p. 115.
[470] *Bihar al-Anwar*, vol. 25, p. 24;and vol. 15, p. 23.

not know are our enemies, and our followers are the people who take heed and are the people of reason.'"[471]

Hadith 25: The Qur'an

Jabir narrates from Imam al-Baqir ﷺ who said, "No one from the people claimed to have collected the whole of the Qur'an (in a book form) as it was revealed. If anyone makes such a claim, then he is a liar. No one collected this Book and memorized it as Allah revealed it, except Ali b. Abi Talib and the Imams after him."[472]

Hadith 26: The Entire Qur'an

Jabir narrates from Imam al-Baqir ﷺ who said, "No one is able to claim that with him is the whole of the Qur'an, its apparent and hidden essence, except the executors of the will of the Prophet ﷺ."[473]

Hadith 27: The Greatest Name of Allah

Jabir narrates that Imam al-Baqir ﷺ said, "The greatest name of Allah has seventy-three letters. There was only one of these letters with Asif (spoken about in the Qur'an 27:40). He spoke that one letter and the land between him and the throne of the Queen of Sheba sank down so much so that he could reach her throne with his hand and then the land returned to its original state. This happened in the twinkling of an eye. Among the greatest name of Allah there are seventy-two letters with us (the Ahl al-Bayt ﷺ). Allah has kept one letter exclusively for Himself in the knowledge of the unseen. There are no means and no powers except by the Help of Allah, the Most High, the Most Great."[474]

---

[471] *Al-Kafi*, The Book about People with Divine Authority, Chapter 21 'Those whom Allah has called the People of Knowledge in His Book, they are the Imams', Hadith 1, p. 180. A similar narration is mentioned in Hadith 2, but with a varying chain of narrators also from Jabir narrating from Imam al-Baqir ﷺ.

[472] Ibid., Chapter 35, 'No one collected all of the Qur'an Except the Imams and they have the Knowledge of all the Qur'an', Hadith 1, p. 194.

[473] Ibid., Hadith 2, p. 195.

[474] Ibid., Chapter 36, 'The Degree of the Great Names of Allah that are Given to the Imams', Hadith 1, p. 196.

Hadith 28: Fatima 🕮 on the Day of Judgement

Jabir said to Imam al-Baqir 🕮, "May I be sacrificed for you, O son of the Messenger of Allah! Narrate to me a hadith in relation to the superior status of your grandmother, Fatima, so that if I narrate it to the Shi'a (of the Ahl al-Bayt) they will become joyful." Imam al-Baqir 🕮 replied: "When my grandmother will reach the door of Heaven (on the Day of Judgement), she will stop and stare. Allah will say: 'O daughter of My beloved! What are you looking for, when I have ordered you to enter My Heaven?' She will reply: 'O my Lord! I would like that my value is known on a day like this.' Allah will say: 'O daughter of My beloved! Return back and look for anyone in whose heart there is love for you, or love for anyone from your progeny. Take him (or her) by the hand and enter him (or her) into Heaven.'" Imam al-Baqir 🕮 then continued: "By Allah, O Jabir! That day, she will pick up her Shi'a and those who love her, like a bird picks up the good grains from the bad ones. When her Shi'a will walk with her to the door of Heaven, Allah will inspire them to look back. When they look back, Allah will say: 'O My dear ones! What are you looking for, when Fatima, the daughter of My beloved has interceded for you?' They will answer: 'O our Lord! We would like that our value is known on a day like this.' Allah will reply back: 'O My dear ones! Return back, and see who loved you for the love of Fatima; and who fed you for the love of Fatima; and who clothed you for the love of Fatima; and who quenched your thirst for the love of Fatima; and who stopped backbiting against you for the love of Fatima? Take him (or her) by the hand and enter him (or her) into Heaven with you.'" Imam al-Baqir 🕮 said: "By Allah, nobody will remain behind among the people, except for one who doubted, a non-believer (*kafir*) or a hypocrite (*munafiq*)."[475]

Hadith 29: The Holy Spirit

Jabir narrates, "Once I asked Abu Ja'far (Imam al-Baqir) 🕮 about the knowledge of a scholar (an Imam from the Ahl al-Bayt). He said, 'O Jabir, in the Prophets and the executors of their will, there are five spirits. They are: the Holy Spirit, the Spirit of Belief, the Spirit of Life, the Spirit of Power, and

---

[475] *Musnad Fatima al-Zahra*, translated by Haider Ali Haider, Ansariyan Publications, pp. 146-155.

the Spirit of Desire. Through the Holy Spirit, O Jabir, they receive the knowledge of all that is below the Throne, as well as what is below the land.' He then said, 'O Jabir, these four spirits are the kind of spirits that may become affected by events that take place. Only the Holy Spirit is that which does not trifle and wander around.'"[476]

Hadith 30: The Unjust Leaders and their Followers

Jabir states, "Once I asked Abu Ja'far about the words of Allah, '...Certain people consider certain things equal to Allah and love them just as one should love Allah.' (2:165). The Imam said, 'They, by Allah, are friends of so and so and so and so, whom they have taken as their leaders instead of the leaders who are appointed for people by Allah. For this reason He has said, '...Had the unjust been able to reflect upon their condition when facing the torment, they would have had no doubt that to Allah belongs all power and that He is stern in His retribution.' (2:165) 'When the leaders see the torment and lose all of their resources, they will denounce their followers. The followers will say, 'If we had the chance we also would have denounced our leaders.' That is how Allah will show them their regrettable deeds. They will not be able to escape from the hellfire.' (2:166-167)

Then Abu Ja'far said, 'By Allah, O Jabir, they are the unjust leaders and their followers.'"[477]

Hadith 31: Words of Allah ﷻ

Jabir said the following quoting from the Imam ﷺ, "About the words of Allah, 'If they had done what they had been advised to do, [the Imam stated that this referred to acknowledging Ali's divine leadership], then it would have been better for their own good and to strengthen their faith.' (4:66)"[478]

---

[476] *Al-Kafi*, vol. 1, The Book about People with Divine Authority, Chapter 55, The Spirits that Exist in the Imams, Hadith 2, p. 236.

[477] Ibid., Part 4: The Book about People with Divine Authority, Chapter 85, About the unqualified claimant, Supporting Him or Rejecting a Certain or All of the Divine Imams, Hadith 11, p. 344.

[478] Ibid., Chapter 108, Enlightening Points Inferred from the Qur'an about Leadership with Divine Authority, Hadith 28, p. 389.

Imam al-Baqir's 🕮 private meeting with Jabir and revealing to him the secrets of the Ahl al-Bayt 🕮

Imam Ja'far al-Sadiq 🕮 narrates that: "One day my father (Imam al-Baqir 🕮) said to Jabir b. Abdullah, 'I need to speak with you privately.'

When my father 🕮 was alone with Jabir, he 🕮 said to him, 'Tell me about the tablet that my mother Fatima had.'"

Jabir then narrated to Imam al-Baqir 🕮, "Allah is my witness that I went to my lady and leader Fatima, daughter of the Messenger of Allah, to congratulate her on the birth of Imam Husayn. I saw a green tablet in her hand made of green aquamarine. There was something written on it with a light that was brighter than the sun, and the tablet, smelled better than the finest musk. I asked Lady Fatima, 'What is this tablet, O daughter of the Messenger of Allah?'

She replied, 'This tablet is a gift from Allah to my father. My father has ordered me to protect it, so I am doing that. It contains the names of my father, my husband and the names of his successors from sons after him.' I asked her to give it to me so I could make a copy of its contents and she accepted.'"

Imam al-Sadiq 🕮 continued, "Then my father (Imam al-Baqir 🕮) said to Jabir, 'Can you show me the copy that you made?' 'Yes', Jabir replied. So Jabir went to his house and brought a red piece of leather. My father said to him, 'Look at your copy to see if what I say matches your writing' and then Imam al-Baqir 🕮 read out what was on the tablet.

'In the name of Allah, the Most Gracious, the Most Merciful.

This is a letter from Allah, the Most Honourable, the Most Knowing and the Most Wise, which was sent with the Guardian Spirit to Muhammad, the last of the Messengers.

O Muhammad! 'Indeed the number of months with Allah is twelve months in Allah's book (since) the day He created the heavens and the earth. From among these, four are sacred. That is the established religion, so do not be unjust therein to yourselves.' (9:36)

O Muhammad, glorify My Names, be thankful for My Grace, and do not deny My Blessings. Do not desire anyone but Me, nor fear anyone but Me because those who desire anyone other than Me, or fear anyone but Me will be punished in a way that I have never punished anyone else from all of the worlds.

O Muhammad, I have chosen you from among all of the Prophets and I have given preference to your successor, Ali, above all of the successors.

I have made Hasan the container of My knowledge after the time of his father, and I have made Husayn the best of the sons from the first to the last and through Husayn the Divine Leadership will continue.

Ali, the beauty of the worshippers will remain from Husayn, and then it will be Muhammad the one who rips open My knowledge, the one who will invite people to My path through the right methods. Then it will be Ja'far the truthful in his speech and his actions, after whom there will be a deafening conspiracy.

Woe and more woe be upon those who deny My slave and the best of My creation, Musa.

Then Ali, the pleasant, will be killed by a disbeliever who is demon-like, and he will be buried in the city that was built by a righteous slave, next to the worst of Allah's creation.

Then Muhammad, the guide, the one who resembles his blessed grandfather will follow, then Ali the guide to My path, the one who safeguards My sanctity and leads My creation. After him it will be Hasan, the honourable who will leave behind him his son, Muhammad, the one with two names, who will rise at the end of time. There will be a white cloud over him to offer him shade from the sun.

Then a caller will call out with an eloquent voice which will be heard by everyone, everywhere, 'This is the Mahdi of the family of Muhammad.' He will fill the earth with justice, just as it was filled with injustice.'"[479]

The words that were read out by Imam al-Baqir 🖼 from the tablet exactly matched those that Jabir had copied out more than fifty years earlier.

Ayatollah Syed Taqi al-Modarresi's comments on this period of Imam Muhammad al-Baqir 🖼

In his historical review of the various Shi'a movements from the time of the event of Karbala to the occultation of Imam al-Mahdi 🖼, Ayatollah al-

---

[479] *Qaem in the Qur'an*, pp. 84-6.

Modarresi focuses heavily on the role of Imam al-Baqir 🕮 during his period of time. He says the following: "According to the consensus of historians, Imam Muhammad b. Ali al-Baqir 🕮 was the one who deduced (presented) the theory of Divine Imamate in its most complete form. This means that he made evident how there is an obligation of Divine leadership in Islam, who is the Imam, what is the need of an Imam, and his functions and responsibilities. He also made it clear how it is possible for man to reform himself and society.

(In the same period came) the emergence of various doctrines, in particular the Four Schools of Thought - approximately at the end of the period of Imam al-Baqir 🕮. There also were tens of other schools which began and then spread. Thus the Muslim community lived in confusion with ideas very distant to Islam, and became preoccupied with these matters. In that time, there was a need for a person of knowledge like Imam al-Baqir 🕮."[480]

Considering these particular challenges, the role of Jabir in assisting the Imam 🕮 to bring about the truth, and remove such confusions and misinformation, became all the more valuable. It might be for this reason we see the vast majority of Jabir's narrations are theological (*aqa'id*) or exegetical (*tafseer* or *ta'weel*) in nature as opposed to jurisprudentially based.

Assessing Kohlberg's Conclusions

Imam Muhammad al-Baqir's 🕮 narrating from Jabir b. Abdullah is certainly a historical anomaly from the Shi'a perspective. As Kohlberg states, "From purely the chronological point of view it is possible for al-Baqir to have obtained information about the Prophet's life and sayings from Jabir." From the Sunni vantage point, an upcoming jurist and commentator like Imam al-Baqir 🕮 would have needed to refer to Jabir considering his experience and proximity to the Prophet 🕮.

Kohlberg appears to have overlooked or not considered there being a chronology to the al-Baqir-Jabir relationship, as proposed above, instead pursuing a linear understanding of its historicity. By excluding the narrations of Jabir narrating from al-Baqir, and focusing primarily on al-Baqir narrating from Jabir, neither a shift within the paradigm or an

---

[480] *Tareekh al-Islami*, pp. 199-201.

equilibrium between the two sets of traditions can be found. The same can be said by discounting the wider trends of living under the Umayyad tyranny and Jabir's persistence in establishing the authority of the Ahl al-Bayt 🕮.

Three solutions to this unique set of traditions are offered by Kohlberg. The first, owing to Jabir's knowledge of the inner meaning of a particular verse of the Qur'an, as testified to by al-Baqir 🕮, demonstrates the extent of his knowledge entitling him to be narrated from. Given that Imam al-Baqir 🕮 met, interacted and lived along with several other leading elder companions of the Prophet 🕮 and Imam Ali 🕮 such as: Anas b. Malik, Abu Tufail 'Amr b. Wathila, Sahl b. Sa'd al-Saa'dee and Abu Umamah al-Bahili - all prolific narrators who were present at times of revelation or expeditions, it begs the question of why Imam al-Baqir 🕮 only narrated from Jabir? If "extensive knowledge, combined with a position of a renowned companion" were criterion, and given that he was belied by the people of Medina and perceived as being in need of bolstering his reputation, then al-Baqir 🕮 should have narrated from more companions than Jabir alone. But he 🕮 never testified to anyone else's knowledge of *ta'weel* - not just interpretation as some erroneously translate, but rather the primary, true meaning of a verse as intended by God Himself - from a non-infallible except for Jabir. When he was asked by a leading student of his, Zurarah b. A'yun, "What [special relationship] do you have with Jabir that leads you to relate [traditions] on his authority?" Imam al-Baqir 🕮 replied, "Jabir knew the [correct] interpretation (*ta'weel*)." This suggests that had al-Baqir 🕮 found another companion with knowledge of ta'weel he would have quoted from him as well. Kohlberg fails to account for the presence of such possibilities and so misreads the relationship between them. The aggregate of al-Baqir's narrations from Jabir suggest a wide range of knowledge. At times al-Baqir 🕮 was quoting theological, historical, spiritual and exegetical matters. Given his 🕮 position in the eyes of his followers, the Imam 🕮 narrating from Jabir was a tacit endorsement of the extent of the spheres of Jabir's knowledge. Its crown was testifying to his knowledge of ta'weel -something which is reserved for Allah ﷻ and the *Rasikhoona Fi al-'Ilm* – 'those endowed with special knowledge' - a supremely high station in Islamic theory.[481]

The second conclusion offered by Kohlberg is that narrating from Jabir allowed al-Baqir's ﷺ name to be dropped where necessary. This suggests a degree of protectionism at a time that rival sects could be identified by their theological, jurisprudential or social positions. Using Jabir's name may have allowed Imam al-Baqir ﷺ to offer his views on the authority of Jabir, protecting the Ahl al-Bayt ﷺ from retribution. If this is correct, it not only demonstrates the severity of oppression undergone by Imam al-Baqir ﷺ but in this context, how weighty the views of Jabir were in Medina that his testimony could weigh equally or greater than the other sects or movements. Jabir's words were weighty enough to be the source of one historical movement known as the Baqiriyyah, who based on a narration said to have been transmitted by Jabir, believed al-Baqir ﷺ to have not died, but rather to have gone into concealment, and that he was the awaited al-Mahdi and Saviour of Mankind.[482] Whilst there may be merit to this conclusion, it still considers Imam al-Baqir's ﷺ narrating from Jabir in isolation and not the subsequent shift in the opposite. Moreover, so long as Imam al-Baqir ﷺ was reliant on Jabir to rehabilitate his own reputation, he would never be able to lead the Muslim Ummah or his own family the Ahl al-Bayt ﷺ. Whilst Jabir was referred to as an authority, there was never a sect created behind him nor did he attempt to lead any group. Imam al-Baqir ﷺ oversaw the Alawite revolutions of the time and was considered the leader of the Ahl al-Bayt ﷺ in opposing the tyrant Banu Umayyad rule. To then consider Imam al-Baqir's ﷺ role with Jabir so one dimensionally excludes all other historical knowledge about the Imam ﷺ.

In the next conclusion Kohlberg notes Imam al-Baqir's ﷺ usage of Jabir's position to regain favour in the Medinan community. Wary of pseudo-scholars, views that drew the wrath of the government and were sources of violence, the people of Medina objected to al-Baqir ﷺ narrating directly from the Prophet ﷺ and Imam Ali ﷺ. Kohlberg understood this point well and invoked the usage of dissimulation or *taqiyyah* by al-Baqir ﷺ stating

---

[481] For further reading on *ta'weel* refer to *Usul al-Tafseer wa al-Ta'weel* of Kamal al-Hayderi; and vol. 1 of *Mutashabiha al-Qur'an wa Mukhtalifahu* by Ibn Shahr Ashoob.

[482] Al-Nawbakhti, Hasan b. Musa, *Firaq al-Shi'a*, p. 31.

that: "Al-Baqir was Jabir's mentor and not vice versa. Often times, Imam al-Baqir 🕮 would correct Jabir on various points and his corrections would automatically be amended. In one narration in which al-Baqir quoted from Jabir, he was made to add, 'And I did not refute Jabir.' [Prophet] Muhammad 🕮 is alleged to have told Jabir, 'Do not teach them [the Imams], for they are more knowledgeable than you.' Kohlberg does not entertain the idea that this practice was purposeful or strategic. Given Jabir's specific knowledge of al-Baqir's authority and experience of the evolving Medinan community, it is probable that this alliance was furtive and predetermined. Al-Baqir 🕮 and Jabir were astute in their caution and gradual shifting of what Medina saw in their relationship. Kohlberg also does not place his collection of narrations in a chronology, and therefore does not offer Jabir as a means of al-Baqir's 🕮 establishment as a Divine or rightful Imam.

The final solution to these unique narrations would be to deny their existence, or to suggest that their order may have been switched in the chain of narrations. This would be a problematic solution to the question of its place in the hadith corpus considering the numerous narrations of its nature and also supporting narrations, such as Imam al-Sadiq 🕮 explaining the dilemma faced by Medina in accepting his father's narrations and Zurarah's question to al-Baqir 🕮 as to why he transmits from Jabir.

Notwithstanding a radical solution, Kohlberg's first and third conclusions appear consistent with historical narratives and Shi'a doctrine. It does however, exclude a central element of the Shi'a doctrine in the Imams 🕮 perfection of decision making to reflect their circumstances and knowledge of the unseen. When considering these factors, the al-Baqir-Jabir relationship must be advantageous towards their mutual goals and not devoid of precise calculation. Kohlberg has however, raised points not necessarily studied before him and brought to light a delicate and fundamental issue overlooked by many a Shi'a scholar too. Seeing the question of these narrations through the lens of an evolution of events provides a fifth, most correct solution and that is that Jabir played the most pivotal role in establishing the Imamate of Imam al-Baqir 🕮.[483] This was purposeful, rooted in wisdom and avoiding both the rejection of Medina as

---

[483] Kohlberg, E. (1975), '*An Unusual Shi'i Isnad,*' Israel Oriental Studies 5, 1975, pp. 142-9.

a centre of learning and the wrath of government. It is well known that from here Imam al-Baqir ☷ lay the foundation for the first university in Islam, led by his son Imam as-Sadiq ☷. None of this would have been possible without Jabir's bringing to light the position of Imam al-Baqir ☷ in the way in which he did.

Another Effect of the Acceptance of Imam al-Baqir ☷ by the People of Medina

As introduced in this section, the people of Medina rejected Imam al-Baqir ☷ for his narrating from Prophet Muhammad ☷ directly. Through Jabir's efforts to demonstrate the Divine authority of the Imam ☷, the people of Medina changed their attitude and began accepting Imam al-Baqir's ☷ quoting of the Prophet ☷ by virtue of his position and knowledge. They now understood that an Imam ☷ could narrate from another infallible without having met them, as their speech is one, consistent with the other, and they were supremely aware of one another.

Given that the people were now able to understand this important aspect of theology, this allowed the subsequent Imams ☷ to be able to narrate from the Prophet ☷ or an earlier Imam ☷ without rejection or misunderstanding of this practice. This is often found in collections of Hadith literature. For example, Mufaddhal b. 'Umar narrates from Imam Ja'far al-Sadiq ☷, who said: "Amir al-Mo'mineen Ali ☷ would often say, 'I am the supervisor of Allah and will determine who should go to Paradise and who should go to Hell. I am the greatest criterion, the possessor of the staff (of Musa) and the *miysam* (marking seal). All of the angels, the spirit and the messengers have acknowledged the existence in me of all of the matters that they had acknowledged in Prophet Muhammad ☷. I am held responsible for all such matters for which Prophet Muhammad ☷ was held responsible. Such are my responsibilities to Allah, the Lord.'"[484]

This is another result of Jabir's efforts towards securing the proper understanding of the rights and positions of the Imams of Ahl al-Bayt ☷.

---

[484] *Al-Kafi*, The Book about People with Divine Authority, Chapter 14, 'Imams are Like the Cornerstone of the Earth,' Hadith 1, p. 163.

Jabir Narrating the Visitation Rights of Imam Ali ☝ from Imam Muhammad al-Baqir ☝

Due to the hatred towards Imam Ali ☝ created by the Banu Umayyah- for a long time after his martyrdom, the holy gravesite of Imam ☝ had been kept secret in order to protect it from desecration- be it verbal or of any other type. As the political situation began to shift during the period of Imam al-Baqir ☝ and Imam al-Sadiq ☝, companions began to inquire about its location. The Imams ☝ would visit the holy gravesite with their followers, teaching them the etiquettes and practices.[485]

Among the best recitations at the holy grave of Imam Ali ☝ is the *ziyarat* known as Ziyarat Ameenullah, which has been narrated by Jabir on the authority of Imam al-Baqir ☝ who stated that Imam Zayn al-Abideen ☝ stood at the tomb and recited the following:

"Peace be upon You, O the trustee of Allah on His earth, and His Proof over His servants. Peace be upon you, O Amir al-Mo'mineen. I bear witness that you strived in the way of Allah what is due, and you acted upon His Book, and followed the ways of His Prophet, blessings of Allah be on him and his family, until Allah called You to His side. So He took you to Him by His choice, and made incumbent upon your enemies the proof, with what you have of the considerable proofs, over all of His creations. O Allah, then make my soul: satisfied with Your decree, pleased with what You have destined for me, fond of Your remembrance and supplications, loving Your chosen friends, (let me be) well-liked on Your earth and in Your heavens, patient when You send down afflictions, grateful for Your gracious blessings, remembering Your abundant bounties, yearning for the happiness of meeting with You, equipped with piety for the day of Your reward, avoiding the manners of Your enemies, diverted from the (love of this) world by Your remembrance and Your praise."

Then the fourth Imam ☝ while resting his cheek on the grave of Imam 'Ali ☝ would recite:

---

[485] For the narrations see *Kamil al-Ziyarat*, Chapter 9 on The Location of the Grave of Amir al-Mo'mineen ☝, and Chapter 10 on The Reward for the Visitation of Amir al-Mo'mineen.

"O Allah, the hearts of those who humble themselves before You, are full of love. The paths of those who desire You are fixed. The signs for those who seek You are clear. The hearts of those who know You, are empty of other than You. The sounds of those who call You rise to You, and the gates of answers are open for them. The prayer of the one who whispers to You is answered. The repentance of the one who turns to You is accepted. The tears of the one who weeps in Your fear are dealt with mercifully. Help is available for the one who cries for help from You, and assistance is given generously to the one who seeks it. Your promises for Your servants are fulfilled. The errors of the one who seeks to reduce them, are reduced. The actions of the doers (of good deeds), are preserved with You, and the provision for Your creatures comes down. The promises of increase (in provision) reach them, the sins of those who seek forgiveness are forgiven. The needs of Your creatures are fulfilled. The rewards of the beseechers are available in plenty with You. The promises of increase are continuous. Wholesome food is prepared for the hungry, and drinks are filled for the thirsty. O Allah, so answer my prayer, and accept my praise. Unite me with my friends, for the sake of Muhammad, and Ali, and Fatima, and Hasan, and Husayn 🕮. Surely You are, the Master of my bounties, the object of my desires, the goal of my hopes, in my ultimate end and my stable abode. (O Allah), You are my God, my Lord, and my Master. Forgive (the sins of) our guardians, keep away our enemies from us, and divert them from troubling us. Let the word of Truth become manifest and make it supreme, and let the word of falsehood be refuted and make it low, Surely You have power over all things."[486]

Imam al-Baqir 🕮 is narrated to have then said, "Indeed, any one of our adherents who pronounce these words at the tomb of Amir al-Mo'mineen 🕮 or the tomb of any one of the Imams 🕮, will certainly have one's prayer lifted up on a ladder of light, carrying the seal of the Holy Prophet's ring, and it will be kept safe until it will be delivered to the Riser from Muhammad's Household (Imam al-Mahdi 🕮), who will receive the reciter of that prayer with good tidings, greetings, and honour."[487]

---

[486] Reference: http://www.duas.org/ziaratamenullah.htm
[487] *Mafatih al-Jinaan*, p. 698; *Misbah al-Mutahajjid*, p. 738; *Misbah al-Zaaer*, p. 474; and the *Mazaar* of Agha Jamaal Khwansaari, p. 98 with slight difference.

Chapter 14

A Collection of Narrations from Jabir

Introduction

As mentioned earlier, Jabir is considered to be one of Islam's most prolific narrators, be it about the Qur'an, from the Holy Prophet ﷺ or the Imams of Ahl al-Bayt ﷺ. Through them, he acquired great wisdom and insight and would teach what he learned. Jabir would also offer his advice to those attending his classes. For example, it is narrated that he used to say, "Attain knowledge, then acquire forbearance, then get more knowledge, then learn to practice and act according to the knowledge, then rejoice."[488]

A full eighty years in the service of the Holy Qur'an, the Messenger of Allah ﷺ and the immaculate family of the Prophet ﷺ ensured a blossoming of faith, knowledge and insight, to such an extent that when Jabir spoke, people gathered and trusted his speech. Therefore, Jabir would regularly hold seminars and lessons in the Masjid of the Prophet ﷺ.[489]

In this chapter we will mention some of the narrations by him.

---

[488] The Arabic text of this passage reads:

تعلموا العلم ثم تعلموا الحلم ثم تعلموا العلم ثم تعلموا العمل بالعلم ثم ابشروا

Reference: *Qasas al-Sahaaba wa al-Tabi'in*, p. 81.
[489] *Tahdhib al-Tahdhib*, vol. 2, p. 43; *Al-Isaba*, vol. 1, p. 214; *The Life of Imam Muhammad al-Baqir*, p. 490.

Hadith 1: Parents of Ammar

Jabir narrates that when the Prophet ﷺ passed by Ammar b. Yasir and his parents Yasir and Sumayya who were being tortured, he said, "O family of Yasir, know the glad tidings that your promised abode will be Paradise!" [490]

Hadith 2: Do not Eat with your Left Hand

Jabir narrates, "The Prophet ﷺ said, 'Do not eat with your left hand for Satan eats with his left hand.'"[491]

Hadith 3: Best Prayer

Jabir narrates, "The Prophet ﷺ was asked: 'Which prayer is best?' He said: 'That with the longest *qunut* (supplication).'"[492]

Hadith 4: Abandoning the Prayer

Jabir reports, "The Messenger of Allah ﷺ said, 'Between a person and disbelief (*kufr*) is abandoning the prayer.'"[493]

Hadith 5: Fasting on a Journey

Jabir states, "Allah's Apostle ﷺ was on a journey and saw a crowd of people and a man was being shaded by them. He asked, 'What is the matter?' They said, 'He (the man) is fasting.' The Prophet said, 'It is not righteousness that you fast on a journey.'"[494]

---

[490] Haythami, vol. 9, p. 293; *Hayat al-Sahaaba*, vol. 1, p. 301.
[491] *Sahih Muslim*, Book of Drinks (Kitab al-Ashriba), Hadith 5007.
[492] *Sunan Ibn Majah*, The Chapter of Establishing the Prayers and the Sunnah Regarding Them, Hadith 1421.
[493] Ibid., Hadith 1078.
[494] *Sahih al-Bukhari*, vol. 3, Book 31, Hadith number 167.

Hadith 6: Best Remembrance and Supplication

Jabir reports: "I heard the Messenger of Allah ﷺ saying, 'The best way to celebrate the remembrance (*dhikr*) of Allah is to say: '*La ilaha illallah*' and the best supplication (*du'a*) is '*Al-Hamdu Lillah.*'"[495]

Hadith 7: Intercession of the Prophet ﷺ

Jabir narrates from the Prophet ﷺ, "Whoever says the following supplication when he hears the call to prayer (*adhaan*), my intercession for him will be permitted on the Day of Resurrection: 'O Allah, Lord of this perfect call and the prayer to be offered. Grant Muhammad ﷺ the privilege of intercession and eminence, and resurrect him to the praised position that You have promised.'"[496]

Hadith 8: Spending in the Way of Allah ﷺ

Jabir states that the Prophet ﷺ said, "A person who spends in the way of Allah while he remains at home shall be rewarded with 700 dirhams for every dirham that he spends. But a person who goes out in the path of Allah and spends for His pleasure shall be rewarded with 700,000 dirhams for every dirham that he spends. The Prophet ﷺ then recited the verse 'Allah multiplies rewards for whomsoever He wills.'" (2:261)[497]

Hadith 9: Never Said No

Jabir narrates, "The Messenger of Allah ﷺ would never say 'no' in refusal to anything that was asked from him."[498]

---

[495] *Sunan Ibn Majah*, Kitab al-Adab, Baab Fadhl al-Hamideen, Hadith 3800; *Mustadrak Ala Al-Sahihayn*, Kitaab al-Dua wa al-Takbeer wa al-Tahleel wa al-Tasbeeh wa al-Dhikr, Hadith 1895.

[496] The Arabic text of this passage reads:

اللَّهُمَّ رَبَّ هَذِهِ الدَّعْوَةِ التَّامَّةِ، وَالصَّلاةِ الْقَائِمَةِ، آتِ مُحَمَّدًا الْوَسِيلَةَ وَالْفَضِيلَةَ، وَابْعَثْهُ مَقَامًا مَحْمُودًا الَّذِي وَعَدْتَهُ

Reference: *Sunan Ibn Majah*, Chapters on the Adhaan and the Sunnah of it, Hadith 722.

[497] *Jaami' al-Fawaa'id*, vol. 2, p. 3; *Hayaat al-Sahaaba*, vol. 1, p. 482.

[498] *Al-Bidaayah wa al-Nihaayah*, vol. 6, p. 42.

Hadith 10: Seeking Knowledge

Jabir states, "Do not seek knowledge in order to show off in front of the scholars, or to argue with the foolish; and do not choose the back seat in a gathering of knowledge (purposely distancing yourself from it haughtily), for whoever does that, the Fire awaits him."[499]

Hadith 11: Best Marriage

Jabir narrates, "I attended the marriage ceremony of Imam Ali ☙ and Lady Fatima ☙ and I have not witnessed a better marriage than theirs. The matting on which we sat was stuffed with the bark of a date palm and we were served raisins and dates to eat. Her bedding on her first night was a sheepskin."[500]

Hadith 12: Ring on Right Hand

Jabir narrates, "The Prophet ﷺ used to wear a ring on his right hand."[501]

Hadith 13: Dua for the Last Friday

Jabir narrates, "I went to the Prophet ﷺ on the last Friday of the month of Ramadaan. As soon as he saw me he said, 'This is the last Friday of the month of Ramadaan, therefore bid it farewell. A person who recites this supplication on this day will get either one of these two good things: Either he will live until the next month of Ramadaan, or the Lord will grant him pardon and mercy.' He ﷺ then taught me the supplication which is: 'O Allah, do not make this month of Ramadaan as the last period of our fasting; and if You have decided it as so, then make me a recipient of Your Mercy and do not make me among the sinners.'"[502]

---

[499] *Sunan Ibn Majah*, The Book of the Sunnah, Hadith 254.

[500] Haythami, vol. 9, p. 209.

[501] *Shamaa'il*, Chapter of the Prophet Wearing a Ring, Tirmidhi, Hadith 4.

[502] The Arabic text of this passage reads as follows:

اَللّٰهُمَّ لَا تَجْعَلْهُ آخِرَ الْعَهْدِ مِنْ صِيَامِنَا إِيَّاهُ فَإِنْ جَعَلْتَهُ فَاجْعَلْنِي مَرْحُوماً وَلَا تَجْعَلْنِي مَحْرُوماً

Reference: Amili, al-Hurr al-, *Wasa'il al-Shi'a*, vol. 10, p. 365.

Hadith 14: The Illuminating Light of Fatima 🌸

Imam Hasan al-Askari 🕊 reports from his fathers, who quote Jabir b. Abdullah al-Ansari, who is narrated to have said, "The Messenger of Allah 🌸 stated: 'When Allah created Adam and Hawwa, they walked through paradise and asked, 'Who could be better than us?' At that moment, they saw an image of a radiant woman, the like of which they had never seen before. From this woman there was an illuminating light that beamed so bright that it almost blinded the eyes. They asked, 'O Lord, who is this?' Allah 🌸 answered, 'This is the image of Fatima, the leader of your female descendants.'"[503]

Hadith 15: Facing the Qiblah

Jabir states, "Abu Sa'id al-Khudri narrated to me, that he bears witness that the Messenger of Allah 🌸 forbade facing the *qiblah* (direction of *Ka'bah*) when defecating or urinating."[504]

Hadith 16: The Blessed Ones

Jabir narrates from Prophet Muhammad 🌸, "Blessed are those who are patient during his (Imam al-Mahdi's 🕊) lengthy occultation. Blessed are those who stay steady in their love for him. They are those whom Allah describes in His book as 'those who believe in the unseen' (2:3). 'They are the party of Allah. Verily the party of Allah are the successful ones.' (58:22)" [505]

Hadith 17: The Path of Allah 🌸

Jabir narrates, "We were with the Prophet 🌸 and he drew a line in the sand. He then drew two lines to its right and two to its left. Then he put his hand on the middle line and said: 'This is the path of Allah.' Then he recited the verse 'And verily, this (Allah's religion) is My straight path, so follow it and

---

[503] *Lisan al-Mizan*, vol. 3, p. 346.
[504] *Sunan Ibn Majah*, The Chapter on Purification and its Practices, Hadith 320.
[505] *Tafseer al-Burhan*, vol. 1, p. 125.

follow not other paths, for they will separate you away from His path.'
(6:153)"[506]

Hadith 18: Sleeping too Much

Jabir reports, "The Messenger of Allah ﷺ said, 'The mother of Prophet
Sulaiman b. Dawud ﷺ said to him, 'O my son, do not sleep too much at
night, for sleeping too much at night will leave a man poor on the Day of
Resurrection.'"[507]

Hadith 19: Seeking the Best from Allah

Jabir mentions, "The Messenger of Allah ﷺ used to teach us the *istikharah*,
just like he used to teach us a surah of the Qur'an. He said: 'If anyone of you
is deliberating about a decision one has to make, then let him pray two units
of non-obligatory prayer, then say the following supplication and mention
your needs:

'O Allah, I seek Your guidance (in making a choice) by virtue of Your
knowledge, and I seek ability by virtue of Your power, and I ask You of Your
great bounty. You have all of the power, while I have none; and You know,
while I do not know. You are the Knower of hidden things. O Allah, if in
Your knowledge, if this matter (then it should be mentioned by name) is
good for me and for my religion, my livelihood and my affairs, both in this
world and in the Hereafter - then ordain it for me, make it easy for me, and
bless it for me. But if in Your knowledge, it is bad for me, then turn it away
from me and turn me away from it, and ordain for me the good wherever it
may be and make me pleased with it.'"[508]

---

[506] *Sunan Ibn Majah*, The Book of the Sunnah, Hadith 11.
[507] Ibid., The Chapter on Establishing the Prayers and the Sunnah Regarding Them,
Hadith 1332.
[508] *Sunan Ibn Majah*, The Chapter on Establishing the Prayers and the Sunnah
Regarding Them, Hadith 1383. The Arabic text of this passage reads:

اللَّهُمَّ إِنِّي أَسْتَخِيرُكَ بِعِلْمِكَ وَأَسْتَقْدِرُكَ بِقُدْرَتِكَ وَأَسْأَلُكَ مِنْ فَضْلِكَ الْعَظِيمِ فَإِنَّكَ تَقْدِرُ وَلَا أَقْدِرُ وَتَعْلَمُ وَلَا
أَعْلَمُ وَأَنْتَ عَلَّامُ الْغُيُوبِ اللَّهُمَّ إِنْ كُنْتَ تَعْلَمُ أَنَّ هَذَا الْأَمْرَ خَيْرٌ لِي فِي دِينِي وَمَعَاشِي وَعَاقِبَةِ أَمْرِي أَوْ قَالَ
عَاجِلِ أَمْرِي وَآجِلِهِ فَاقْدُرْهُ لِي وَيَسِّرْهُ لِي ثُمَّ بَارِكْ لِي فِيهِ وَإِنْ كُنْتَ تَعْلَمُ أَنَّ هَذَا الْأَمْرَ شَرٌّ لِي فِي دِينِي وَمَعَاشِي
وَعَاقِبَةِ أَمْرِي أَوْ قَالَ فِي عَاجِلِ أَمْرِي وَآجِلِهِ فَاصْرِفْهُ عَنِّي وَاصْرِفْنِي عَنْهُ وَاقْدُرْ لِيَ الْخَيْرَ حَيْثُ كَانَ ثُمَّ أَرْضِنِي

Hadith 20: The Prophet's ﷺ Prayers

Jabir narrates, "The Prophet ﷺ used to offer the *nawafil* (supererogatory prayers), even while riding, and facing a direction other than that of the qiblah."[509] Jabir also mentions that the Prophet ﷺ would face East if possible, but for compulsory prayers would dismount and ensure that he faced the Ka'bah.[510]

Hadith 21: Five Daily Prayers

Jabir narrates that the Prophet ﷺ said, "The similitude of the five daily prayers is like an overflowing river passing by the gate of your house. A person who washes oneself five times a day from that river will have no filthiness remain on him."[511]

Hadith 22: Saving Oneself from the Fire

Jabir reports from the Prophet ﷺ, "There is no action more effective in saving oneself from the fire of hell than the remembrance of Allah (*dhikr*). Someone asked, 'Not even fighting in the path of Allah?' The Prophet ﷺ replied, 'Not even fighting in the path of Allah unless one fights until his sword breaks.'"[512]

Hadith 23: Remembrance of Allah ﷻ

Jabir states that the Prophet ﷺ came to the community and said, "O people, Allah has groups of angels who descend and remain amongst the gatherings where the remembrance of Allah (*dhikr*) is taking place on the earth. You should therefore eat from the gardens of Paradise." The companions asked the Prophet ﷺ, "Where are the gardens of Paradise?" The Prophet ﷺ responded, "They are the gatherings of *dhikr*. You should spend part of your day in the remembrance of Allah and regularly remind yourself of Him. A person who wishes to know one's status in Allah's estimation should see

---

[509] *Sahih al-Bukhari*, The Chapter on Shortening the Prayers, Hadith 199.
[510] Ibid., Hadith 203.
[511] *Sahih Muslim*, The Book of Prayers, Book 4, Hadith 1411.
[512] Haythami, vol. 10, p. 74.

what Allah's status is in His estimation. This is because Allah only grants a servant that status in His sight that the servant grants to Allah in his sight."[513]

Hadith 24: Recitation of Surahs before Sleeping

Jabir narrates, "The Prophet ﷺ would not go to sleep until he had recited Surah al-Sajdah and Surah al-Mulk."[514]

Hadith 25: Cleanliness

Jabir narrates, "The Prophet ﷺ visited us and he saw an unkempt, untidy man whose hair was disheveled, so he said, 'Did this man not find anything with which to tame his hair?' He then saw another man who was wearing dirty clothes, so he said, 'Did this man not have any water to wash his clothes?'"[515]

Hadith 26: First Thing Allah ﷻ Created

Jabir states, "I said to the Prophet ﷺ, 'What was the first thing created by Allah?' He replied, 'The Divine light of your Prophet, O Jabir. Allah created it and then He created from it every goodness.'"[516]

Hadith 27: Spending the Night

Jabir reported the Messenger of Allah ﷺ as saying, "Behold, no person should spend the night with (in the company of) a married woman, except if he is married to her or he is her mahram (someone from the kin who it is prohibited to marry)."[517]

---

[513] Ibid., vol. 10, p. 77.
[514] *Hayaat al-Sahaaba* , vol. 3, p. 329.
[515] *Sunan Abi Dawud*, Hadith 4062.
[516] *Bihar al-Anwar*, vol. 25, p. 21.
[517] *Sahih Muslim*, Book 26, The Book of Salutations and Greetings (Kitab al-Salaam) Hadith 5399.

Hadith 28: An Equal Response

Jabir b. Abdullah reported that: "Some people from among the Jews said to Allah's Messenger ﷺ Abul-Qasim! *As-Samu 'Alaykum*, whereupon he replied: '*Wa 'Alaykum.*' 'Aisha was enraged and asked him (Allah's Apostle ﷺ) whether he had not heard what they had said. He ﷺ said, 'I did hear and I retorted to them (and what I invoked upon them will receive response from Allah), but (what they invoked upon us) will not be answered.'"[518]

Hadith 29: Two Types of Brethren

Jabir narrates on the authority of Abi Ja'far al-Baqir ﷺ that a man went to Basra to see the Commander of the Faithful Imam 'Ali ﷺ and said, "O Commander of the Faithful! Please inform me about my brethren." The Commander of the Faithful ﷺ replied, "There are two types of brethren: sincere ones and hypocrites. The sincere brethren are similar to one's hands, wings, and property. Once you find a sincere brother, do not hesitate to help him with your life and wealth. Be friends with his friends and be an enemy to his enemies. Cover up his flaws, and express his good deeds. However, you who are asking should know that such friends are as scarce as red matches are. Then about the hypocrites, you should only associate with them on the surface as they do with you. You should not expect anything else from them. Treat them just as they treat you in terms of being polite and talking pleasantly with them."[519]

Hadith 30: People are of Two Groups

Jabir narrates on the authority of Abi Ja'far al-Baqir ﷺ that the Messenger of Allah ﷺ said, "People are in two groups: those who get relieved by others and those from whom others are relieved. Those who get relieved are the believers. Once they die they are relieved of this world and its calamities. Those from whom others get relief are the unbelievers. Once they die, the trees, animals and many of the people will become relieved of them."[520]

---

[518] Ibid., Hadith 5388.
[519] *Al-Khisal*, al-Sadooq, On 'two' numbered characteristics, Hadith 55.
[520] Ibid., Hadith 21.

Hadith 31: What the Prophet ﷺ Feared the Most

Jabir b. Abdullah said that the Messenger of Allah ﷺ as having said, "What I am most afraid of for my nation is unattainable aspirations and unreachable hopes. Aspirations hinder one from the truth and unreachable hopes will make one forget the Hereafter. The life in this world will end while the life in the Hereafter is still ahead of you. Each life has its own children. Try to be among the children of the Hereafter if you can. Try not to be from the children of this world. Today you are alive, can do things and there is no Reckoning. However, tomorrow you will die and will be in the World of Reckoning where you cannot do anything.[521]

Hadith 32: Remember Satan in Three Situations

Jabir said that Abi Ja'far al-Baqir ﷺ said, "When Nuh ﷺ prayed to his Lord - the Honorable the Exalted Allah - and cursed his nation, Satan said, 'O Nuh! I am indebted to you and wish to give you a reward.' Nuh said, 'I swear by Allah that you do not owe me anything. What could it be?' Satan replied, 'I am indebted to you since you did me a favour by your praying to Allah to drown everyone in your nation. Now until there comes another generation, no one is left for me to lead him astray.' Nuh said, 'Yes. What reward do you want to give me?' Satan replied, 'Remember me in three situations where I am the closest to my servants: whenever one gets angry; whenever a person wants to judge between two people; and remember me whenever you are left alone with an unfamiliar (non-*mahram*) woman."[522]

Hadith 33: Three Things That will Complain on the Day of Judgement

Jabir says, "I heard the Messenger of Allah ﷺ say: 'Three things will complain to the Honourable, Exalted Allah on the Day of Resurrection: the Qur'an; the *masjid*, and my household. The Qur'an will say, 'O Lord! They misinterpreted me and tore me up.' The *masjid* will say, 'O Lord! They left me unused and wasted me.' Finally, my household will say, 'O Lord! They

---

[521] Ibid., Hadith 62.
[522] On 'three' numbered characteristics, Hadith 140.

killed us. They deported us. They made us homeless." The Prophet ﷺ continued: 'I will sit down to judge this case.' However, Allah - may His Majesty be Exalted – will say, 'I deserve more to do this.'"[523]

Hadith 34: Allah Forgives one who Takes it Easy in Four Issues

Jabir b. Abdullah said that the Messenger of Allah ﷺ said, "The Honourable, Exalted Allah will forgive one who takes it easy whenever he sells, buys, judges or has a demand."[524]

Hadith 35: Five Exclusive Things for the Prophet's ﷺ Nation

Jabir b. Abdullah quotes the Messenger of Allah ﷺ as having said: "My nation has been granted five things in the month of *Ramadan* which have not been granted to the followers of any of the previous prophets. First of all, the Honourable, Exalted Allah would take a look at his nation on the first night of the month of *Ramadan*. He will never torture those upon whom He looks. Secondly, the smell of the mouth of those who fast is better than the smell of musk to the Honourable, Exalted God. Thirdly, the angels pray and ask for their forgiveness day and night. Fourthly, the Honourable, Exalted One orders Paradise to ask for Allah's forgiveness for Muhammad's nation and to adorn itself the Almighty's servants so that the hurt and harm of this world is removed from them once they see it. The fifth is that they will all be forgiven on the last night of the month of *Ramadan*."

Someone said, "O Prophet of Allah! How about the Night of Power (*Laylatul Qadr*)?" The Prophet ﷺ replied, "Have you not seen that labor workers are paid off when they finish their work?"[525]

---

[523] Ibid., Hadith 232.
[524] On 'four' numbered characteristics, Hadith 6.
[525] Ibid., Hadith 102.

Hadith 36: Nine Things Granted to the Followers of Ali b. Abi Talib 🕮

Jabir b. Abdullah al-Ansari said, "One day I was with the Prophet 🕮 when suddenly he turned his face towards Ali b. Abi Talib 🕮 and said, "O Aba al-Hasan! Do you want me to give you glad tidings?" (Imam) Ali 🕮 replied: "Yes, O Prophet of Allah!" The Prophet 🕮 continued, "Allah - may His Majesty be Exalted - informed me through Jibra'il that He granted nine things to your lovers and your followers. They will have: gentle treatment at the time of death; a companion at times of fear; light at times of darkness; security at the time of resurrection; justice at the time of reckoning; permission to pass through the passage (to Heaven); entry to Heaven before other people; the light (of their faith) will be shining in front of them and on their right side."[526]

Hadith 37: A Servant in the Fire of Hell for Seventy Lifetimes

Jabir narrates that Abi Ja'far al-Baqir 🕮 said, "A servant of Allah will stay in the fire for seventy lifetimes - each lifetime being seventy years. Then he will call out to the Honourable, Exalted Allah by Muhammad and his Holy Household to have mercy upon him. Then the Honourable, Exalted Allah will reveal to Jibra'il to go to His servant and take him out (of Hell). Then Jibra'il will ask, 'O my Lord! How can I descend into Hell?' Allah will say, 'I shall make the fire cool and (a means of) safety for you.' Jibra'il will ask, 'O my Lord! I do not know where he is?' Allah will reply: 'He is imprisoned in a pit.' Jibra'il will cover up his face, descend into Hell and pull him out.

Then the Honourable, Exalted Allah will say, 'O My servant! For how long did you stay in the Fire and call out to Me?' The servant will reply, 'O my Lord! You know best.' Allah will answer: 'I swear by My Majesty that I will forgive all of the sins of My servants who call Me through Muhammad and his Holy Household to have mercy upon them - all that only they themselves and I know about. I forgive your sins today.'[527]

---

[526] Ibid., On 'nine' numbered characteristics, Hadith 2.
[527] Ibid., On 'seventy' numbered characteristics, Hadith 9.

Hadith 38: What is Recorded on the Door of Paradise

Jabir narrates that Messenger of Allah ﷺ said, "2,000 years before the creation of the heavens and the Earth it was recorded on the door of Paradise, '*La illaha illa Allah 'Muhammadan Rasul Allah Ali Akhu Rasul Allah*' meaning that: 'There is no god but Allah, Muhammad is Allah's Prophet, and Ali is the brother of Allah's Prophet.'"[528]

---

[528] Ibid., On 'one thousand or more' number characteristics, Hadith 1.

Chapter 15

Death of Jabir b. Abdullah al-Ansari

Jabir's life can be seen as the epitome of a life spent in service of the Holy Thaqalayn that is the Qur'an and the Ahl al-Bayt 🕮. He had seen before him the foundations of Islam and been a part of them through his commitment and belief. He also saw its growth from a religion of worship of the One God, a road towards piety, social reform and intellectual inquiry - to it becoming an empire and pawn in the hand of corruption, murder and greed. Jabir also witnessed the Divine leadership of five Imams 🕮 after the Prophet 🕮 and the way that they steered Islam throughout its shifting circumstances.

Being the last living companion of Prophet Muhammad 🕮 gave Jabir a unique and prestigious position in the community. It also allowed him to reflect deeply upon the lives, actions and deaths of each of the companions that went before them. Companions like Ammar b. Yasir who died on the battlefield; Abu Dharr who was excommunicated and left in the harshest of circumstances to live out his last days; and 'companions' like Mu'awiyah b. Abi Sufyan who rose up against the just and Divine Imams 🕮 pulling other companions towards themselves. Therefore, Jabir was able to make a choice about what kind of death he desired.

Much of the last years of his life were spent seeking knowledge and further development at the nurturing hands of Imam Muhammad al-Baqir 🕮. As part of that preparation, many discussions included issues of old age, attitude towards life, sickness and death. For example, Jabir narrates from Imam al-Baqir 🕮, "Whoever carries the *janaaza* (coffin/burial procession) from any of its four sides, Allah will forgive that person forty of his great sins."[529]

Jabir also appeared to increase his mentioning of Imam al-Mahdi 🕮, calling towards his Divine and just rule as a means of reminding the community that the tyrants in charge will never be successful anyhow. For example, it is narrated that: "The Messenger of Allah 🕮 has said, 'There will be caliphs after me, and after the caliphs, there will be emirs and after the emirs there will be tyrant kings. Then the Mahdi from my household will rise. He will fill the earth with justice as it was replete oppression."[530]

Imam al-Baqir 🕮 used to come and visit Jabir regularly out of respect for his companionship with the Messenger of Allah 🕮 and companionship to the Imams of Ahl al-Bayt 🕮. Jabir also used to come to Imam al-Baqir 🕮 at both parts of the day (morning and evening) to learn from him. This continued until one day when they met, Imam al-Baqir 🕮 looked at him and said, "O Jabir, execute your will because soon you will be travelling to your Lord."

Then Jabir began to cry and said, "O my master, how do you know about that, this was a pledge which had been given to me by the Messenger of Allah 🕮." The Imam 🕮 replied, "I swear by Allah, O Jabir, that Allah has given me the knowledge of what has happened (in the past), what is happening now, and what shall happen until the Day of Judgement."[531]

Towards Paradise: The End of His Life and Death

During the Marwanid dynasty, Hajjaaj b. Yusuf al-Thaqafi ruled Iraq and Khorasan (Iran) from 75-95 A.H. In the preceding years, the only Muslim lands independent of Marwanid rule was Hijaz (Mecca and Medina), which was ruled by Abdullah b. Zubayr. In order to capture it, the then Caliph Abdul Malik b. Marwan, sent Hajjaaj in 73 A.H. to conquer Mecca, the second Umayyad military expedition to conquer Hijaz after the infamous attack known as the Battle of Harra Waaqim which took place on the 27th of Dhu al-Hijjah, 63 A.H.[532] Following the first attack, catapults and other

---

[529] *Wasaa'il al-Shi'a*, vol. 3, p. 153.

[530] Al-Majlisi, *Bihar al-Anwar*, vol. 51, The Book of Occultation, p. 164.

[531] *Noor al-Absaar*, Sheikh Muhammad Mahdi al-Mazandarani, p. 44.

[532] For further reading, refer to *Ansab al-Ashraf* of Al-Baladhuri, vol. 4 p., 31; *Tareekh al-Ya'qubi*, vol. 2, p. 250; *Tareekh al-Tabari*, vol. 4, p. 368.

defensive features were installed forcing Hajjaaj to extend a lengthy blockade against the people Mecca eventually capturing the city.

Subsequently, Hajjaaj turned his attention to Medina in the year 74 A.H. When he arrived to the city, amongst his first targets were the remaining companions of Prophet Muhammad ﷺ who would no doubt reject and fight the city's capture. Therefore, Hajjaaj physically attacked many of the remaining companions including Malik b. Anas, Sahl b. Sa'ad and Jabir b. Abdullah al-Ansari.[533] Al-Tabari says: "(Hajjaaj) was completely disregarded in the city by the companions of the Prophet ﷺ. He (Hajjaaj) tied them by the neck. Muhammad b. 'Imraan b. Abi Dhi'b states regarding Jabir b. Abdullah al-Ansari that he had his hands tied."[534]

By this time Jabir had again lost his sight and was in his late eighties or early nineties. As much as Jabir, a warrior never shy of martyrdom, wanted to rise up, it was out of his capacity. In fact anyone who rose up would immediately have been put to death as per the famous statement of Abdul Malik that: "I swear by God, if anyone enjoins me to fear Allah, I will break his neck."[535]

Hajjaaj was known to have tortured Jabir b. Abdullah. Historian Ibn Khallakaan states, "Many a story has been recounted about the massacre and torture done by Hajjaaj that were unparalleled."[536] Suyuti wrote, "He massacred countless numbers of the Prophet's ﷺ companions and the second generation of Muslims let alone others.[537] He even made gashes on the neck of Anas b. Malik and others." During this period many uprisings against Hajjaaj occurred under various banners including the mainstream Muslims, Shi'ites and Khawarij.

Hajjaaj took a particular scorn with the Shi'a of Imam al-Baqir ﷺ. The Imam ﷺ is narrated to have said that the words 'Shi'a of Ali' was less

---

[533] *Tareekh al-Tabari*, vol. 5, p. 292; *Tareekh al-Khulefa*, p. 215.
[534] The Arabic text of this passage reads:

استخف فيها باصحاب رسول الله ، فختم في اعناقهم ، فذكر محمد بن عمران بن ابي ذئب حدثه عمن رأى جابر بن عبد الله مختوما في يد.

[535] The Arabic text of this passage reads:

والله لا يأمرني أحد بتقوى الله بعد مقامي هذا إلا ضربت عنقه.

Tareekh al-Khulefa, p. 218
[536] *Wafayat al-A'yan*, vol. 2, p. 31.
[537] *Tareekh al-Khulefa*, p. 221.

tolerable to Hajjaaj than the words polytheist or atheist.[538] Hajjaaj would summon the Shi'as to Iraq for as little as publicly announcing that Imams Hasan 🕮 and Husayn 🕮 were the descendants of Prophet Muhammad 🕮.[539] The family of the Prophet 🕮 and his closest followers were so harshly treated that they even faced starvation.[540]

Understanding the pressures and tortures that Hajjaaj laid upon Jabir also has a significant role in the belief system (*aqa'id*) of the Muslims. In a lengthy narration in which Imam Ali b. Musa al-Ridha 🕮 details who should be disavowed and why, he 🕮 mentions about the attacks on companions like Jabir, stating that: "It is also obligatory to disavow (perform *bara'a* with) those who fought against the Commander of the Faithful (Imam Ali 🕮), killed the Ansar, the Muhajireen, the noble ones and the good doers from the past. As well friendship (*tawalla*) with the Commander of the Faithful (Imam Ali 🕮), and with those who followed the way of the Prophet 🕮 and who did not change their way... is obligatory. Further, the friendship with their followers who have been guided along their path - may Allah be pleased with them – is also obligatory."[541]

In fact, Imam Ja'far al-Sadiq 🕮 names Jabir as one of those companions obligated to love, saying, "It is obligatory to hate all of those who murdered the members of the household of the Prophet 🕮. It is obligatory to love those believers who did not turn away from the religion after the demise of the Prophet 🕮 such as: Salman al-Farsi; Abu Dharr al-Ghiffari; Miqdaad b. al-Aswad al-Kindi; Ammar b. Yasir; Jabir b. Abdullah al-Ansari; Hudhayfah b. al-Yaman; Abi al-Haytham b. Tayhan; Sahl b. Hanif; Abi Ayoob Al-Ansari; Abdullah b. Samit; Ibadat b. Samit; Khuzayma b. Thabit Dhu al-Shahadatayn; Abi Sa'id al-Khudri; and others who followed their way and acted as they did. It is obligatory to love those who used them as their models and followed them."[542]

It was in this state of physical and political pressure that Jabir had one of his last, but most profound, interactions with Imam al-Baqir 🕮. Throughout

---

[538] *Sharh Nahj al-Balaghah*, Ibn Abi al-Hadeed, vol. 2, p. 44.
[539] Ibn Khallakaan, *Wafayaat al-A'yan*, vol. 6, p. 147.
[540] Ibid., vol. 7, p. 106.
[541] Al-Sadooq, *Uyoon Akhbar al-Ridha*, vol. 2, Chapter 35, Hadith 1, p. 262.
[542] *Al-Khisal*, al-Sadooq, On 'One to One Hundred' numbered characteristics, Hadith 13.

his life, Jabir had demonstrated acquiring knowledge and submitting to the advice and traditions of the Ahl al-Bayt ﷺ. Even in his nineties, when many halt their spiritual development, Jabir continued his thirst for the presence of an Imam ﷺ and acting upon what he was guided towards.

Imam al-Baqir ﷺ narrates that he was with Jabir when the latter breathed a heavy sigh. The Imam ﷺ asked him, "O Jabir, what was the reason for such a sigh, is it because of this world?" To which Jabir replied in the affirmative. Imam al-Baqir ﷺ responded, "O Jabir, enjoyments of this world are seven: Food, drink, clothing, marriage, modes of transportation, aroma and sounds.

As for eating, the tastiest thing is honey, and that comes from the spit of a bee. As for drinking, the sweetest thing is water, and it is available enough to allow one to travel on the face of the earth. As for clothes, the best kind is silk, which is the saliva of a worm. As for marriage, the best marriage is with a beautiful wife but even then you will have trouble with her. What one wants is what is best in a woman, and not what is most ugly in her. As for a means of transport, the best thing is a horse and even that shall die. As for aroma, the best smell is musk which is the blood from the navel of a deer. As for sounds, the best is music and songs which are sinful.

Which of these things described does an intelligent person sigh over?"

Jabir responded, "I swear by Allah, the world never entered my heart again after this."543 544

It was from the oppression, torture and affliction upon an elderly Jabir that ultimately caused his demise, and in the year 78 A.H. Allah ﷻ concluded this great companion's service to Islam and called him back to His Mercy.

According to *al-Isti'aab*, Jabir died in the year 74 A.H., while it has also been said that he died in the years 77 and 78 A.H. It has been further elaborated in *al-'Isaba* that he passed away in the year 73 A.H., while in al-Mustadrak of al-Hakim with reference from Abi Nai'm it says that he passed away in the year 79 A.H. Sheikh al-Tusi in his *Rijal* states that Jabir died in the year 78 A.H. and this is the most reliable.

It has been narrated in *al-'Isaba* from Ali b. al-Madini that Jabir willed that Hajjaaj does not recite his funeral prayer (*Salat al-Mayyit*). This is not just because of the oppression against him and other companions, but rather

---

543 The Arabic text of this passage reads:

عن الامام الباقر عليه السلام:

أنه رأى جابر بن عبد الله وقد تنفّس الصعداء ، فقال عليه السلام : ياجابر ، علام تنفّسك ؟ أعلى الدنيا ؟ فقال جابر : نعم .

فقال عليه السلام له : ياجابر ، ملاذّ الدنيا سبع : المأكول والمشروب و الملبوس و المنكوح و المركوب و المشموم و المسموع .

فألذّ المأكولات العسل ، وهو بصق من ذبابة .

وأحلى المشروبات الماء ، وكفى بإباحته سياحته على وجه الأرض .

وأعلى الملبوسات الديباج ، وهو من لعاب دودة .

و أعلى المنكوحات النساء ، وهو مَبال في مبال ، و مثال لمثال ، وإنما يُراد أحسن مافي المرأة لا أقبح ما فيها.

و أعلى المركوبات الخيل ، وهي قواتل .

و أجلّ المشمومات المسك ، وهو دم من سرة دابة (يقصد الغزال).

و أجلّ المسموعات الغناء والترنم ، وهو إثم ..

فما هذه صفته لم ينتفس عليه عاقل .

قال جابر : فوالله ماخطرت الدنيا بعدها على قلبي .

Bihar al-Anwar, vol. 75, p. 11.

544 A similiar narration between Jabir and Imam Ali ﷺ is recorded:

قال جابر بن عبد الله الانصاري: تبعتُ أمير المؤمنين عليه السلام فتنفّستُ الصعداء ، فالتفت إليّ وقال: يا جابر ماهذا التنفس ؟ على الدنيا ملاذها خمس :مأكول ومشروب وملبوس ومركوب و منكوح ! فألذّ المأكول العسل ، وهو ريق الذبابة . وألذّ المشروب الماء ، وكفى برخصته وإباحته .وألذّ الملبوس الديباج ، وهو لعاب دودة .وألذّ المركوب الدواب ، وهي قواتل .وألذّ المنكوح النساء ، وهنّ مبال لمبال ؛ انما يراد أحسن مافي المرأة لا أقبح ما فيها. !

because of Hajjaaj's oppression towards the Ahl al-Bayt 🕮 and his aim in life to destroy Islam. By having Hajjaaj recite his funeral prayer it would have been perceived that Jabir ended his life endorsing Hajjaaj, or that matters were forgiven, or it would have given legitimacy to him in the eyes of the Muslims. Despite Jabir's request Hajjaaj still attended his funeral. Abbas b. 'Uthman who was the ruler of Medina [in that time] conducted his funeral prayer, and it is said that Jabir died at the age of 94.

There are differences of opinion as to whether he was the last companion of the Prophet 🕮 to die. It is mentioned in al-Kashi's narration that he was the last remaining companion of the Messenger of Allah 🕮, and Ibn Asakir said that he was the last of the companions in Medina to have died. Similar to this in *Tahthib al-Tahthib*, and in *al-Isaba*, al-Baghawi narrated from 'Tareeq Abi Hilal (Abi Hilal's path) from Kitada who said that: "The last of the Messenger of God's 🕮 companions who died in Medina were Jabir, and Sahil b. Sa'ad."[545] It is mentioned in *Usd al-Ghaba* that he was the last one to die in Medina of those who had witnessed al-Aqaba, and this is the most correct view.[546]

---

[545] *Qasas als-Sahaaba wa al-Tabi'in*, pp. 98-9.
[546] Ibid., p. 99; *A'yan al-Shi'a*, vol. 4, p. 45.

Conclusion

The purpose of this book was to collect the contributions of Jabir b. Abdullah al-Ansari and to appreciate his influence on Islam's intellectual and cultural development. By doing so this could be a point of reference in understanding his role and stances as one of the great members of early Islamic history and so revive his efforts in preserving the religion of Allah ﷻ.

The noble companions of Prophet Muhammad ﷺ enjoy a special status among the Muslims, and their lives serve as a source of understanding the wider history of revelation, and the changes that Islam brought to Arabia. Inseparable from the story of prophethood and revelation, the success of Islam rested on their struggles and sacrifices, at times being amongst the harshest of conditions. In periods of ease and victory, they were tested with moral and civil trials.

Jabir was no ordinary companion. He was a witness to the Prophet's ﷺ expansion of Islam beyond Mecca, and was part of the Ansar who welcomed the Prophet ﷺ to Medina, and is unanimously recognized by Muslim scholars to be among the pre-eminent servants of early Islam. Uniquely proximate to and favoured by the Prophet ﷺ, he often shared time in solitary with the Messenger of Allah ﷺ and had private access to the Ahl al-Bayt ﷺ. This was not the case for a majority of the companions. The more Jabir demonstrated capacity and loyalty, the more he was given intimate access - even to the secrets of the Ahl al-Bayt ﷺ, often becoming the first or only companion to be a part of something, such as narrating Hadith al-Kisaa, Ziyarat Amecnullah, being the first to visit Karbala, or seeing the preserved tablet of Lady Fatima ﷺ. No other companion matched in observing these fervent or distinguished moments. He is surely a manifestation of the verse of the Holy Qur'an: "And those foremost (in Islamic faith and the very first to embrace Islam) will be foremost (in paradise). These will be those nearest to Allah, in the gardens of delight." (56:10-12)

These prestigious points result in an obligation for the Muslim community to love and serve Jabir and his legacy. Imam Muhammad al-Baqir ﷺ used to often say: "Love those who love the family of the Prophet ﷺ even if they are scavengers."[547]

Anas b. Malik narrates that Jabir b. Abdullah greatly served him when they travelled together on a journey. Jabir said, "I saw the Ansar give great services to the Prophet ﷺ and therefore I serve every person from the Ansar whom I see."[548] In light of these two statements, this work was also intended to be a show of love, effort toward and service to Jabir b. Abdullah al-Ansari.

Having appreciated the aggregate of his contributions and achievements, three narrations beautifully summarize Jabir's lofty position and description. The first one speaks about the perfection of a few companions and how close to the station of prophethood they reached.

Imam Ja'far al-Sadiq ﷺ is narrated to have said, "No one other than a Prophet or his successor or a true believer, whose strength of faith Allah has already tested, can have a whole army of intelligence, with all of its entire range of characteristics. However, certain followers of ours and friends may acquire a few of these characteristics so that they may reach perfection, repulse the army of ignorance and purify themselves from evil. In such a case they could step at a high degree and reach the level of the Prophets and the successors of the Prophets. This progress can be made only after knowing with certainty, intelligence and its armies, and ignorance and its armies."[549] It is for this reason Jabir was granted knowledge of the *ta'weel* of the Qur'an.

The second narration speaks about a few of the companions, such as Jabir, who were the masters of narrations and supremely accurate in their transmission of the Qur'an and Prophetic practices. Imam Ali ﷺ categorizes the narrators of *ahadith* into four: "The first is 'A hypocrite who only pretends to be a Muslim. He does not consider it a sin and offence to lie and purposefully mentions a narration of the Prophet ﷺ while it is not a narration.' The second is 'One who heard narrations from the Prophet ﷺ but

---

[547] *Bashaaratu al-Mustafa li Shi'ati Murtadha*, Section 1, p. 76.
[548] *Kanz al-Ummal*, vol. 7, p. 136.
[549] *Al-Kafi*, Part 1, The Book of Intelligence and Ignorance, Hadith 14.

did not preserve it the way it should have been preserved and thus is uncertain about it.' The third group of narrators are those who 'Heard from the Messenger ﷺ something that contained a command, but later the Prophet prohibited it, and the man did not have any knowledge about such a prohibition; or he heard a prohibition and then the Prophet made it a commandment but the man did not know about such a commandment.'"

The final group describes and includes the great companion Jabir b. Abdullah al-Ansari. Owing to the fact that he was so trustworthy and accurate with his speech, Prophet Muhammad ﷺ conveyed his salutations through him to Imam al-Baqir ﷺ. Did not other companions live long enough to meet Imam al-Baqir ﷺ? Why were they not asked to fulfil this great honour but only Jabir was asked? Moreover, in order to prove his own Divine leadership (*Imamate*), why did Imam Muhammad al-Baqir ﷺ - who requires no additional evidence other than his own knowledge and character that he ﷺ was Allah's ﷻ chosen representative to the universe - continuously narrate from Jabir, had it not been for his sublime reputation, truthfulness and accuracy in narrating from the Ahl al-Bayt ﷺ.

Imam Ali ﷺ continues, "The last and fourth kind of narrator is 'The one who does not ascribe a lie to the Messenger of Allah ﷺ, who in fact hates lies, has consciousness of Allah ﷻ and respect for His Messenger ﷺ. He has not forgotten anything and he has preserved the narration the way it should have been preserved. He speaks it exactly the way that he heard it without any addition or omission. He knows that which was abrogating and that which was abrogated. He has practiced according to the abrogating and he has rejected the abrogated.'"[550]

The third narration describes the relationship between an Imam ﷺ and his devoted follower. Imam Ali ﷺ said, "Where are they, the intimate friends of Allah and how many are they? They are very few, but are of great respect before Allah ﷻ. They follow the Divine, guiding leaders of religion, and establish in their own selves the discipline of the Imams ﷺ and practice their way of life. In such conditions knowledge will lead them to true belief, and their souls will then accept the call of the leaders of knowledge. They are the followers of the scholars. They only accompany the worldly people

---

[550] *Al-Kafi*, vol. 1, Part 2, The Book on the Excellence of Knowledge, Chapter 21, The Differences in the Hadith, Hadith 1, pp. 47-9.

in obedience to Allah ﷻ and His friends. They maintain secrecy to be part of their religion for fear of their enemies. Their scholars and followers live quietly and silently under the rule of the government of falsehood, waiting for the government of Truth. How fortunate it is for them due to their patience in the matters of their religion in their peacetime! How strong is the desire to see them in the time of the dominance of their government? Allah ﷻ will soon bring us together with them in Paradise along with their parents, children and spouses who had been of the good doers."[551]

It was Jabir's mastery over the *ahadith*, and perfection of his soul that lead him to contribute his most important benefaction to Islam, after his service to the Prophet ﷺ, which was establishing the Imamate of Imam Muhammad al-Baqir ﷺ in Medina, the city which would become the base for Islamic knowledge and the first university of the Muslim nation. As such, his narrations run into the thousands, forging a distinct influence on the collection, dissemination and systematization of Islam until today. The intricate synthesis between al-Baqir ﷺ and Jabir is certainly unique in the history of Islam and demonstrates their cooperation, understanding of their circumstances and mutual influence over Medina generally and the Shi'a specifically. It is worth noting again that arguably no other companion had such a sustained influence over the city of Medina, apart from the first three Caliphs, like Jabir such that they looked to him as a resort against tyrants, a verification of the *sunnah* and a teacher of many Islamic sciences.

This brings us to the final purpose of the book which was to reflect on the taking of Jabir as a source of guidance in its absolute sense or whether he is a source of guidance by virtue of whom he sought guidance from. The Salafi school of thought relies on a particular narration as central to their doctrine, narrated by Abdullah bin Mas'ood who apparently states the Prophet ﷺ said, "The best of people are my generation, then those who follow them, then those who follow them."[552] It is evident that Jabir would have known such a narration, given his proximity to the Prophet ﷺ and that he travelled across the Muslim world to hear, collect and narrate *ahadith*

---

[551] *Al-Kafi*, vol. 1, Part 4, The Book about People with Divine Authority, Chapter 79, Select Hadith about Imam al-Mahdi ﷺ, Hadith 3, pp. 304-5.
[552] *Al-Salafiyyah*, Dr. Muhammad Sa'eed Ramadan al-Bouti, pg. 11. The Arabic of this reads:

خير الناس قرني ،ثم الذين يلونهم ،ثم الذين يلونهم

and that it would have been referring to him as part of the first generation of Muslims. Yet clearly he did not believe in nor act upon this so-called narration. He was that earliest generation, the very first whom Islam flourished through. Yet he gave great preference to Imam's Husayn ☾, Zain al-Abideen ☾ and especially al-Baqir ☾ above his own self and implored the rest of the Ummah to do the same, citing narration after narration of the Prophet ﷺ as evidence. If Jabir then is to be our guide yet he took the Ahl al-Bayt ☾ as his guide, this means that we too must do the same. This of course calls into question the authenticity of the narration, given that Jabir did not see greatness in terms of the sequence of generations, but rather whom Allah ﷻ gave preference to, whichever generation they come from. It is for this reason the Qur'an asks, "Then is He who guides to the Truth (worthier) to be closely followed or he who finds no guidance (for himself or others) unless he is guided? What (plea) have you; how do you judge?" (10:35)

Dr. Shari'ati observed that: "In order to understand any religion, one must study its God, its Book, its Prophet ﷺ and the best individuals whom it nurtured and raised." Indeed there can be no greater testimony to the one that it has raised and nurtured than Jabir b. Abdullah al-Ansari.

To this end, the Prophet ﷺ is narrated to have said to his companions, "The most beloved and closest of you to me is the one who meets me in the condition that he left me."[553] Jabir accomplished this. He will meet the Prophet ﷺ in the same condition that he left him in - in service to Allah ﷻ, the Prophet ﷺ, the Ahl al-Bayt ☾ and the Holy Qur'an. And to preserving these and illuminating the way for us to serve them, we are grateful to Jabir. For if we were to remove, forget or lose this example and contribution, a gaping hole would be left in the true face of Islam, one which may be irreparable.

For the reward of Jabir and those who this work is dedicated to, please recite a Surah al-Fatiha.

Jaffer Ladak

Shawwal, 1438 A.H.

---

[553] Haythami, vol. 10, p. 253.